ASPEN PUBLISHERS

E-Z RULES® FOR NEGOTIABLE INSTRUMENTS

UCC Articles 3 and 4
With Other Selected UCC Provisions

Jack S. Ezon, Esq.
Jeffrey S. Dweck, Esq.

Wolters Kluwer
Law & Business

AUSTIN BOSTON CHICAGO NEW YORK THE NETHERLANDS

Aspen Publishers
Attn: Permissions Department
76 Ninth Avenue, 7th Floor
New York, NY 10011-5201

To contact Customer Care, e-mail customer.care@aspenpublishers.com, call 1-800-234-1660, fax 1-800-901-9075, or mail correspondence to:

Aspen Publishers
Attn: Order Department
PO Box 990
Frederick, MD 21705

Printed in the United States of America.

1 2 3 4 5 6 7 8 9 0

ISBN 978-0-7355-7199-0

Library of Congress Cataloging-in-Publication Data

Ezon, Jack S.
E-Z rules for negotiable instruments (UCC articles 3 and 4) : with other selected UCC provisions / Jack S. Ezon and Jeffrey S. Dweck.
p. cm.
Includes bibliographical references and index.
ISBN 978-0-7355-7199-0 (alk. paper)
1. Negotiable instruments—United States—Outlines, Syllabi, etc. 2. Checks—United States—Outlines, Syllabi, etc. I. Dweck, Jeffrey S. II. Title.

KF957.E96 2008
346.73'096—dc22 2008035659

Cover Illustration: Vasily Kafanov/Images.com

Note: E-Z Rules are not a substitute for the actual text of the UCC, and should not be quoted or cited to. E-Z Rules is meant to be used as a quick reference and guide to understanding Articles 3 and 4 of the UCC, and cannot completely replace them. In addition, the "overview" for each section of the "Roadmap to Negotiable Instruments" is not meant to be a comprehensive teaching tool. It is merely meant to remind the reader of certain key points.

About Wolters Kluwer Law & Business

Wolters Kluwer Law & Business is a leading provider of research information and workflow solutions in key specialty areas. The strengths of the individual brands of Aspen Publishers, CCH, Kluwer Law International and Loislaw are aligned within Wolters Kluwer Law & Business to provide comprehensive, in-depth solutions and expert-authored content for the legal, professional and education markets.

CCH was founded in 1913 and has served more than four generations of business professionals and their clients. The CCH products in the Wolters Kluwer Law & Business group are highly regarded electronic and print resources for legal, securities, antitrust and trade regulation, government contracting, banking, pension, payroll, employment and labor, and healthcare reimbursement and compliance professionals.

Aspen Publishers is a leading information provider for attorneys, business professionals and law students. Written by preeminent authorities, Aspen products offer analytical and practical information in a range of specialty practice areas from securities law and intellectual property to mergers and acquisitions and pension/benefits. Aspen's trusted legal education resources provide professors and students with high-quality, up-to-date and effective resources for successful instruction and study in all areas of the law.

Kluwer Law International supplies the global business community with comprehensive English-language international legal information. Legal practitioners, corporate counsel and business executives around the world rely on the Kluwer Law International journals, loose-leafs, books and electronic products for authoritative information in many areas of international legal practice.

Loislaw is a premier provider of digitized legal content to small law firm practitioners of various specializations. Loislaw provides attorneys with the ability to quickly and efficiently find the necessary legal information they need, when and where they need it, by facilitating access to primary law as well as state-specific law, records, forms and treatises.

Wolters Kluwer Law & Business, a unit of Wolters Kluwer, is headquartered in New York and Riverwoods, Illinois. Wolters Kluwer is a leading multinational publisher and information services company.

IMPORTANT NOTE

All rules follow the format of the Uniform Commercial Code. Where the actual subsection of the rule is used, it is enclosed between parenthesis "( )." All other numbers and letters are produced by E-Z Rules and therefore, should not be cited to when discussing a rule. "E-Z Rules bullets" have been added in addition to the official sub-sections found in the actual code in order to make the substance more comprehensive.

For example, in § 3-103 there are four sections, referred to in E-Z Rules as (a)–(d). These are actual sections used in the U.C.C. and may be referred to, for example, as "subsection (a)." Under subsection (a) there are eleven subsections, (1)–(11). Since these are surrounded by parentheses, these, too, may be referenced by their names (ex: "§ 3-103(a)(1)"). Under § 3-103(a)(6), however, there are items labeled "a," "b," "c," and so forth. Since these are not enclosed in parenthesis, they are not the numbers the letters used by the Uniform Commercial Code.

USING E-Z RULES FOR NEGOTIABLE INSTRUMENTS

Why E-Z Rules?

Welcome to ***E-Z Rules***, a new way of presenting rules and laws, designed to put the "ease" into *legalese*!

E-Z Rules translates the confusing statutory language of the UCC into plain and simple English. ***E-Z Rules*** are designed to give you quick access to important information you often need, without the unnecessary strain of dissecting long, monotonous, statutory texts. And remember, ***E-Z Rules*** does this WITHOUT EXCLUDING ANY KEY POINTS OF THE ACTUAL RULE OR STATUTE!

What Is the E-Z Rules Format?

E-Z Rules is easy to use. It has been carefully tailored to meet the needs of both the law student and today's active law firm. In order to take full advantage of the ***E-Z Rules*** system, it would be beneficial to review some of its features:

- The rules are **boldly** titled for quick spotting.
- ***E-Z Rules*** is laid out so that the entire substance of a rule or statute could be grasped at a single glance.
- All rules follow the format of the Uniform Commercial Code. Where the actual subsection of the rule is used, it is enclosed between parenthesis "( )." All other numbers and letters are produced by ***E-Z Rules*** and therefore, should not be cited to when discussing a rule. "***E-Z Rules*** bullets" have been added in addition to the official sub-sections found in the actual code in order to make the substance more comprehensive.

For Example, in § 3-103 there are four sections, referred to in ***E-Z Rules*** as (a)–(d). These are actual sections used in the U.C.C. and may be referred to, for example, as "subsection (a)." Under subsection (a) there are eleven subsections, (1)–(11). Since these are surrounded by parentheses, these, too, may be referenced by their names (ex: "§ 3-103(a)(1)"). Under § 3-103(a)(6), however, there are items labeled "a," "b," "c," and so forth. Since these are not enclosed in parenthesis, they are not the letters used by the Uniform Commercial Code.

When the actual subsection letter or number of the rule is used, it is enclosed between parentheses. These are actual sections used in the UCC and may be called, for example, "subsection (1)."

All other numbers and letters, not enclosed in parentheses, are produced by *E-Z Rules*. They are not the letters or numbers used in the UCC and, therefore, should not be cited to when discussing a rule.

§3-103: Definitions

(a) The following definitions apply to Article 3:
- (1) **"Acceptor"** — A Drawee who has *accepted* a Draft
- (2) **"Drawee"** — A Person Ordered in a Draft to make Payment (e.g. Bank)
- (3) **"Drawer"** — The Person ordering Payment—either by *Signing* or being *identified* in a Draft
- (4) **"Good Faith"** — Requires both:
  - a. Honesty In Fact
  - and b. The Observance of *Reasonable Commercial Standards of Fair Dealing*
- (5) **"Maker"** — A Person who *signs* or is *identified* in a Note as the Person undertaking to pay
- (6) **"Order"**
  - a. An "Order" is a written instruction to pay Money
  - b. To be effective, the Order must be *Signed* by the Person giving the Order
  - c. The Order may be addressed to anyone (this includes the Person giving the instruction, one or more persons jointly or in the alternative).
  - d. An authorization to pay, alone, will not be considered an Order unless the Person authorized to pay is actually *Ordered* to pay
- (7) **"Ordinary Care"**
  - a. A Person Engaged in Business—Reasonable Commercial Standards (prevailing in the location and business that the Person is in)
  - b. A Bank — Reasonable Commercial Standards do not require a Bank to examine an Instrument if:
    - i. Failure to examine does not violate the Bank's prescribed procedures
    - and ii. The Bank's procedures do not vary unreasonably from general banking usage (not disapproved by Articles 3 or 4)
    - and iii. The Bank takes the Instrument by automated means for processing Collection or Payment

- Key words and phrases are emphasized with either **bold**, *italic*, or under-line. This not only helps in making the rules easier to understand, but has been proven to help the user focus in on pivotal words or phrases, which may otherwise go unnoticed. In addition, certain words have been abbreviated in order to facilitate quicker reading.
- All defined terms begin with a Capital Letter, in order to remind the reader to check the definition the term before applying the statute.
- The Uniform Commercial Code, Articles 3 and 4 were last amended in 2002. Since the revised version of Articles 3 and have not yet been adopted by most states, E-Z Rules follows the pre-2002 Code in the main text, but has noted the differences between the former and the revised versions in shaded text.

Shading is used to explain differences betweeen the pre-2002 version of the Code and the 2002 amended version.

§4-207: Transfer Warranties

(a) **Warranties:**
The following warranties are made to a Transferee and *any subsequent* Collecting Banks by a Customer or Collecting Bank when it transfers an Item for a Settlement or other Consideration:
- (1) **Entitlement to Enforce:** The warrantor is a Person is Entitled to Enforce the Item (see §3-301)
- and (2) **Authentic and Authorized Signatures:** All Signatures on the Item are Authentic and Authorized
- and (3) **No Alterations:** The Item has not been altered
- and (4) **No Defense of Recoupment:** The Item is not subject to a defense or claim in recoupment (as per §3-305(a)) of any party (which can be asserted against the warrantor).
- and (5) **No Knowledge of Insolvency:** The warrantor has no knowledge that the Maker, Acceptor, or Drawer (in the case of an Unaccepted Draft) is involved in Insolvency Proceedings (see §1-201(22)).

Revised Article 3 (2002) adds:
- and (6) **Remote Consumer Item:** With respect to a remotely-created consumer item, that the person on whose account the item is drawn authorized the issuance of the item in the amount for which the item is drawn.

- The most significant differences between the versions are indicated in shaded boxes, as below.

§ 3-309: Enforcement of Lost, Destroyed, or Stolen Instruments:

(a) A Person not in possession of an Instrument is entitled to enforce the Instrument if:
- (i) The Person was in possession of the Instrument and was entitled to enforce it when he lost possession.
- and (ii) The loss of possession was not the result of a Transfer by the Person or a Lawful Seizure.
- and (iii) The Person cannot readily obtain possession of the Instrument because it was *either:*
  - a. Destroyed
  - or b. Lost (i.e.—its whereabouts cannot be determined)
  - or c. In the *Wrongful Possession* of a Person:
    - 1. Whose identity is unknown
    - or 2. Who cannot be found
    - or 3. Who is not amenable to service of process

Amended Revised Article 3-309(a)

(a) A Person not in possession of an Instrument is entitled to enforce the Instrument if:
- (1) The Person seeking to enforce the Instrument either:
  - (A) Was entitled to enforce the Instrument when he lost possession.
  - or (B) Has acquired ownership (directly or indirectly) of the instrument from a person who was entitled to enforce the instrument when it lost possession.
- and (2) The loss of possession was not the result of a Transfer by the Person or a Lawful Seizure.
- and (3) The Person cannot readily obtain possession of the Instrument because it was *either*:
  - a. Destroyed
  - or b. Lost (i.e.—its whereabouts cannot be determined)
  - or c. In the *Wrongful Possession* of a Person:
    - 1. Whose identity is unknown
    - or 2. Who cannot be found
    - or 3. Who is not amenable to service of process

Note: E-Z Rules are not a substitute for the actual text of the UCC, and should not be quoted or cited to. E-Z Rules is meant to be used as a quick reference and guide to understanding Articles 3 and 4 of the UCC, and cannot completely replace it. In addition, the "overview" for each section of the "Roadmap to Negotiable Instruments" is not meant to be a comprehensive teaching tool. It is merely meant to remind the reader of certain key points.

ACKNOWLEDGMENTS

ABBREVIATIONS USED IN E-Z RULES FOR NEGOTIABLE INSTRUMENTS

BIOC	Buyer in the Ordinary Course
BOL	Bill of Lading
BOP	Burden of Proof
CIF	Cost, Insurance, Freight
C&F	Cost & Freight
DOT	Document of Title
GFP	Good Faith Purchaser
FOB	Freight on Board
HDC	Holder in Due Course
HDN	Holder by Due Negotiation
L/C	Letter of Credit
S/I	Security Interest
U.C.C.	Uniform Commercial Code
W/R	Warehouse Receipt

SUMMARY OF CONTENTS

Part One

E-Z RULES™

ROADMAP TO NEGOTIABLE INSTRUMENTS

One of the most beneficial features of E-Z Rules is its **Roadmap to Negotiable Instruments.** This section consists of an overview of the key topics of Articles 3 and 4 with the relevant rules or sections alongside. The "Roadmap" places all sections needed for a given topic at your fingertips. Please note that the overview appears in a different typeface than the text of the rule. Also note that where only a portion of a rule is included in the overview, its title is not bolded.

The Roadmap will be most beneficial to readers who are looking to analyze problems. Using the Roadmap as a checklist will help the reader break down a problem and "attack" it in a comprehensive and organized fashion and in accordance with the rules.

Studying the Roadmap will also help the reader grasp the concepts behind Articles 3 and 4 and get an overall picture of the relevant law.

The Roadmap is one of the most beneficial features of E-Z Rules, and we strongly recommend using it.

Part One
CONTENTS TO ROADMAP TO NEGOTIABLE INSTRUMENTS

I. USING AND UNDERSTANDING ARTICLE 3 AND ARTICLE 4

A. THE UCC:

OVERVIEW

The Uniform Commercial Code ("UCC") governs many commercial transactions throughout the United States.

What makes the UCC so powerful and important is the fact that every state has adopted at least some portion of it. Many states, however, make minor changes to the original UCC provisions, and it is therefore imperative to check the applicable jurisdiction's version of the UCC.

The UCC is divided into 11 "Articles," dealing with a variety of commercial law issues such as Secured Lending, Sales of Goods, Shipping, Letters of Credit, Checking, Banking, and Negotiable Instruments.

- Article 3 of the UCC deals with NEGOTIABLE INSTRUMENTS. Related to Article 3 is Article 4, which deals with BANK COLLECTIONS.

Scope of this book:

- This book deals with commercial paper, but primarily focuses on Negotiable Instruments.
- Generally, there are three types of commercial paper:
  - *Money paper*—which is an Instrument payable in Money (example: Checks, Promissory Notes)
  - *Commodity paper*—which is an Instrument payable in goods (example: warehouse receipt, Bill of Lading) (docs of title, letters of credit)
  - X *Investment paper*—which is an Article 8 Instrument representing an interest in a security (example: bond certificate, certificated security)
- Investment paper is beyond the scope of this book and will not be discussed further.
- This book briefly describes certain forms of commodity paper, and includes relevant sections from Article 7, which deals with Documents of Title. Letters of Credit will also be discussed.
- Non-negotiable Instruments are generally covered by contract law. This book will discuss the differences between Negotiable and Non-negotiable Instruments, but will not discuss the substantive legal issues concerning Non-negotiable Instruments.

B. APPLICABILITY OF ARTICLE 3:

OVERVIEW

Article 3 applies only to Negotiable Instruments; therefore, it is important to first decide whether an Instrument is a Negotiable Instrument before proceeding to apply Article 3 rules to a transaction (see § 3-102). Section 3-104(a) sets out the general requirements for an Instrument to be considered "negotiable" (see "REQUIREMENTS FOR NEGOTIABLE INSTRUMENTS" below).

Negotiability refers mostly to the FORM of the Instrument.

Keep in mind the UCC's policy goals of Negotiation:

- Free Negotiation — The UCC wants the creation of a Negotiable Instrument to be as **formal** and **free from defense** as possible to make the Instruments *truly Negotiable* (i.e., so that the "price" of the N/I (its face Value) will be predictable).
- Formalism — The UCC wants the creation of N/Is to be formal so people do not unintentionally make them.
- Cash Money is perfectly negotiable (but note, cash money is not governed by Articles 3 or 4).

Negotiable Instruments and Checks: Remember that Checks are only one form of Negotiable Instrument (See "TYPES OF NEGOTIABLE INSTRUMENTS" below). Checks are governed by other special rules, including Article 4 and "Regulation CC" (which is discussed later).

Applicability of Article 4: Article 4 defines rights between the parties of a Bank deposit and collection transaction. Since Banks are often parties to Negotiable Instrument transactions (especially Check transactions), Article 4 often plays a role in understanding the law under Article 3.

Relevant Section: § 3-102

§ 3-102: Subject Matter:

(a) **Scope Deleted**

1. This Article applies to Negotiable Instruments.
2. This Article does NOT apply to:
    a. Money
    b. Payment Orders (governed by Article 4A)
    c. Securities (governed by Article 8).

(b) **Subject to Article 4 and 9: Deleted** If there is a conflict between this Article and Article 4 or 9, Articles 4 and 9 govern.

(c) **Overriding Laws:** The following supersede any inconsistent provision of this Article (to the extent of the inconsistency):

1. Regulations of the Board of Governors of the Federal Reserve System
2. Operating Circulars issued by the Federal Reserve Banks.

II. CHARACTERISTICS OF A NEGOTIABLE INSTRUMENT

A. GENERAL BACKGROUND:

OVERVIEW

The Negotiable Instrument is governed primarily by Articles 3 and 4. This special body of law was created to promote the use of Negotiable Instruments in place of cash. Since cash is often so bulky and quite easy to steal, the use of a Negotiable Instrument in a transaction can be very helpful. Today, most people do business with Negotiable Instruments. Paying bills by Check or Money Order is an example of using a Negotiable Instrument in a typical, daily transaction.

HDC

- The most important element of Negotiable Instrument law is the "Holder in Due Course" ("HDC") rule, which protects a Person who takes an Instrument (for Value and in Good Faith) from "personal defenses" to Payment of the Instrument. This "HDC" rule is intended to assure people taking the Negotiable Instrument that it is almost as safe as taking cash. Without the HDC rule, a Person taking the Negotiable Instrument as Payment would have to worry if anyone else had any rights of setoff or other defenses for not paying it (see "HOLDER IN DUE COURSE").

B. NEGOTIABLE AND NON
I

OVERVIEW

Keep in mind that not all instruments are Negotiabl
with the words "I Promise to pay Stephanie $1,0
since it is payable only to Stephanie; Stephanie ca
because the Promissor only promises to pay Ste
ever Stephanie orders the Promissor to pay on her behalf. To do this, the Note would either have to say "to the Order of Stephanie" or "to Stephanie or Order").

Differences between Negotiable and Non-negotiable Instruments:

- **Assignability:**
  - Negotiable Instruments cannot be assigned; rather, they are *Negotiated*; Rules of Negotiation are governed generally by Article 3, and specifically in § 3-201 (see "NEGOTIATION" below).
  - Non-negotiable Instruments, like contracts and certain *promissory notes* are *assignable*. The rules of assignment are governed generally by common law and § 9-404, § 9-405, and § 9-406 of the UCC. Assigned instruments and contracts are normally subject to the claims and defenses of prior parties (§ 9-318(1)):
    - For example, under § 9-404, a buyer may purchase goods from a seller on "credit." This credit will create a security interest in the goods. The seller of the goods may assign the buyer's debt to a third-party creditor (in order to get immediate Money):
    - The creditor will pay the seller for the Value of the buyer's debt for the goods.
    - The creditor will obtain the seller's security interest in the buyer's goods.

Holder in Due Course Rules: Holder in Due Course ("HDC") rules apply only to Negotiable Instruments. The HDC exception is what makes N/Is so useful and powerful, since it protects a Person who takes the Instrument (for Value and in Good Faith) from most defenses to Payment of the Instrument (see section on "HOLDER IN DUE COURSE" below).

Defenses:

- If the Buyer is not satisfied with the goods, he may refuse to pay the creditor for the amount of the loan, thereby asserting a "defense" against the seller (e.g., § 2-601's "Perfect Tender Rule").
- In such a case, the creditor cannot force the buyer to pay; instead, the creditor must sue the seller for the "defense" amount.

Setoffs:

- In a similar credit situation between the buyer and the seller, the buyer may refuse to pay the entire amount of the loan to the seller because the seller owes the buyer Money from another transaction. This is known as a "*setoff.*"

...ditor must sue the seller for the "setoff" amount and cannot force ...uyer to pay him for the "setoff" amount—***unless*** the amount of the ...etoff" accrued *before* the buyer received notice of the assignment of the debt.

Relevant Sections: §9-404, §9-405, §9-406

§9-404: Rights Acquired by Assignee; Claims & Defenses Against Assignee:

(a) **Defenses Against Assignees:** Unless the Account debtor has made an enforceable agreement not to assert defenses or claims arising out of a sale (as per (b) and (e) below), the rights of an assignee are subject to:

(1) **Contractual Terms:** All terms of the contract between the Account debtor and assignor, *including* any claim or defense arising from the contract

and (2) **Setoffs of Defenses or Claims** (outside contact): Any other defense or claim that the Account debtor has against the assignor, as long as it accrues *before* the Account debtor received notification of the assignment.

(b) **Setoffs for Amounts Owed to Assignee:** The claim of an Account debtor against an assignor may be asserted against an assignee under (a), but *only* to *reduce* the amount the Account debtor owes (subject to (c) and except as provided in (d)).

(c) **Exception for Individuals:** This section is subject to the law (other than this article) which establishes a different rule for an Account debtor who

1) Is an *Individual*

and 2) Who incurred the obligation primarily for personal, family or household purposes.

(d) **Omission of Required Statement in Consumer Transaction:** If a record evidencing the Account debtor's obligation is required by law to include a statement to the effect that the *account debtor's recovery against an assignee* (with respect to claims and defenses against the assignor) *may not exceed amounts paid by the Account debtor*, and such record does not include such statement, it will be deemed to contain such statement for purposes of an Account debtor asserting a claim against an assignee.

(e) **Inapplicability to Health-Care-Insurance Receivable:** This section does not apply to an assignment of a health-care-insurance receivable.

§ 9-405: Modification of Assigned Contract:

(a) <u>**Effect of modification of assigned contract:**</u>

a. Any modification of or substitution for the contract will be effective against the assignee if it is <u>*made in Good Faith*</u>.
b. The assignee acquires the assignor's corresponding rights under the modified or substituted contract.
c. The assignment may provide that such a modification or substitution is a breach by the assignor.

(b) **Applicability:** Section (a) above will only apply <u>*to the extent that*</u> the right to payment has:

(1) Not been fully earned by performance under an assigned contract

or (2) Been fully earned by performance <u>*and*</u> the Account debtor has not received notification of the assignment under § 9-406(a).

(c) **Exception for Individuals:** This section is subject to other laws which establish a different rule for an Account debtor who

1) Is an individual

and 2) Who incurred the obligation primarily for personal, family, or household purposes.

(e) **Inapplicability to Health-Care-Insurance Receivable:** This section does not apply to an assignment of a health-care-insurance receivable.

§ 9-406: Discharge, Restrictions, and Proof of Assignment:

(a) **Discharge of Account Debtor; Effect of Notification:**

1. An Account debtor (on an account, chattel paper or Payment Intangible) may <u>*discharge*</u> its obligation by paying the *assignor* <u>until</u>, *but not after*, the Account debtor received a notification.
2. <u>Requirements for notification:</u>
   a. Authenticated by the assignor or assignee
   and b. States that the amount due (or to become due) has been assigned
   and c. Payment is to be made to the assignee
3. <u>Effect of notification:</u> After receiving such notification, the Account debtor may discharge its obligation by paying the assignee.
   - It can no longer discharge its obligation by paying the assignor.

(b) **Ineffective Notification:** Notification is ineffective under (a) if

(1) It does not *reasonably identify* the rights assigned.

or (2) An agreement between the Account debtor and the assignor (i.e., the seller of the payment intangible) specifically limits the Account debtor's duty to pay a person other than the seller (and such limitation is effective under law (other than this Article)).

or (3) The notification notified the Account debtor to make less than the full amount of any installment or other periodic payment to the assignee (at the option of the Account debtor), *even if:*

(A) Only a portion of the receivable has been assigned.

or (B) A portion has been assigned to another assignee.

or (C) The Account debtor knows that the assignment to the assignee is limited.

(c) **Proof of Assignment:**

1. An assignee shall *seasonably* furnish reasonable proof of an assignment upon request by the Account debtor.
2. If the assignee does not comply with giving notice, then the Account debtor may discharge its obligation by paying the assignor (even if it received notification under (a) above).

(d) **Term prohibiting assignment ineffective:** A term in any Promissory Note or contract between an Account debtor and an assignor is *ineffective* if it:

(1) Prohibits the assignment of an account by:

a. Prohibiting assignments

b. Restricting assignments

c. Requiring the consent of the Account debtor or person obligated under the Promissory Note to the assignment

or d. Prohibiting the creation of an S/I in a general intangible for money due or to become due

or (2) Provides that a default, breach, or other claim will occur upon:

a. Assignment

b. Transfer

c. Creation, attachment, perfection, or enforcement of a security interest

(e) **Exceptions:** Subsection (d) does not apply to the sale of a Payment Intangible or Promissory Note.

(f) **Ineffectiveness of Legal Restriction on Assignment:** A rule of law that prohibits, restricts, or requires consent (by Account debtor or a governmental body) to the transfer, assignment, or creation of an S/I in a payment intangible, will be *ineffective* to the extent that the law:

(1) Prohibits the assignment of an account by:
   a. Prohibiting assignments
   b. Restricting assignments
   c. Requiring the consent of the Account debtor or person obligated under the Promissory Note to the assignment
   or d. Prohibiting the creation of an S/I in a general intangible for money due or to become due

or (2) Provides that a default, breach, or other claim will occur upon:
   a. Assignment
   b. Transfer
   c. Creation, attachment, perfection, or enforcement of a security interest

(g) **No Waiver:** An Account debtor may not waive or vary its option under Subsection (b)(3) above.

(h) **Exception for Individuals:** This section is subject to other laws which establish a different rule for an Account debtor who is an individual and who incurred the obligation primarily for personal, family, or household purposes.

(i) **Inapplicability to Health-Care-Insurance Receivable:** This section does not apply to an assignment of a health-care-insurance receivable.

C. REQUIREMENTS FOR NEGOTIABLE INSTRUMENTS:

General Requirements for Instrument to Be Negotiable: (§ 3-104(a))

OVERVIEW

In Order to be a Negotiable Instrument, the Instrument must be:

1) An **Unconditional Promise** or Order to pay (as per § 3-106)
2) In **Writing** (as per § 3-103(a)(6),(9))[1]
3) **Signed** (as per § 3-401)
4) A Sum Certain/**Fixed amount** (including interest and other charges (§ 3-104(a))
5) Payable in **Money** (defined in § 1-201(24) (as per § 3-107))
6) Payable on Demand or at a **Specified Time** (§ 3-108; § 3-115)
7) **Free from any other Promises** (§ 3-104(a)(3))[2]
8) Payable to **"Bearer" or "Order"** (§ 3-104(a)(2))[3]

Refer to the following pages for a more detailed discussion of the requirements for N/Is

Relevant Section: § 3-104

§ 3-104: Negotiable Instrument:

(a) **Requirements of a Negotiable Instrument** (except as provided in (c) and (d)):

(1) Must be payable *"to Bearer" or "to Order"* either at the time it:

a) Is Issued

or b) First comes into Possession of a Holder

and (2) Must be Payable either *on Demand* or *at a definite time*

and (3) Must not undertake or instruct the promisor (or Person Ordering Payment) to do *anything other than pay*, except that the promise may also include:

(i) An undertaking or power to give, maintain, or protect collateral to secure Payment

---

[1] Note that Revised Article 3 (2002) changes the requirement of a "Writing" to a "Record."

[2] Former 3-112.

[3] Former 3-104(1).

or (ii) An authorization or power to the Holder to
- a) Confess judgment on collateral
- or b) "Realize on" collateral
- or c) Dispose of collateral

or (iii) A waiver of the benefit of any law intended for the advantage or protection of an obligor.

4) Must be an *Unconditional Promise or Order* to pay
5) Must Promise a *fixed amount*
6) Must Promise/Order to pay *Money* (with or without interest or other charges described in the Promise or Order)

(b) **"Instrument"** — refers to a Negotiable Instrument

(c) **Negotiable Instrument and Check**

An Order is a Negotiable Instrument and a Check if it:

1) Meets all the requirements of 3-104(a) (except for § 3-104(a)(1) — where there is no need to say "Order" or "Bearer")

and 2) Otherwise falls within the definition of "Check" (as per 3-104(f)).

(d) **Promise or Order Not an N/I:** A Promise or Order is not an Instrument if:

1) It is not a Check.

and 2) It contains a *Conspicuous Statement* (however expressed) that either:
- a) The Promise or Order is not Negotiable.
- or b) The Promise or Order is not an Instrument governed by Article 3.

and 3) This statement appears on the Promise or Order *either* at the time:
- a) It is Issued.
- or b) It first comes into possession of a holder.

(e) **Notes and Drafts:**

1) An Instrument is a "**Note**" if it is a *Promise.*
2) An Instrument is a "**Draft**" if it is an *Order* (example: a Check).
3) A Person may treat an Instrument as either a Draft or a Note if it falls within the definition of both.

(f) **"Checks"** —

1. A Check is:
   - (i) A Draft — other than a Documentary Draft (see § 4-104), Payable on Demand and drawn on a Bank
   - or (ii) A Cashier's Check — or Teller's Check
2. An Instrument may be a Check even if it is referred to as something else on its face (example: the Check says it is a "Money Order").

(g) **"Cashier's Check"**—A Draft in which both the Drawer and the Drawee are the same Bank (or branches of the same Bank).

(h) **"Teller's Check"**—A Draft drawn by a Bank, either:

(i) On another Bank
or (ii) Payable at or through a Bank

(i) **"Traveler's Check"**—An Instrument that is:

(i) Payable on Demand
and (ii) Drawn on or payable at or through a Bank
and (iii) Designated by the term *"Traveler's Check"* (or by a substantially similar term)
and (iv) Requires a countersignature (by the Person whose specimen signature appears on the Instrument) as a condition to Payment

(j) **"Certificate of Deposit"**—

1. A Certificate of Deposit is an Instrument containing an acknowledgment by a Bank that:
   a. A Sum of Money has been received by a Bank
   and b. The bank promises to repay that sum of Money
2. A Certificate of Deposit is a Note of the Bank

1) Unconditional Promise:

OVERVIEW

A reference on an Instrument to other agreements or documents does not, *itself*, destroy its negotiability.

- Although separate agreements may affect the rights of the parties to a particular transaction, such separate agreements/documents will have no effect on a subsequent HDC. (example: *"I Promise to pay $100 to you or your order. This Note is made pursuant to our sales contract of April 5, 1990"* will have no effect on subsequent HDCs).
- Negotiability will be destroyed only if the Promissory Note is made *"subject to"* the outside agreement.
- Writing "*pursuant to*" or "*in accordance with*" an outside agreement (§ 3-117) on an Instrument will not destroy its negotiability.[4]

Source of Money—An Instrument will be Negotiable even if it restricts Payment to a particular source of funding (§ 3-106).[5] (but non-neg under pre-Rev)

Relevant Sections: § 3-106, § 3-103(a)(9), § 3-117

§ 3-106: Unconditional Promise or Order:[6]

(a) **"Unconditional Promise or Order"**

1. Except as provided in this section, a Promise or Order is considered *Unconditional* (for purposes of § 3-104(a)) unless it states:
   - (i) An Express Condition to Payment
   - or (ii) That the Promise or Order is *subject to* or *governed by* another **writing** (no effect on HDC)
   - or (iii) That the *rights and obligations* of the Promise are stated in another **writing**
2. A reference to another **writing** does not, *itself*, make a Promise or Order conditional

---

[4] Note that Revised Article 3 (2002) changes the requirement of a "Writing" to a "Record."

[5] Under the former Article 3, if an Instrument limits the source from which funds to pay the Note come, the Note is Non-negotiable (see former 3-105(2)(b)) (example: an Instrument saying "Pay to the Order of Bearer from Account # 8233" would not be Negotiable (under the former Article 3; *rationale:* a Check represents a Promise to pay from all of Drawer's assets. Thus, with a Check, if there are not enough funds in an Account, the Payee may go after the Drawer's other assets)).

[6] In states adopting Revised Articles 2, 3, and 4 (2002), the requirement for a writing is replaced with a requirement for a "record," which could include anything recorded in a tangible or electronic medium and retrievable in tangible form (as per § 3-103(a)(14)).

(b) **Not Considered Conditional:** The following examples will not make a Promise or Order become conditional:

(i) Referencing another **writing** stating rights with regard to:
a) Collateral
or b) Prepayment or acceleration of Payment

or (ii) Limiting Payment to a particular fund or source (e.g., limiting a Check to Money in particular Bank Account)
↳ (but not under pre-Rev)

(c) **Co-signatures not Conditional:**

1. If, as a condition to Payment, a Promise or Order requires a *countersignature* by a Person whose sample signature appears on the Instrument, the Instrument will not be considered conditional (for purposes of §3-104(a)), *even if the Note requires the countersignature as a condition for Payment.*
2. Failure to Countersign:
   a) The failure of a Person (whose sample signature appears on the Note) to countersign an Instrument is a defense to the Issuer's obligation to pay the Instrument.
   b) Failure to countersign will not prevent a *transferee* of the Instrument from becoming a Holder of the Instrument.

(d) **Statements Allowing Issuer to Assert Defenses Not Conditional:**

1. A Promise or Order will not be made conditional (for the purposes of §3-104(a)) if it:
   a) Contains a statement subjecting the rights of a holder or transferee to the Issuer's claims or defenses against the Original Payee
   and b) The statement was required by applicable statutory or administrative law
   and c) The statement was made at the time the Promise or Order either:
      i) Was first Issued
      or ii) First came into possession of a holder
2. If an Instrument contains the above statement, there can never be a Holder in Due Course of that Instrument.

§3-103(a)(9): Definitions:

(a) The following definitions apply to Article 3:

* * *

(9) **"Promise"** —
a) A Written undertaking to pay Money
b) Must be *Signed* by the Person undertaking to pay.

c) An acknowledgment of an obligation, alone, is not a promise to pay; the obligor must specifically *undertake* to pay the obligation.

§ 3-117: Other Agreements Affecting Instrument:

a) A Party's obligation to pay an Instrument may be modified, supplemented, or nullified by a separate agreement (e.g., security agreement, mortgage) of the obligor and the Person Entitled to Enforce the Instrument so long as:

1. The Instrument is Issued (or the obligation incurred) *in reliance* on the agreement.

or 2. The Instrument is Issued (or the obligation incurred) as *part of the same transaction* giving rise to the agreement. (Note: In this case the Instrument may not be a Negotiable Instrument—see § 3-104 and § 3-106.)

b) The Agreement will be a valid defense to Payment of the Instrument to the extent the agreement modifies, supplements, or nullifies the obligation. (Note: This defense is not good against a subsequent Holder in Due Course of the Note that took it without notice of the agreement (see § 3-117, Off. Comm. 1).)

c) This section is subject to applicable law regarding exclusion of proof of contemporaneous or previous agreements (parol evidence rule).

2) Signature: (§ 1-201(39))

OVERVIEW

The Person writing the N/I is known as the "**Maker**," "**Issuer**," or "**Drawer**."

- The Maker's actual signature is not necessary to make the Instrument negotiable; any mark made with the *"intent to authenticate"* will suffice as a signature (i.e., the Maker can sign by marking an "x" if he intends the "x" to act as a signature).
- Location of signature: The signature need not appear on the signature line; it may be anywhere on Instrument (as long as it was made with intent to authenticate the Instrument; but note, signatures not on the signature line should make a subsequent Holder suspicious for purposes of determining HDC status).
- An *authorized* agent may sign the Drawer's name on the Instrument (§ 3-402(a)).
- Unauthorized signatures (example: forgeries) are signatures made by an unauthorized Person (§ 1-201(43)). These include forgers and agents acting without appropriate authority. The UCC holds the forger himself liable as Drawer (see "FORGERY" below).

Relevant Sections: § 3-401, § 3-402, § 3-403, § 1-201(39), § 1-201(43)

§ 3-401: Signature:

(a) **Liability on an Instrument:**

A Person will be liable on an Instrument only if:

(i) The Person has *Signed* the Instrument.
or (ii) A Representative has Signed it for the Person (and such signature is binding on the represented Person under § 3-402).

(b) **Method of Signature:**

A signature may be made by:

(i) Any of the following means:
a) Manually
or b) By use of a machine or device
and (ii) The use of:
a. A name (including a trade or assumed name)
or b. Any of the following if they are *executed or adopted* by a Person with a *present intention to authenticate a writing*:
1) Word
or 2) Mark
or 3) Symbol

§ 3-402: Signature by Representation:

(a) **Represented Person Bound**

1. A Person whose name is Signed by a Representative is bound to the same extent he would be if the signature were on a simple contract if:
   a) The Person acting (or purporting to act) as a Representative signs the Instrument.
   and b) Such Person either:
      1) Signs the name of the Represented Person
      or 2) Signs his own name.
2. If the Represented Person is bound (under the law of agency), then the following rules apply:
   a) The signature of the Representative is considered to be the *"Authorized signature of the Represented Person."*
   and b) The Represented Person is liable on the Instrument *whether or not he is identified in the Instrument.*

(b) **Liability of the Representative—**

<u>Scope:</u> The liability rules in this section apply if:

a) The Representative signs an Instrument in her own name.
and b) The Representative's signature is considered the *"authorized signature of the Represented Person"* (under § 3-402(a)).
   (1) <u>The Representative is not liable if:</u>
      a) The form of the signature shows *unambiguously* that the signature is made on behalf of the represented Person.
      and b) The Represented Person is identified in the Instrument.
   (2) <u>The Representative Will Be Liable</u>
      a) *To HDC*— The Representative will be liable to a *Holder in Due Course* if:
         1. The HDC took the Instrument <u>without notice</u> that the Representative was not intended to be liable on the Instrument.
         and 2. *Either*:
            (i) The form of the signature <u>does not</u> *unambiguously* show that the signature is made in a Representative capacity.
            or (ii) The represented Person is not identified in the Instrument.
      b) *To Non-HDC*— The Representative will be liable to non-HDCs, *unless* he can prove that the original parties did not intend the Representative to be liable on the Instrument.
      c) Subsection 3-402(b)(2) is subject to § 3-402(c).

(c) **Checks—** The Representative Signer is not liable on a Check if:

1. The signature is an "authorized signature of the Represented Person."

and 2. The Representative signs with his own name (as Drawer of a Check).

and 3. The Representative does not indicate his status as a Representative (i.e., no need to indicate status).

and 4. The Check is payable from an Account of the Represented Person.

and 5. The Represented Person is identified on the Check.

FORGER held liable as maker/DR

§ 3-403: Unauthorized Signature:

(a) **Unauthorized Signature Ineffective:** An Unauthorized signature is <u>**ineffective**</u> unless:

1) Otherwise provided in Article 3 or 4
2) The signature is effective to impose liability upon the signer in favor of a Person who in **Good Faith**:
    a) Takes it for Value
    or b) Pays the Instrument
3) **"<u>Ratification</u>":** The Unauthorized signature may be retroactively adopted by the Person whose name is Signed.
    - Ratification may be found from conduct or express statements.

(b) **Multi-Person Signatures:**

If an organization requires more than one signature to constitute the organization's authorized signature, the signature is deemed unauthorized if *any* of the required signatures are absent.

(c) **Liability:** Civil or criminal liability for persons making Unauthorized signatures is not affected by any provision of this Article which makes the Unauthorized signature effective for the purposes of this Article.

§ 1-201(39): "Signed":

Includes any symbol executed or adopted by someone *intending* to authenticate a writing.

§ 1-201(43): "Unauthorized":

1. An Unauthorized signature is made without actual, implied, or apparent authority.

2. A Forgery is a type of Unauthorized signature.

3) *Specified Time of Payment:*

OVERVIEW

The time of payment must be specified or ascertainable at the time the N/I is written.

Instrument Presumed Payable on Demand: If no time for Payment is specified, the Instrument will be presumed to be "Payable on Demand" (as per § 3-108).

Acceleration Clauses do not affect negotiability.

An *Extension Clause* destroys negotiability only if it does not state the extended date.

Relevant Section: § 3-108

§ 3-108: Payable on Demand or at a Definite Time:

(a) **"Payable on Demand"** — An Instrument will be considered *"Payable on Demand"* if:

(i) It states that it is payable *either*:

a. "On Demand"

or b. "At Sight"

or c. It otherwise indicates at the will of the Holder

or (ii) It does not state any time for Payment *

(b) **"Payable at a Definite Time"**

1. An Instrument will be considered *"Payable at a Definite Time"* if:

a. It is payable on the lapse of a *definite period of time* after Sight or Acceptance of the Promise or Order

or b. At *either:*

1. A Fixed Date (or dates)

or 2. At a time *readily ascertainable* at the time the Promise or Order is Issued

2. Payment at the defined time may be subject to the rights of:

(i) Prepayment

or (ii) Acceleration

or (iii) Extension at the option of the Holder

or (iv) Extension to a further definite time *either*:

a. At the option of the Maker or Acceptor

or b. Automatically upon the occurrence of a specified event

(c) **Payable upon Demand and Fixed Date**—If an Instrument is payable both upon a Fixed Date or upon Demand (made any time before the fixed date):

1. The Instrument will be considered *"Payable on Demand"* until the Fixed Date.
2. The Instrument will be considered *"Payable at a Definite Time"* on the fixed date if demand for Payment is not made before that date.

4) *Fixed Value:*

OVERVIEW

The amount payable on the Negotiable Instrument must be *"ascertainable"* at the time it is Negotiated; Thus, the following examples would be acceptable:

- "This Instrument is to pay $500"
- "This Instrument is to pay $500 + 3% interest"
- "This Instrument is to pay $500 + interest" (interest rate will be calculated according to § 3-112).

Contradictory Terms

- **Words Prevail:** If the numbers and words contradict each other, the words will prevail (as per § 3-114).
- **Handwriting Prevails**: over both typewritten and pre-printed terms.

Relevant Sections: § 3-112, § 3-114

§ 3-112: Interest:

(a) **Assumption of Interest Free Instrument:** Unless the Instrument provides otherwise,

(i) An Instrument is not payable with Interest.

and (ii) If the Instrument provides for interest, it will be payable from the *Date of the Instrument* (as per § 3-113).

(b) **Terms of Interest:**

1. Method of Stating Interest: Interest may be stated in an Instrument as *either*:
   a. A *Fixed* or *variable* amount of Money
   or b. A *Fixed* or *variable* rate (or rates) of Interest
2. Amount of Interest: the amount of interest on the Instrument may:
   a. Be stated or described in the Instrument in any manner
   or b. Refer to information not contained in the Instrument
3. Interest Rate not Ascertainable: If the interest rate is not ascertainable from its description in the Instrument, the interest rate shall be the *judgment rate* in effect:
   a. At the time interest first accrues
   and b. At the place of Payment

§ 3-114: Contradictory Terms of an Instrument:

If an Instrument contains contradictory terms:

a. Handwritten terms will prevail over typewritten and printed terms.

b. Typewritten terms will prevail over printed terms.

c. Words will prevail over numbers.

5) Money:

OVERVIEW

The Instrument must be payable in "Money" (as defined in § 1-201(24)) (Thus, an Instrument that Promises to pay in $500 worth of wool is not a Negotiable Instrument (this may be a Document of Title, and may also be enforceable under general contract law (see "DOCUMENTS OF TITLE" below).

An Instrument may be payable in foreign currency (§ 3-107).

Relevant Sections: § 1-201(24), § 3-107

§ 1-201(24): "Money":

1. A medium of exchange authorized or adopted by a domestic or foreign government.
2. "Money" includes any monetary unit of account established by an inter-governmental organization or by agreement between two or more nations (example: The European ECU).

§ 3-107: Instrument Payable in Foreign Money:

Unless the Instrument otherwise provides, an Instrument that states a payable amount in foreign Money may be paid *either*:

a) In foreign Money

or b) In an equivalent dollar amount, to be calculated by using the current Bank-offered *spot rate:*

1. For the Purchase of dollars

and 2. At the place where Payment is actually made

and 3. On the day Payment of the Instrument is actually made

6) *Payable to "Bearer" or "Order":*

OVERVIEW

The N/I must *either* be:

1. Payable to "*Bearer*" (i.e., anyone who possesses the Instrument may enforce it)

or 2. Payable to the *"Order"* of an "Identified Payee" (example: "Pay to the Order of Celia" is okay since Celia can *Indorse* the Check to Susan, thereby "Ordering" the Maker of the Instrument to pay Susan instead of Celia; "Pay to Celia" is not sufficient for purposes of creating a Negotiable Instrument)

Exception for Checks: A Check is the only type of Negotiable Instrument that does not need the words "to the Order of" or "to Bearer" (§ 3-104(c))[7]

Bearer Instruments: Instruments are Payable to Bearer if they are drawn payable to:

(1) "Bearer"

or (2) "Cash"

or (3) Any other indication not specifying the Payee

Conflicting Terms: If an Instrument has Bearer **and** Order language, it will be considered a *Bearer Instrument* (§ 3-109).[8]

Relevant Sections: § 3-103(a)(6), § 3-109, § 3-110, § 3-104(c)

§ 3-103(a)(6): Definitions:

(a) The following definitions apply to Article 3:

* * *

(6) **"Order"**

a) An "Order" is a written instruction to pay Money.

b) To be effective, the Order must be *Signed* by the Person giving the Order.

c) The Order may be addressed to anyone (this includes the Person giving the instruction, one or more persons jointly, or in the alternative).

---

[7] Note: this was not the case in the former Article 3.

[8] According to the former Article 3, it would be construed as an Order Instrument (see former 3-110(3)).

d) An authorization to pay, alone, will not be considered an Order unless the Person authorized to pay is actually *Ordered* to pay.

§ 3-109: Payable to Bearer or to Order:

(a) **Payable to Bearer:** A Promise or Order is Payable to Bearer if it:

(1) Indicates that:
a) It is "Payable to Bearer"
or b) It is "Payable to the Order of Bearer"
or c) It otherwise indicates that the Person in possession of the Promise or Order is entitled to Payment
or (2) Does not state a Payee
or (3) Indicates that it is:
a) "Payable to Cash"
or b) "Payable to the Order of Cash"
or c) It otherwise indicates that it is not payable to an identified Person

(b) **Not Payable to Bearer:**

1. A Promise or Order that is not Payable to Bearer is Payable to Order if it is payable *either*:
   (i) To the Order of an Identified Person (e.g., "To the order of John Doe")
   or (ii) To an Identified Person or Order (e.g., "To John Doe or order")
2. A Promise or Order that is not Payable to Order is payable to the identified Person.

(c) **Indorsement's Effect on to Whom Instrument Is Payable:**

1. An Instrument Payable to Bearer may become Payable to an Identified Person if it is *specially Indorsed* to the Identified Person (as per § 3-205(a)).
2. An Instrument made Payable to an Identified Person may become Payable to Bearer if it is Indorsed "in Blank" (as per § 3-205(b)).

§ 3-110: Identification of Person to Whom Instrument Is Payable:

(a) **Signer's Intent:**

1. The Person to whom an Instrument is payable is determined by the intent of the Person signing the Instrument as Issuer

or on behalf of the Issuer (whether or not that Person is authorized).

2. The Instrument is payable to the Person intended by the signer, even if that Person is identified in the Instrument by another name (example: David Drawer, president of Corporation owes money to the cleaning lady, Joan Smith, who often goes by the nickname Jane Smith. An impostor, also named Jane Smith came to David to get the Check; since David never saw Jane, he gave it to the impostor. However, David Intended to make Payment to Jane Smith, the cleaning lady, and not Jane Smith, the thief. Thus, Jane Smith, the impostor, is not a holder. Since David Drawer's intent controls, the name appearing on the Instrument is intended to be for Jane the cleaning lady. It is not properly payable to Jane the impostor.).
3. If more than one Person signs the Instrument and they do not all intend for the same Person to be Payee, the Instrument will be payable to any of the persons intended by one or more of the signers.

(b) **Automated Signatures** (i.e., Check-writing machines): The Payee will be determined by the intent of the Person supplying the name of the payee to the machine (whether or not authorized to do so).

(c) **Identification of Payee and Holder:**

i) Determining Payee: A Person to whom an Instrument is payable may be identified *in any way*, including:
   a) Name
   b) Identification number
   c) Account number
   d) Office (e.g., President, Treasurer)

ii) Determining Holder:
   (1) **Instruments Payable to a Person or Account:**
      a. *PAYABLE TO AN ACCOUNT* (if the Account is Identified only by an Account Number): The Instrument is payable to the Person to whom the Account is payable.
      b. *PAYABLE TO PERSON AND ACCOUNT NUMBER*: The Instrument will be Payable to the *Named Person*, whether or not that Person owns the specified Account.
   (2) **Instruments Payable to a Representative:**
      (i) *PAYABLE TO A TRUST, ESTATE, or TRUSTEE or REPRESENTATIVE of a trust or estate*: The Instrument is payable to the trustee, Representative, or successor of either (whether or not the beneficiary is named).

(ii) PAYABLE TO AN AGENT OR REPRESENTATIVE OF IDENTIFIED PERSON: The Instrument is Payable to the represented Person, or the Representative and the Representative's successor.

(iii) PAYABLE TO A FUND OR ORGANIZATION *that is not a legal entity*: The Instrument is Payable to a Representative of the Members of the Fund/Organization.

(iv) *PAYABLE TO AN OFFICE OR A PERSON DESCRIBED AS HOLDING AN OFFICE*: The Instrument is Payable to the named Person, the incumbent of the office, or a successor of the incumbent.

(d) **Payable to Two or More Persons**:

1. Payable to multiple Persons *alternatively* (e.g., Esther or Lauren): It is Payable to any of them (and may be negotiated, discharged, or enforced by any of them in possession)

2. Payable to multiple Persons jointly (e.g., Esther and Lauren): It is payable to all of them (and may be negotiated, discharged, or enforced only by all of them together).

3. Presumption of alternative payability: If the Instrument is not clear whether it is payable to multiple parties Alternatively or jointly, it will be presumed alternatively.

§ 3-104(c): Negotiable Instrument:

(c) **Negotiable Instrument and Check**

An Order is a Negotiable Instrument and a Check if it:

1) Meets all the requirements of 3-104(a) (except for § 3-104(a)(1) — where there is no need to say "Order" or "Bearer")

and 2) Otherwise falls within the definition of "Check" (as per 3-104(f)).

D. TYPES OF NEGOTIABLE INSTRUMENTS:

draft = order to 3p to pay obligation

Note = maker promises to pay

OVERVIEW

Negotiable Instruments are divided into two general categories: Drafts and Notes (see § 3-104 Off. Comm. 4).

1) A **Draft** is an Instrument that is an Order to a third party to pay the obligation.
2) A **Note** is an Instrument that is a Promise by the Maker to pay the obligation.

Types of Negotiable Instruments:

1) **Drafts** (§ 3-104(c)-(j))
   - A Draft is a N/I Ordering a third party, known as a *"Drawee"* (usually a "Payor Bank"), to pay.
   - The most common type of Draft is the Check (a Check is a Draft with a Bank as Drawee).
   - The *Drawer* (i.e., Maker) is the one who signs the Draft (see "PARTIES TO THE CHECK" below)
   - The *Payee* (person obtaining the Check) will be personally liable on a Draft if she *Indorses* it (§ 4-315).
   - There are circumstances when the Drawee (*Payor* Bank) does not have to Honor a Check (see § 4-402, and "PROPERLY PAYABLE" below).
   - Rejected Drafts: If a Drawee denies Payment, the *Holder* of the Draft may sue either the *Drawer* or *Indorser* (as discussed later, it is usually best to sue the Drawer).
   - When dealing with Checks, Article 4 must be examined, since it supersedes Article 3 (§ 4-102) (Article 4 applies *only* when dealing with Drafts payable at a Bank).
2) **Checks**:—Checks are Drafts in which a Bank is the Drawee (i.e., the "Payor Bank") (See section on "CHECKS" below).
3) **Certified Checks**:
   - When a Bank *certifies* a Check, it accepts liability on it.
   - The Bank is the only one liable on a Certified Check.
   - A Bank has no obligation to certify a Check (§ 3-409(d)).
   - A Bank's refusal to certify a Check is not considered a Dishonor (§ 3-409(d)).
   - **Dishonoring Certified Checks:** (§ 3-411) (see "DISHONOR" below)
4) **Teller's Checks**—(§ 3-104): A Teller's Check is a Check written by one Bank to another (or with another Bank as the Payor Bank).
5) **Cashier's Checks**:
   - A Cashier's Check is a Check between branches of the same Bank (in which the Payor Bank and Payee are the same Bank).
   - Delivery of a Cashier's Check in exchange for another Check is considered a "*Final Settlement*" (§ 4-213(c)).
   - The Person paying for the Cashier's Check is known as the ***Remitter*** (not a Drawer)

- Banks remain liable on a Cashier's Check ((under § 3-414; § 3-415); The best security for the Bank is to take cash for a Cashier's Check, and not another Check (which may be Dishonored); the bank may also immediately debit the remitter's account).

6) **Certificates of Deposit:** are considered to be Drafts (see § 3-104 Off. Comm. 4).

7) **Promissory Note:**
   - A Promissory Note is an *unconditional* Promise to pay.
   - Unlike Drafts, the "*Payor*" himself is the signer.

Relevant Section: § 3-104

§ 3-104: Negotiable Instrument:

(a) **Requirements of a Negotiable Instrument** (except as provided in (c) and (d)):

(1) Must be *payable "to Bearer" or "to Order"* either at the time it:
- a) Is Issued
- or b) First comes into Possession of a Holder

and (2) Must be Payable either *on Demand* or *at a Definite Time*

and (3) Must not undertake or instruct the promisor (or Person Ordering Payment) to do *anything other than pay*, except that the promise may also include:
- (i) An undertaking or power to give, maintain, or protect collateral to secure Payment
- or (ii) An Authorization or power to the Holder to
  - a) Confess judgment on collateral
  - or b) "Realize on" collateral
  - or c) Dispose of collateral
- or (iii) A Waiver of the benefit of any law intended for the advantage or protection of an obligor.

4) Must be an *Unconditional Promise or Order* to pay

promise = a written undertaking to pay $, signed by person undertaking to pay
order =

5) Must Promise a *fixed amount*

6) Must Promise/Order to pay *Money* (with or without interest or other charges described in the Promise or Order)

(b) **"Instrument"** — refers to a Negotiable Instrument

(c) **Negotiable Instrument and Check**

An Order is a Negotiable Instrument and a Check if it:

1) Meets all the requirements of 3-104(a) (except for § 3-104(a)(1) — where there is no need to say "Order" or "Bearer")

and 2) Otherwise falls within the definition of "Check" (as per 3-104(f)).

(d) **Promise or Order Not an N/I:** A Promise or Order is not an Instrument if:

1) It is not a Check.

and 2) It contains a *conspicuous statement* (however expressed) that either:

a) The Promise or Order is not Negotiable.

or b) The Promise or Order is not an Instrument governed by Article 3.

and 3) This statement appears on the Promise or Order *either* at the time:

a) It is Issued.

or b) It first comes into possession of a holder.

(e) **Notes and Drafts:**

1) An Instrument is a "**Note**" if it is a *Promise.*
2) An Instrument is a "**Draft**" if it is an *Order* (example: a Check).
3) A Person may treat an Instrument as either a Draft or a Note if it falls within the definition of both.

(f) **"Checks"** —

1. A Check is:

(i) A Draft—other than a Documentary Draft (see § 4-104), Payable on Demand and drawn on a Bank

or (ii) A Cashier's Check—or Teller's Check

2. An Instrument may be a Check even if it is referred to as something else on its face (example: the Check says it is a "Money Order").

(g) **"Cashier's Check"** — A Draft in which both the Drawer and the Drawee are the same Bank (or branches of the same Bank).

(h) **"Teller's Check"** — A Draft drawn by a Bank, either:

(i) On another Bank

or (ii) Payable at or through a Bank

(i) **"Traveler's Check"** — An Instrument that is:

(i) Payable on Demand

and (ii) Drawn on or payable at or through a Bank

and (iii) Designated by the term *"Traveler's Check"* (or by a substantially similar term)

and (iv) Requires a countersignature (by the Person whose specimen signature appears on the Instrument) as a condition to Payment

(j) **"Certificate of Deposit"** —

1. A Certificate of Deposit is an Instrument containing an acknowledgment by a Bank that:

a. A Sum of Money has been received by a Bank

and b. The bank promises to repay that sum of Money

2. A Certificate of Deposit is a Note of the Bank

III. NEGOTIATION AND INDORSEMENT

A. NEGOTIATION:

OVERVIEW

Normally, a **Derivation Rule** applies to transactions, dictating that one may not sell or give away more than he has (example: If Stacey rents a TV from Andrea, Stacey can't sell the TV to Steven in Fee Simple Absolute).

The **Negotiation Rule** is the exception to the Derivation Rule, and applies when a second-hand Purchaser is *either* a "*Holder in Due Course*" or a "*Buyer in the Ordinary Course.*"

Elements of a Negotiation (§ 3-201)

1) Instruments Payable to Bearer: Transfer of possession is all that is required to negotiate a "Bearer" Instrument.
2) Instruments Payable to an Identifiable Person—require two actions for Negotiation:
   a. Transfer of possession
   and b. **Indorsement** by the Person identified in the Instrument (see "INDORSEMENTS")

Negotiation cannot be made by the Issuer (i.e., the Drawer or Maker).

(For special Negotiation rules applying to a Holder in Due Course See "HOLDER IN DUE COURSE" below.)

Relevant Section: § 3-201

§ 3-201: Negotiation:

(a) **Negotiation** is the transfer of possession of an Instrument, *whether voluntary or involuntary,*

1. BY: A Person other than the Issuer
2. TO: A Person who thereby becomes a Holder

(example: Instrument is Payable to Bearer and it is stolen by thief or is found by finder; Either thief or finder can become the Holder of the Instrument when possession is obtained)

(b) **Requirements for Negotiation:**

1. Instruments Payable to an Identifiable Person (except for Negotiation by Remitter):
   - Negotiation requires *both*:
     a. Transfer of Possession of the Instrument
     and b. Indorsement of the Instrument by the Holder (i.e., the Instrument cannot be forged)
2. Instruments Payable to Bearer: May be negotiated by transfer of possession alone

B. INDORSEMENT:

OVERVIEW

An Indorsement is a signature by a Person (other than the Maker) on the Instrument for the purpose of Negotiating the Instrument (§ 3-204).

Indorsements are needed only to Negotiate instruments that are payable to an Identified Person.

Types of Indorsements: There are several different types of Indorsements the Identified Person can make:

1) Blank Indorsement: This Indorsement consists of nothing but the Indorser's signature. The Blank Indorsement turns the Instrument into a "Bearer" Instrument (example: Signed: "*Lucy Ricardo*") (see § 3-205(b)).
2) Special Indorsement is an Indorsement that identifies the Indorsee (i.e., the new Payee) (example: Signed: *"Lucy Ricardo—for Ethel Mertz"*) (see § 3-205(a)).
3) Anomalous Indorsement is an Indorsement made by a Person who is not a Holder. These Indorsements do not affect negotiability. The only effect an Anomalous Indorsement has is that it makes the Anomalous Indorser liable (§ 3-205(d)). Anomalous Indorsers are typically Sureties or Guarantors of the Instrument (under § 3-419); (§ 3-205 Off. Comm. 3).
4) Restrictive Indorsement is an Indorsement that restricts negotiability of the Instrument (example: "Lucy Ricardo—Pay to Fred in trust for Ethel" or "Lucy Ricardo—for Deposit only") (§ 3-206; see also § 3-205 Off. Comm. 2).

Indorsement Rules:

- **Forgeries**: A forged Indorsement has the same effect as no Indorsement (i.e., no title passes and subsequent possessors cannot become Holders, since Negotiation will not occur without a valid Indorsement (§ 3-203(c))).
- **Multiple Identified Parties**:
  - If the Indorsement is made to multiple parties jointly (example: Joe and John), both parties must Indorse the Instrument (§ 3-110(d)).
  - If the Instrument is made available to multiple parties *alternatively* (i.e., John or Joe), then only one party need Indorse (§ 3-110(d)).
  - *Presumption*: If the Instrument is not clear whether it is payable to the parties jointly or alternatively, it is *presumed to be alternatively*.
- **If the required Indorsements are not made, title will not Transfer** (and the Instrument would not be deemed negotiated), and subsequent possessors cannot qualify as "Holders."

Restrictive Indorsements Rules: (§ 3-206)

- Restrictive Indorsements do not prevent someone from obtaining HDC status (see § 3-206(e)).
- In order to become an HDC, the Holder (usually the Bank) must obey the restrictions on the Indorsement.

- If the Depositary Bank does not obey such restrictions, it is considered "*converting*" from the Indorser (§ 3-420; § 3-206(c)(2));
- The Payor Bank and other Collecting Banks will be protected from conversion (under § 3-206(c)(4)).

Indorsement to Banks: See "BANKS AS HOLDER IN DUE COURSE" for special rules and exceptions relating to Indorsements to Banks.

Relevant Sections: § 3-204, § 3-205, § 3-206, § 3-203, § 3-110(d), § 3-420

§ 3-204: Indorsement:

(a) **"Indorsement"**

1. An Indorsement is a signature that is made for the purpose of
   - (i) Negotiating the Instrument.
   - or (ii) Restricting Payment of the Instrument.
   - or (iii) Incurring Indorser's liability on the Instrument.
2. The Indorsement may be alone or accompanied by other words.
3. **When a signature may not be an Indorsement:**
   - a) Indorsements do not include signatures by the *Maker*, *Drawer*, or *Acceptor*.
   - b) Regardless of the signer's intent, a signature (and its accompanying words) will be considered an Indorsement *unless* there is an unambiguous indication that the signature was not made for the purpose of Indorsement, from looking at:
     - 1) The words accompanying the signature.
     - or 2) Terms of the Instrument.
     - or 3) Place of the signature (e.g., not on the back of the instrument, where Indorsements are normally made).
     - or 4) Other circumstances.
4. A paper affixed to an Instrument is considered part of the Instrument for purposes of determining whether a signature is made on the Instrument.

(b) **"Indorser"** — a Person making an Indorsement

(c) **Holders by Indorsement:**

An Indorsement that transfers a security interest in an Instrument is effective as an *unqualified Indorsement*, when determining whether a transferee of the Instrument is a Holder.

(d) **When Holder's Name Differs from Stated Name:**

1. If an Instrument is payable to a Holder under a name different than the holder's, the holder may Indorse:
   a) In the name stated in the Instrument.
   or b) In the Holder's actual name.
   or c) Both.
2. A Person taking the Instrument (for Value or collection) may require the holder to sign both names.

§ 3-205: Types of Indorsements:

(a) **"Special Indorsements":**

1. A Special Indorsement identifies the Person to whom an Instrument (payable to an identified Person or to Bearer) is payable (e.g., "Pay to Mary Jones" or "Pay to the order of Mary Jones").
2. Special Indorsements make an Instrument an Order Instrument.
3. Special Indorsements may be negotiated only by the identified Person (as per § 3-110, since they are considered Order Instruments).

(b) **"Blank Indorsement":**

1. Indorsements that are not "Special Indorsements" (i.e., those not identifying a payee) are considered Blank Indorsements.
2. Instruments that have Blank Indorsements become Bearer instruments.

(c) **Converting Indorsements:** A Blank Indorsement may be converted into a Special Indorsement by writing, above the signature, words that identify the Person to whom the Instrument is made payable.

(d) **"Anomalous Indorsement":**

1. An Indorsement made by a Person who is *not the holder* of the Instrument is an Anomalous Indorsement.
2. An Anomalous Indorsement does not affect the manner in which the Instrument may be negotiated.

§ 3-206: Restrictive Indorsement:

(a) **Indorsement Prohibiting Further Transfer or Negotiation**:

An Indorsement **cannot** prevent further transfer or negotiation of an Instrument by:

a) Limiting Payment to a particular Person
or b) Specifically prohibiting further transfer or negotiation (e.g., "Pay to Mary Smith only")

(b) **Indorsement Stating a Condition:**

1. An Indorsement stating a condition to Payment to the Indorsee does not affect the rights of the Indorsee.
2. The Person paying the Instrument (or taking it for Value or collection) may disregard the condition. No rights or liabilities will be affected by disregarding it.

(c) **Indorsements for Deposit:**

A. Scope: This subsection applies to instruments with the following Indorsements:
   (i) Those described in § 4-201(b)
   (ii) *"For deposit,"* or *"For collection,"* (or other words indicating a purpose to collect Payment for a particular Account) (in blank or to a particular Bank)

B. The following rules apply to the Indorsements described above:
   (1) *A Person* (other than a Bank) who purchases such an Indorsed Instrument will have **Converted** it, *unless:*
      a. The Indorser receives the amount paid for the Instrument.
      or b. The amount paid for the Instrument is applied consistently with the Indorsement.
   (2) *A Depositary Bank* that purchases the Instrument or takes it for collection will **Convert** it *unless:*
      a. The Indorser receives the amount paid by the Bank for the Instrument.
      or b. The amount paid for the Instrument is applied consistently with the Indorsement.
   (3) *A Payor Bank*
      a. The Payor Bank **Converts** the Instrument if it:
         1. Is also the Depositary Bank.
         or 2. Takes the Instrument for immediate Payment over the counter (from a Person other than a Collecting Bank).
      b. The Payor Bank will not be liable for conversion if:
         1. The Indorser receives the amount paid for the Instrument.
         or 2. The amount paid for the Instrument is applied consistently with the Indorsement.
   (4) Except as otherwise provided in (3), a Payor Bank or Intermediary Bank may disregard the Indorsement, and is not liable if the proceeds are not received

by the Indorser or applied consistently with the Indorsement.

(d) **Indorsements to Trustee/Fiduciary**

i) **Scope**:

1) The Following rules apply if an Instrument has an Indorsement containing words indicating that Payment is to be made to an agent, trustee, or other fiduciary, *for the benefit of the Indorser or another Person.*

2) The following rules do not apply to Indorsements made for deposit (under § 3-206(c)).

ii) **Rules Regarding Indorsements to Fiduciaries:**

(1) A Person receiving an Instrument which indicates that Payment is to be made to an agent may pay the Indorsee of the Instrument, without worrying that the Indorsee has breached a fiduciary duty to the Indorser, if:

a) The Person is *either:*

1. Purchasing the Instrument

or 2. Taking the Instrument from the Indorsee *for collection or Payment*

and b) There is no notice of a breach of fiduciary duty (as per § 3-307)

(2) Notice

a) A subsequent transferee or Person paying such an Instrument will not be deemed to have notice unless it knows that the fiduciary dealt with the Instrument or its proceeds in breach of fiduciary duties (see § 3-307).

(e) The above restrictions do not prevent a Person from becoming an HDC unless the Person is a *converter* (under (c)) or has notice or knowledge of a breach of fiduciary duty (as stated in(d)).

(f) **Defense to Payment:**

The Obligor has a defense in an action to enforce Payment of an Instrument if Payment would violate a valid Restrictive Indorsement (under this section).

§ 3-203: Transfer of Instruments; Rights Acquired by Transfer:

(a) **Time of Transfer** — An Instrument is transferred when it is delivered if:

1) The purpose of the delivery is to give the receiver the right to enforce the Instrument.

and 2) The Person delivering it is not the Issuer (i.e., Maker or Drawer (See § 3-105)).

(b) **Rights of the Transferee** ("Shelter Provision")—The transferee will acquire the following rights by transfer (whether or not the Instrument is negotiated):

1) Any rights of the transferor to enforce the Instrument
2) Any rights of the transferor as an HDC, *unless* the transferee engaged in fraud or illegality affecting the Instrument

(c) **Transfer Without Indorsement:**

1) A transferee will have the right to obtain an *unqualified Indorsement* from the transferor if:
   a) The Instrument is transferred for Value, even if transferor did not Indorse the Instrument.
   and b) The parties don't otherwise agree.
2) In such a case the transferee does not become a Holder because the transferor did not Indorse it. (But note: the transferee can still have the rights of a HDC pursuant to § 3-203(b), above.)
3) Negotiation will not be deemed to have occurred until the transferor makes the Indorsement.

(d) **Transfer of Less Than the Entire Instrument** (Note: Value will be deemed given even if the Instrument is sold at a discount.)

1) Negotiation will not occur if the transferor purports to transfer *less than* the entire Instrument.
2) The transferee obtains no rights under Article 3; he obtains the rights of a *partial assignee*.

§ 3-110(d): Identification of Person to Whom Instrument Is Payable:

(d) **Payable to Two or More Persons**:

1. Payable to multiple Persons *alternatively* (e.g., Esther or Lauren): It is Payable to any of them (and may be negotiated, discharged, or enforced by any of them in possession).
2. Payable to multiple Persons jointly (e.g., Esther and Lauren): It is payable to all of them (and may be negotiated, discharged, or enforced only by all of them together).
3. Presumption of alternative payability: If the Instrument is not clear whether it is payable to multiple parties alternatively or jointly, it will be presumed alternatively.

§ 3-420: Conversion of an Instrument:

(a) **Grounds for Conversion**

1) The law applicable to conversion of personal property also applies to instruments (i.e., common law and other statutes).
2) An Instrument is also converted if:
   a) A transferee takes it, without Negotiation, from a Person not Entitled to Enforce the Instrument (i.e., a forgery or missing Indorsement).

   or b) A Bank makes or obtains Payment for a Person not Entitled to Enforce the Instrument or receive Payment.
3) An action for conversion of an Instrument may not be brought by:
   (i) The Issuer or Acceptor of the Instrument

   or (ii) A Payee or Indorsee who did not receive delivery of the Instrument either:
      1. Directly

      or 2. Through delivery to an agent or a co-payee

(b) **Amount of Liability**

1. The amount of liability in (a) is *presumed* to be the *amount payable on the Instrument.*
2. Recovery may not exceed the amount of the plaintiff's interest in the Instrument.

(c) **Representative's Liability:**[9]

A Representative (other than a Depositary Bank) will be liable only for the amount of any proceeds not paid out to a Person not entitled to enforce the Instrument, if:

1) The Representative dealt with the Instrument or its proceeds in **Good Faith.**

and 2) The Representative dealt with an Instrument on behalf of someone not entitled to enforce an Instrument.

and 3) The Representative is not a Depositary Bank.

[9] Former § 3-419 only allowed a Depositary Bank to sue under its capacity as a Depositary Bank, and not a trustee.

IV. HOLDER IN DUE COURSE (§ 3-302)

A. SPECIAL PROPERTY RIGHTS OF AN INNOCENT OWNER:

OVERVIEW

A recurring theme throughout the UCC is the concept of the "Innocent Owner." The term "Innocent Owner" is an E-Z Rules term created to denote the many types of people who may take greater rights in property than the Person selling the property.

The UCC affords special rights to *"Innocent Owners"*:

- Normally, a **Derivation Rule** applies to all transfers of property. According to this rule, a Person may acquire only the property rights of the Person it received the property from (i.e., the Seller cannot sell more than he owns) (example: If Seller only owns 50% of his car, he cannot sell the *entire* car to Buyer; Seller may sell only his 50% interest in the car. Thus, under normal conditions, even if Buyer thought he was buying the entire car, he will have rights only in 50% of the car).
- Under certain circumstances the UCC allows certain parties to take *more* rights than what the Seller had. Such parties can usually take their property *free from all other interests* in it (except for rightful claims of ownership (example: a good faith purchaser cannot acquire good title to stolen goods)).

The following are the five types of **Innocent Owners** afforded such special property rights under the UCC:

- ***Holder in Due Course***—referred to in Articles 3 and 4 (regarding Checks and other Negotiable Instruments).
- ***Holder by Due Negotiation***—referred to in Article 7 (regarding Warehouse Receipts and other Documents of Title) (see "HOLDER BY DUE NEGOTIATION" below).
- ***Bona Fide Purchaser***—referred to in Article 8 (regarding Securities).
- ***Good Faith Purchaser***—referred to in Articles 2 and 6 (regarding the Sale of Goods and Bulk Sales).
- ***Buyer in the Ordinary Course of Business***—referred to in Articles 2 and 9 (regarding the Sale of Goods and Security Interests).

For purposes of Commercial Paper issues, the relevant types of Innocent Owners are:

- The Holder in Due Course

and

- The Holder by Due Negotiation (which is discussed under Documents of Title).

Of the five types of Innocent Owners, only a Holder in Due Course can take free of the rightful claim of someone to the Instrument (§ 3-306).

B. THE HOLDER IN DUE COURSE:

OVERVIEW

HDC Requirements (§ 3-302)

1. The Instrument must be **NEGOTIABLE** (under § 3-104 — § 3-109)

and 2. The transferee must become a **HOLDER** (through Negotiation)

and 3. The transferee must take the Instrument **IN DUE COURSE**, which requires:
   - a. **Value**
   - and b. **Good Faith**
   - and c. **No Notice of a Claim, Defense**, unauthorized signature, or alteration

"Shelter Rule" — A transferee may become an HDC *without* the above requirements by taking the Instrument by *transfer* from an HDC (as per § 3-203) (since the Negotiation Rule gives the transferee whatever title the transferor had) *unless*:

- The transferee is involved in fraud/illegality with respect to the Instrument (§ 3-203)

or
- There is no Indorsement on an Order Instrument (§ 3-201)

Note: Once the HDC chain is broken, a subsequent Holder must fulfill the § 3-302 requirements (listed above) to become an HDC.

Transferor as Holder: Section 3-201(a) transfers the rights of the Indorser to the Indorsee through Negotiation. Section 3-203(b) allows a transferee to "inherit" the transferor's right to enforce the Instrument (including the rights of an HDC, if the transferor was an HDC).

Negotiation with an HDC — The Negotiable Instrument must first be negotiated to someone who qualifies as an HDC under the rules of § 3-302 in order for the "*Shelter Rule*" to take effect:

- An Instrument with a forged Indorsement can't be negotiated (§ 3-203(c))
- An Instrument that is negotiated by fraud is still valid

The initial Payee (i.e., the Person taking the Instrument from the Drawer) cannot become an HDC.

Defenses against an HDC: Holders In Due Course ("HDCs") take free of almost all defenses and setoffs asserted against an Instrument. The only defenses an HDC will take subject to are those listed in § 3-305(a)(1), sometimes called "*Real Defenses*" (as per § 3-305(a)(1) and § 3-305(b)) (see also section on "DEFENSES" below).

- Non-HDCs will be subject to any § 3-305 defenses that the Drawer has against the Payee (see § 3-306), in addition to any claims to the Instrument (as per § 3-306)

"Real Defenses" include (see § 3-305):

1. Infancy — only if State law makes a contract void *or* voidable if made by an infant
2. Incapacity — only if State law renders a contract void (voidable is not enough) if made by a Person without capacity
3. Illegality — only if State law renders a contract void (voidable is not enough) if illegal
4. Duress — only if state law renders a contract Void (voidable is not enough) if made under duress
5. Fraud in Factum — This defense applies when a Person is *induced* to sign something he does not know is an Instrument (whereas *"personal fraud"* arises from a misrepresentation underlying the contract (i.e., "Fraud in the Inducement"))
6. Discharge in Insolvency Proceedings
7. Discharges known to the HDC (usually a personal defense; see below for more detail)
8. Accommodation Party known to the HDC — An Accommodation Party is a form of surety. A surety may assert most defenses available to the person whose obligation the surety is guaranteeing.
9. Material Alteration
10. Forgery — The owner of the Check will not be liable to pay the Check if someone else forged his signature since he will not be considered the Drawer (see § 3-401 and § 3-402).

Relevant Sections: § 3-302, § 3-203, § 3-305, § 3-306

§ 3-302: Holder in Due Course:

(a) A Holder is a **Holder in Due Course** (subject to § 3-302(c) and § 3-106(d)) if:

(1) The Instrument looks authentic — the Instrument when issued or negotiated to the Holder:

a. Does not bear apparent evidence of forgery or Alteration

or b. Is not otherwise so irregular or incomplete as to call into question its authenticity

(2) The Holder takes the Instrument:

(i) For **Value**

and (ii) In **Good Faith**

and (iii) Without notice that the Instrument *either:*

a. Is Overdue

or b. Has been dishonored

or c. Belongs to a series of instruments, in which there is an uncured default with respect to the Payment of another Instrument in that series and (iv) Without Notice that the instrument contains an unauthorized signature or has been altered

and (v) Without Notice of any claim to the Instrument (as described in § 3-306)

and (vi) Without Notice that any party has a defense or claim in recoupment (as described in § 3-305(a))

(b) **Notice of Discharge**

1. Notice of discharge of a party (other than in an insolvency proceeding) is not an adequate notice of a defense under § 3-302(a) (above).
2. However, discharge is effective against a Person who became an HDC with Notice of the discharge.
3. Public Filing or recording of a document does not, itself, constitute notice of a:
   a) Defense
   or b) Claim in recoupment
   or c) Claim to the Instrument

(c) **People Who Do Not Qualify as HDCs:**

1. A Person does not acquire rights of an HDC in an Instrument if he takes the Instrument:
   (i) By *either:*
      a) Legal process
      b) Purchase in a bankruptcy, execution, or creditor's sale (or similar proceeding)
   or (ii) By Purchase as part of a bulk transaction, not in the *Ordinary Course of Business* of the transferor
   or (iii) As the successor in interest to an estate or other organization
2. This section does not apply to the extent that the Person's transferor or predecessor in interest has rights as an HDC.

(d) **Partial Performance:**

If a Promise of performance (that is consideration for an Instrument under § 3-303(a)(1)) has been only *partially* performed, the holder may assert rights as a HDC only to the following fraction of the amount payable under the Instrument:

(Face Value of the Instrument) × **Amount already paid** / **Total Value Promised** (example: if discounted)

(example: Susan purchased a $1,000 Note at a discount, for $900 from Steve. If Susan is an HDC, but has only paid $500, she may only assert her rights as an

HDC for $555.55 (which equals ($1000) x ($500/$900)). This formula is designed to reward the holder with a ratable portion of the bargained-for profit).

(e) **Security Interest in Instrument:**

The Person Entitled to Enforce the Instrument may assert rights as an HDC only up to the amount of the unpaid, secured portion of the Instrument (at the time of enforcement of the Instrument) if:

(i) The Person Entitled to Enforce the Instrument has only a security interest ("S/I") in the Instrument

and (ii) The Person obliged to pay the Instrument has, against the Person who granted the S/I, *either*

a) A Defense

or b) A Claim in recoupment

or c) A Claim to the Instrument

(f) **Notice:** In order to be effective, notice must be received at a time and manner that gives a *reasonable opportunity* to act on it.

(g) This section is subject to any law (state statutory and case law and any other similar law that may evolve in the future) limiting the status of an HDC in particular classes of transactions.

§ 3-203: Transfer of Instruments; Rights Acquired by Transfer:

(a) **Time of Transfer**—An Instrument is transferred when it is delivered if:

1) The purpose of the delivery is to give the receiver the right to enforce the Instrument.

and 2) The Person delivering it is not the Issuer (i.e., Maker or Drawer (see § 3-105)).

(b) **Rights of the Transferee** ("Shelter Provision")—The transferee will acquire the following rights by transfer (whether or not the Instrument is negotiated):

1) Any rights of the transferor to enforce the Instrument

2) Any rights of the transferor as an HDC, *unless* the transferee engaged in fraud or illegality affecting the Instrument

(c) **Transfer Without Indorsement:**

1) A transferee will have the right to obtain an *unqualified Indorsement* from the transferor if:

a) The Instrument is transferred for Value, even if transferor did not Indorse the Instrument.

and b) The parties don't otherwise agree.

2) In such a case the transferee does not become a Holder because the transferor did not Indorse it. (But note: the transferee can still have the rights of a HDC pursuant to §3-203(b), above.)
3) Negotiation will not be deemed to have occurred until the transferor makes the Indorsement.

(d) **Transfer of Less Than the Entire Instrument** (Note: Value will be deemed gievn even if the Instrument is sold at a discount)

1) Negotiation will not occur if the transferor purports to transfer *less than* the entire Instrument.
2) The transferee obtains no rights under Article 3; he obtains the rights of a partial assignee.

§3-305: Defenses and Claims in Recoupment:

(a) Except as otherwise provided in this subsection, the right to enforce the obligation of a party to pay an Instrument is subject to:

(1) Certain Defenses (These are sometimes referred to as "Real" Defenses):
- (i) *Infancy*—of the obligor (to the extent it is a defense to a simple contract)
- or (ii) *Duress, lack of legal capacity, illegality*— of the Transaction (which under other law would nullify the obligor's obligation; Note: the obligation must be void, not merely voidable)
- or (iii) *Fraud in the inducement*—fraud that caused the obligor to sign the Instrument not knowing the character or essential terms of the Instrument (nor having a reasonable opportunity to learn of its character or essential terms)
- or (iv) *Discharge*—of the obligor in an insolvency proceeding

and (2) Other Defenses (These are sometimes referred to as "Personal" Defenses):
- i) Obligor's defenses as stated elsewhere in Article 3
- or ii) Other defenses available to the obligor under Payment of a simple contract (e.g., Failure of consideration, fraud as to the underlying subject matter)

and (3) Claims in Recoupment:
- a) A claim in recoupment of the obligor will arise against the original Payee of the Instrument if the claim arises from the transaction that gave rise to the Instrument.
- b) The claim of the obligor may be brought only
  - 1) Against a transferee of the Instrument
  - and 2) To reduce the amount owing on the Instrument at the time the action is brought (i.e., to enter a right to setoff).

(b) **Right of a Holder in Due Course:**

The HDC's right to enforce an Instrument is subject only to the "Real Defenses" stated in § 3-305(a)(1) (above), but not those stated in (a)(2) or (a)(3).

(c) **Obligor Using People's Defenses:**

1. An obligor cannot use another Person's defenses (3-306) against the Person entitled to Payment of the Instrument *unless* the other Person:
   a) Is joined in the action
   and b) Personally asserts the claim against the Person Entitled to Enforce the Instrument.
2. Lost/Stolen Instruments: An obligor is not obligated to pay the Instrument if:
   a) The Person seeking enforcement does not have the rights of an HDC.
   and b) The obligor proves that the Instrument is a lost or stolen Instrument.

(d) **Actions to Enforce an Instrument Against an Accommodation Party**

The Accommodation Party may assert all defenses as the Accommodated Party (original obligor), except:

1. Infancy and Lack of Legal Capacity (§ 3-305(a)(1))

and 2. Discharge in Insolvency proceedings (§ 3-305(a)(3))

Revised Article 3 (2002) adds:

(e) **Consumer Transaction:** If law (other than this Article) requires that an Instrument include a statement to the effect that the "*rights of a holder or transferee are subject to a claim or defense that the issuer could assert against the original payee,*" and the Instrument does not include such a statement:

(1) The Instrument has the same effect as if it included such a statement

and (2) The Issuer may assert all claims and defenses that would have been available if the statement were included

and (3) Claims may be asserted against the holder or transferee as if such statement were included.

(f) This section is subject to law other than this article that establishes a different rule for consumer transactions.

§ 3-306: Claims to an Instrument: (Claims of ownership)

a) A Non-HDC takes an Instrument subject to *any claim of a property or possessory right* in the Instrument or its proceeds, including:

1. Claims to rescind a negotiation

or 2. Claims to recover the Instrument or its proceeds

b) A Holder in Due Course (HDC) takes free of the claim to the Instrument.

1) Holder:

OVERVIEW

One may become a Holder of an Instrument through **Negotiation** (see § 1-201(20); and section on "NEGOTIATION"):

- *Bearer Instrument*—The Holder must have the Instrument in his possession.

or

- *Identified Instrument*—The Holder must be identified in the Instrument (on the front or in a Special Indorsement) and take possession.
  - Special Indorsements (§ 3-205(a))—Only the identified Person can be a Holder by taking possession of it (unless the Indorsement is forged; § 3-403(a)).
  - Blank Indorsement (§ 3-205(b))—Only possession is needed to become a Holder (the Check becomes a Bearer Check once it is Indorsed in blank).

A Person cannot be a Holder if a necessary signature or Indorsement is forged (§ 3-403(a)).

Negotiation Requirements (§ 3-201) (see also "NEGOTIATION"):

- Instruments Payable to Bearer—Transfer of possession is good enough for Negotiation
- Instruments Payable to an Identifiable Person—Require 2 actions:
  - Transfer of possession

  and
  - **Indorsement** by the Person identified in the Instrument (see "INDORSEMENTS")

Relevant Sections: § 3-205(a), § 3-205(b), § 3-201

§ 3-205: Types of Indorsements:

(a) **"Special Indorsements":**

1. A Special Indorsement identifies the Person to whom an Instrument (payable to an identified Person or to Bearer) is payable (e.g., "Pay to Mary Jones" or "Pay to the order of Mary Jones").
2. Special Indorsements make an Instrument an Order Instrument.
3. Special Indorsements may be negotiated only by the identified Person (as per § 3-110, since they are considered Order Instruments).

(b) **"Blank Indorsement":**

1. Indorsements that are not "Special Indorsements" (i.e., those not identifying a payee) are considered Blank Indorsements.
2. Instruments that have Blank Indorsements become Bearer instruments.

§ 3-201: Negotiation:

(a) **Negotiation** is the <u>Transfer of Possession</u> of an Instrument, *whether voluntary or involuntary,*

1. BY: A Person other than the Issuer
2. TO: A Person who thereby becomes a Holder

(example: Instrument is Payable to Bearer and it is stolen by thief or is found by finder; Either thief or finder can become the Holder of the Instrument when possession is obtained)

(b) **Requirements for Negotiation:**

1. <u>Instruments Payable to an Identifiable Person</u> (except for Negotiation by Remitter):
   - <u>Negotiation requires *both:*</u>
     a. Transfer of Possession of the Instrument
     and b. Indorsement of the Instrument by the Holder (i.e., the Instrument cannot be forged)
2. <u>Instruments Payable to Bearer:</u> May be negotiated by Transfer of Possession alone

2) In Due Course:

OVERVIEW

1) **VALUE** (§ 3-303)—
   - To become a Holder in Due Course, the Holder must have *actually* given Value for the N/I ((§ 3-302(d)).
     - The HDC can assert her rights only up to the amount of Value she *actually* gave (example: If you only gave $40,000 for a $60,000 N/I and Promise to pay the remaining $20,000 later, you are an HDC only up to the $40,000, which is the Value you actually gave)).
   - If an Instrument is purchased at a *discount*, the amount of the claim which the Holder may assert her rights as an HDC will be pro-rated as follows (§ 3-302(d)):

$$\text{(Face Value of the Instrument)} \times \frac{\text{Money paid already}}{\text{Discounted Price}}$$

   - Note: "Value" as defined in § 1-201(44) **does not apply** to Articles 3 and 4 (see § 3-303 Off. Comm. 1 and § 1-201 Off. Comm. 44).
2) **GOOD FAITH**—Articles 3 and 4 require *both* (§ 3-103(a)(4)):
   1. Honesty in Fact

   and 2. The observance of *Reasonable Commercial Standards* of fair dealing.[10]
3) **NO NOTICE of a Claim or Defense**—Notice will be deemed given in the following cases:
   - Adverse Claim—this includes instruments that are:
     - Overdue/Stale (a Check is stale after 90 Days (§ 3-304(a)(2)))
     - Dishonored
     - Part of a series (or installments) in which there is an uncured default
     - Subject to other claims
     - Subject to defenses of a party (in § 3-305)
   - Notice by Suspicion—Notice that is apparent on the Instrument (example: the Instrument seems irregular or not authentic); a suspicious-looking instrument can often put a Person on notice of a potential outstanding claim.

Relevant Sections: § 3-303, § 1-203, § 1-201(19), § 3-103(4)

§ 3-303: Value and Consideration:

(a) **"Value"**—An Instrument is issued or transferred for **Value** if:

(1) It is issued or transferred for a *promise of performance* (only to the extent the Promise has been performed)

[10] Under former Article 3, only Honesty in Fact was required to establish Good Faith.

or (2) A transferee acquires an S/I or other lien on the Instrument (other than a judicial lien)

or (3) It is issued or transferred as Payment or security of a pre-existing ("antecedent") claim (against any Person), whether or not the claim was due

or (4) It is issued or transferred in exchange for an N/I

or (5) It is issued or transferred in exchange for an irrevocable obligation to a third party by the Person taking the Instrument

(b) **"Consideration"**—any consideration sufficient to support a simple contract.

1. The Drawer/Maker has a defense if the Instrument is issued without consideration.
2. If an Instrument is issued for a *promise of performance*, the Maker/Drawer has a defense *to the extent* the Promise has not been performed (and is due).
3. If an Instrument is issued for Value (as stated in (a)), it will also be considered issued for consideration.

§1-203: Good Faith:

"Every contract or duty within this Act imposes an obligation of Good Faith in its performance or enforcement."

§1-201(19): "Good Faith":

"Good Faith" means honesty in fact in the Conduct or Transaction Concerned (see also §3-103(a)(4) for Negotiable Instruments).

§3-103(4): Definitions:

***

(4) "**Good Faith**"—Requires both:

a) Honesty in fact

and b) The observance of *reasonable commercial standards of fair dealing*

V. DEFENSES

OVERVIEW

Defenses are excuses not to pay an Instrument that may be raised by the Drawer, Indorser, or any other party liable to pay the Instrument.

There are two types of defenses:
- "Real Defenses"—available against all Holders of an Instrument. *Real Defenses* focus primarily on the validity of the Instrument itself, and not the situation leading to its creation.
- "Personal Defenses"—available only against non-HDCs. *Personal Defenses* include all other defenses that would be available in contract actions (such as personal fraud, setoffs, failure of consideration) (see § 3-305(a)(2)) relating to the Instrument.

Only **Real Defenses** may be used against an HDC. An HDC takes free of all "personal defenses." A holder who is not an HDC takes the Instrument subject to rightful claims (example: from a prior holder who lost the Instrument or had it stolen from him) (see § 3-306).

Examples of Personal Defenses:
- Lack of Consideration for an underlying contract
- Personal fraud
- Setoffs
- Breach of Contract
- Breach of Warranty

Real Defenses include (see § 3-305):
1. Infancy—only if State law makes a contract void *or* voidable if made by an infant
2. Incapacity—only if State law renders a contract void (voidable is not enough) if made by a Person without capacity
3. Illegality—only if State law renders a contract void (voidable is not enough) if illegal
4. Duress—only if state law renders a contract void (voidable is not enough) if made under duress
5. Fraud in Factum—this defense applies when a Person is *induced* to sign something he doesn't know is an Instrument (whereas, *"personal fraud"* arises from a misrepresentation underlying the contract) (example: the Signor is told that the Instrument was a tax form).
6. Discharge in Insolvency Proceedings
7. Discharges known to the HDC (usually a personal defense; see below for more detail)
8. Accommodation Party known to the HDC—an Accommodation Party is a form of surety. A surety may assert most defenses available to the person whose obligation the surety is guaranteeing.
9. Material Alteration, to the extent of the altered amount (§ 3-407)
10. Forgery—the owner of the Instrument will not be liable to pay the Instrument if someone else forged his signature, since he is not considered the Drawer (see § 3-401 and § 3-402).

Relevant Sections: § 3-301, § 3-305, § 3-306

§ 3-301: Person Entitled to Enforce Instrument:

a. **"Person Entitled to Enforce"** is *either:*

(i) The Holder of the Instrument

or (ii) A non-Holder in possession of the Instrument — who has the rights of a holder

or (iii) A Person Not in possession of the Instrument — entitled to enforce the Instrument pursuant to § 3-309 (lost/stolen Instrument) or § 3-418(d) (Payment/Acceptance by mistake)

b. A Person may be entitled to enforce an Instrument, even if:

1. The Person is not the owner of the Instrument.

or 2. The Person is in wrongful possession of the Instrument.

§ 3-305: Defenses and Claims in Recoupment:

(a) Except as otherwise provided in this subsection, the right to enforce the obligation of a party to pay an Instrument is subject to:

(1) Certain defenses (These are sometimes referred to as "Real" defenses):

(i) *Infancy* — of the obligor (to the extent it is a defense to a simple contract)

or (ii) *Duress, lack of legal Capacity, illegality* — of the Transaction (which under other law would nullify the obligor's obligation; Note: the obligation must be void, not merely voidable)

or (iii) *Fraud in the Inducement* — fraud that caused the obligor to sign the Instrument not knowing the character or essential terms of the Instrument (nor having a reasonable opportunity to learn of its character or essential terms)

or (iv) *Discharge* — of the obligor in an insolvency proceeding

and (2) Other defenses (These are sometimes referred to as "Personal" Defenses):

i) Obligor's defenses as stated elsewhere in Article 3

or ii) Other defenses available to the obligor under Payment of a simple contract (e.g., Failure of consideration, fraud as to the underlying subject matter)

and (3) Claims in recoupment:
a) A claim in recoupment of the obligor will arise against the original Payee of the Instrument if the claim arises from the transaction that gave rise to the Instrument.
b) The claim of the obligor may be brought only
1) Against a transferee of the Instrument
and 2) To reduce the amount owing on the Instrument at the time the action is brought (i.e., to enter a right to setoff)

(b) **Right of a Holder in Due Course:**

The HDC's right to enforce an Instrument is subject only to the "Real Defenses" stated in § 3-305(a)(1) (above), but not those stated in (a)(2) or (a)(3).

(c) **Obligor Using People's Defenses:**

1. An obligor cannot use another Person's defenses (3-306) against the Person entitled to Payment of the Instrument *unless* the other Person:
   a) Is joined in the action
   and b) Personally asserts the claim against the Person Entitled to Enforce the Instrument.
2. Lost/Stolen Instruments: An obligor is not obligated to pay the Instrument if:
   a) The Person seeking enforcement does not have the rights of an HDC.
   and b) The obligor proves that the Instrument is a lost or stolen Instrument.

(d) **Actions to Enforce an Instrument Against an Accommodation Party**

The Accommodation Party may assert all defenses as the Accommodated Party (original obligor), except:

1. Infancy and lack of legal capacity (§ 3-305(a)(1))
and 2. Discharge in insolvency proceedings (§ 3-305(a)(3))

Revised Article 3 (2002) adds:
(e) **Consumer Transaction:** If law (other than this Article) requires that an instrument include a statement to the effect that the "*rights of a holder or transferee are subject to a claim or defense that the issuer could assert against the original payee,*" and the instruments does not include such a statement:
(1) The Instrument has the same effect as if it included such a statement
and (2) The Issuer may assert all claims and defenses that would have been available if the statement were included

and (3) Claims may be asserted against the holder or transferee as if such statement were included.

(f) This section is subject to law other than this article that establishes a different rule for consumer transactions.

§ 3-306: Claims to an Instrument:

a) A Non-HDC takes an Instrument subject to *any claim of a property or possessory right* in the Instrument or its proceeds, including:

1. Claims to rescind a negotiation

or 2. Claims to recover the Instrument or its proceeds

b) A Holder in Due Course (HDC) takes free of the claim to the Instrument.

VI. LIABILITY AND WARRANTY

A. INTRODUCTION:

OVERVIEW

Signature Rule: A Person will not be liable on an Instrument unless he or she *Signs* or *Accepts* it (§ 3-401).

Types of Liability on a Instrument

- **Suits "on the Instrument":** (Article 3 & 4 claims)
  - Contract—A party to the Negotiable Instrument transaction may sue the Drawer for a Dishonored Instrument under general contract law principles (because the drawer has not paid for goods or services received) and may also sue on the Instrument itself. However, before these claims can be made, the Drawee (i.e., Payor Bank) must first Dishonor the Instrument. Only after dishonor will the Drawer/Maker be liable on the Instrument (§ 3-414).
  - Conversion—Under certain circumstances, the Payee may sue the Drawer for conversion (see "CONVERSION").
- **Suits "off of the Instrument":**
  1) Implied Warranties (Article 3 & 4 claims)—(See "WARRANTIES")
  2) Breach of Contract *(see also*, "CHECKS AS PAYMENT")
     - If a Contract is paid with a Certified Check, the Drawer will be immediately discharged of his obligation to pay (as if paid with cash) (§ 3-310(a)).
     - If a Contract is paid with a non-certified Instrument, the contract obligation of the Drawer is *suspended* (§ 3-310); the obligation under the contract will only be discharged once the Instrument is *Paid* or *Accepted* by the Bank (example: buyer's obligation to pay seller for goods will be suspended until its Check is Dishonored).
     - A *suspended* obligation cannot be the basis for a cause of action until the check is Dishonored (§ 3-310(b)(1)).

Most Common Types of Liability Situations:

- Wrongful Dishonor
- Countermanded Checks
- Forgery, Theft, and Alteration

Relevant Sections: § 3-401, § 3-310

§ 3-401: Signature:

(a) **Liability on an Instrument:**

A Person will be liable on an Instrument only if:

(i) The Person has *Signed* the Instrument.

or (ii) A Representative has Signed it for the Person (and such signature is binding on the Represented Person under § 3-402).

(b) **Method of Signature:**

A signature may be made by:

(i) Any of the following means:

a) Manually

or b) By use of a machine or device

and (ii) The use of:

a. A name (including a trade or assumed name)

or b. Any of the following if they are *executed or adopted* by a Person with a *present intention to authenticate a writing*:

1) Word

or 2) Mark

or 3) Symbol

§ 3-310: Effectiveness of Instruments as Payment:

(a) **Effectiveness of Certified/Bank Checks**

1. Unless otherwise agreed, any of the following Checks may be used to pay off an obligation, and shall discharge the obligation as if Money had been paid:
   a. Certified Check
   b. Cashier's Check
   c. Teller's Check
2. Discharge of an obligation does not affect the obligor's liability as Indorser of the Instrument.

(b) **Effectiveness of Notes and Uncertified Checks**

i) Unless otherwise agreed, if any of the following Instruments are used to pay off an obligation, the obligation will be *"Suspended"* in the amount of the Instrument (to the same extent the obligation would be discharged if paid off with Money):

a) Note

b) Uncertified Check

ii) This rule is subject to (a) above.

iii) Rules for Notes and Uncertified Checks:

(1) Uncertified Checks—

a. The obligation will continue to be "suspended" until:

1) The Check is dishonored (in which case the obligation will be revived).

or 2) The Check is Certified (in which case the obligation will be discharged as per (a)).

or 3) The Check is Paid (in which case the obligation will be discharged as per (a)).

b. Payment or Certification of the Check results in discharge of the obligation in the amount of the Check.

(2) Notes—

a. The obligation will continue to be "suspended" until:

1) The Note is dishonored (in which case the obligation will be revived).

or 2) The Note is Paid.

b. Payment of the Note results in discharge of the obligation in the amount of the Payment.

(3) Dishonor of Check or Note:

a. **Obligee Entitled to Enforce**—If the obligee of the obligation (for which the Instrument was taken) is the Person Entitled to Enforce the Instrument, upon Dishonor he may enforce either:

1) The Instrument

or 2) The obligation (may sue on the underlying obligation, most likely an action in contract)

b. **Instrument of a Third Party**—If an Instrument of a Third Person is Indorsed over to the obligee in Payment of the obligation, the obligee will be discharged; the discharge of the obligor on the Instrument also discharges the underlying obligation (but the instrument may still be enforced against the third person Maker or Drawer) (e.g., buyer delivers to seller an uncertified personal Check of X payable to the Order of buyer in Payment of the price of goods, and buyer Indorses the Check over to seller).

c. This rule (§ 3-310(b)(3)) is subject to (4) (below).

(4) Dishonor of Check or Note:

a. **Non-Obligee Entitled to Enforce**—If the Person Entitled to Enforce the instrument is not the obligee, the obligee may not enforce the "*suspended*" part of the obligation (i.e., the amount reflected in the Instrument).

b. **Obligee Without Possession of the Instrument**—If the obligee is the Person Entitled to Enforce the Instrument but no longer has possession of it (i.e., it was stolen, lost, or destroyed), then the following rules apply:

1. He may not enforce the "*suspended*" part of the obligation (i.e., the amount reflected in the Instrument).

2. The obligee's rights against the obligor are limited to enforcement of the Instrument, to such extent.

(c) **Other Instruments:**

1. The effect of an Instrument being used to pay for an obligation is:
   (i) That stated in §3-310(a)—if the Bank is liable for the Instrument as Maker or Acceptor
   (ii) That stated in §3-310(b)—in all other cases
2. This subsection applies only to instruments not included in §3-310(a) or (b).

B. WARRANTIES:

OVERVIEW

Generally

- Warranties are implied in certain Negotiable Instrument transactions.
- Action must be brought within <u>30 Days</u> after a breach of warranty is discovered (§ 3-416(c); § 3-417(e); § 4-207(d); § 4-208(e)).[11]

Transfer Warranties: (§ 3-416; § 4-207):[12]

- Transfer warranties are made by anyone who transfers the Negotiable Instrument (§ 3-417(a); § 4-208(a)).
- Transfer warranties are made by any transferor *except:*
  1) <u>The Issuer</u>—for the initial transfer (there are no issuance warranties).

  and 2) <u>The Presentor</u>—for the final transfer (i.e., transfer to the Payor Bank; The final transferor will be liable under "Presentment Warranties" (discussed below)).
- **<u>Warranties Made:</u>**
  1) Good Title (i.e., transferor is a creditor, or a "Person Entitled to Enforce the Instrument")
  2) Rightful transfer (i.e., transferor rightfully obtained title to Instrument)
  3) Authentic and Authorized signature and Indorsements
  4) No Alteration
  5) No § 3-305 "*Real*" defenses apply
  6) No knowledge of Maker/Drawer's Insolvency
- **<u>Requirements to Obtain Transfer Warranties:</u>**
  1) There must be a transfer for <u>Consideration</u> (§ 3-416(a); § 4-207(a))

  and 2) The transferor must <u>Indorse</u> the Instrument (§ 3-416(a)).
     - Banks do not have to obtain an Indorsement to get transfer Warranties (§ 4-207).
- If there is no Indorsement the warranty will only run to the immediate transferee. If there is an Indorsement, the warranty will run to all subsequent transferees.

Presentment Warranties:

Presentment Warranties are made by the person transferring the Instrument to the Payor.

- **<u>Presentment Warranties Made:</u>**
  1) Good title (i.e., transferor is a <u>*Person Entitled to Enforce*</u> the Instrument)
  2) Rightful transfer (i.e., transferor rightfully obtained title to the Instrument)
  3) No Alteration
  4) Authorized and Authentic Indorsements
  5) No knowledge that the purported Drawer's signature is unauthorized or forged.

---

[11] Under former Article 4, the time limit to bring an action was limited to a *"reasonable time"* (see former: 4-207(4))

[12] For former Article 3 and 4 Transfer Warranty provisions see former 3-417 and former 4-207.

- *Forgery:*
  - Good title is not affected if the Drawer's signature is forged (It is only affected if an Indorsement is forged, since the Drawer (i.e., the Forger who Signed it) will always be liable on the Instrument).
  - Knowledge of the Drawer's Forgery: If the Presentor (the Person presenting the N/I) knows of the forgery, she has breached her Presentment Warranty (§ 3-417(a)(3)), *unless:*

    1. The Presentor is the Maker/Drawer

    or 2. The Presentor is an HDC and

    a) The Draft has already been accepted (example: a Certified Check)

    and b) The HDC learned of the Drawer's forgery *after* he negotiated it.

Relevant Sections: § 3-416, § 4-207, § 3-417, § 4-208

§ 3-416: Transfer Warranties:

(a) **Warranties:** When a Person transfers an Instrument for consideration, the following warranties are made to a transferee and, if the transfer is by Indorsement, to any subsequent transferees:

(1) **Entitlement to Enforce:** The warrantor is a Person Entitled to Enforce the Instrument.

and (2) **Authentic and Authorized Signatures:** All signatures on the Instrument are Authentic and Authorized.

and (3) **No Alterations:** The Instrument has not been altered.

and (4) **No Defense of Recoupment:** The Instrument is not subject to a defense or claim in Recoupment of any party (which can be asserted against the warrantor).

and (5) **No Knowledge of Insolvency:** The warrantor has no knowledge of any insolvency proceedings of the Maker, Acceptor, or Drawer (in the case of an Unaccepted Draft).

Revised Article 3 (2002) adds:

and (6) **Remote Consumer Item:** With respect to a Remotely-Created Consumer Item, that the person on whose account the Item is drawn authorized the issuance of the Item in the amount for which the Item is drawn.

(b) **Damages for Breach of Warranty:**

1. A Person may recover (from the warrantor) the amount lost as a result of a breach of warranty, if:
   a. The Transfer Warranties under (a) are made to that Person.
   b. The Person took the Instrument in Good Faith.

2. Limitation: The damages cannot exceed the following:

The amount of the Instrument
\+ **Expenses and loss of interest** (incurred as a result of the breach)

(c) **Notice and Disclaimer:**

1. The Warranties in (a) cannot be disclaimed for Checks.
2. If the claimant does not notify the warrantor of the claim for breach of warranty within 30 Days after the claimant has *reason to know* of the breach (and the identity of the warrantor), the warrantor will be discharged of any amount of damages he incurs from the delay in giving notice of the claim (i.e., deductions for failure to mitigate).

(d) **Cause of Action:** A cause of action for breach of warranty (under this section) accrues when the claimant has *reason to know of the breach.*

§ 4-207: Transfer Warranties:[13]

(a) **Warranties:**

The following warranties are made to a transferee and any *subsequent* Collecting Banks by a Customer or Collecting Bank when it transfers an Item for a Settlement or other Consideration:

(1) **Entitlement to Enforce:** The warrantor is a Person Entitled to Enforce the Item (see § 3-301).
and (2) **Authentic and Authorized Signatures:** All signatures on the Item are Authentic and Authorized.
and (3) **No Alterations:** The Item has not been altered.
and (4) **No defense of recoupment:** The Item is not subject to a defense or claim in recoupment (as per § 3-305(a)) of any party (which can be asserted against the warrantor).
and (5) **No knowledge of insolvency:** The warrantor has no knowledge that the Maker, Acceptor, or Drawer (in the case of an Unaccepted Draft) is involved in Insolvency Proceedings (see § 1-201(22)).

Revised Article 3 (2002) adds:
and (6) **Remote consumer Item:** With respect to a Remotely Created Consumer Item, that the person on whose account the Item is drawn authorized the issuance of the Item in the amount for which the Item is drawn.

[13] Note: § 4-207 is almost identical to § 3-416's Transfer Warranty section, except for § 4-207(b).

(b) **Item Dishonored:**

1. If an Item is Dishonored, a Customer or Collecting Bank (which transfers the Item and receives Settlement for it) is obligated to pay the amount due on the Item:
   (i) According to the terms of the Item (at the time it was transferred).
   or (ii) If an Incomplete Item: according to the terms of the Item when completed (as per §3-115 and §3-407).
2. The obligation of a transferor is owed to:
   a) The transferee—who takes the Item in *Good Faith.*
   and b) Any subsequent Collecting Banks taking the Item in *Good Faith.*
3. Transferor Cannot Disclaim: A transferor cannot disclaim these obligations by indorsing the Item *"without recourse"* or otherwise disclaiming liability.

(c) **Damages for Breach of Warranty:**

1. A Person may recover from the warrantor the amount he lost as a result of the breach of warranty, if:
   a. The warranties (in (a) above) are made to him.
   and b. He took the Item in *Good Faith.*
2. Limitation: The damages cannot exceed:

   The amount of the Item
   \+ **Expenses and Loss of Interest** (incurred as a result of the breach)

(d) **Notice and Disclaimer:**

1. The warranties in (a) cannot be disclaimed for Checks.
2. If the claimant does not notify the warrantor of the breach within 30 days after the claimant had *reason to know* of the breach (and the identity of the warrantor), the warrantor will be discharged of any damages he incurs from the delay in notice.

(e) **Cause of Action:** A cause of action for breach of warranty (under this section) accrues when the claimant has *reason to know* of the breach.

§ 3-417: Presentment Warranties:

(a) **Presentment Warranties:**

i) Presentment warranties will be available only if:
   1) An Unaccepted Draft is presented to the Drawee for Payment or Acceptance. The warranties will be made by:
      (i) The Person obtaining Payment or Acceptance.
      and (ii) A previous transferor of the Draft.
   and 2) The Drawee Pays or Accepts the Draft in Good Faith.

ii) The Warranties include:
   (1) **<u>Good Title and Rightful Transfer:</u>** The warrantor is (or was at the time the warrantor transferred the Draft):
      a) A Person Entitled to Enforce the Draft.
      or b) A Person authorized to obtain Payment or Acceptance of the Draft on behalf of a Person Entitled to Enforce the Draft.
   (2) **<u>No Alteration:</u>** The Draft has not been Altered.
   (3) **<u>Authentic and Authorized Signature:</u>** The Warrantor has <u>No knowledge</u> that the Drawer's signature is unauthorized.

(b) **Damages for Breach of Warranty:**

1. A Drawee making Payment may recover from any warrantor (damages for breach of warranty):

   The amount paid by the Drawee
   – **The amount the Drawee received** (or is entitled to receive) **from the Drawer** (because of Payment)
   + **Compensation for expenses and loss of interest** (resulting from the breach)

2. The Drawee's rights are not affected by any failure to exercise Ordinary Care in making Payment.
3. **Defense:** If the Drawee accepts the Draft, the Acceptor may use Breach of Warranty as a defense to the obligation of the Acceptor.
4. If the Acceptor makes Payment for the Draft, he may collect damages as provided in section (b).

(c) **Available Defenses:**

1. <u>Scope:</u> Section 3-417(c) applies if a Drawee asserts a claim for breach of warranty under (a) based on:
   a) An Unauthorized Indorsement of the Draft ((a)(1))
   or b) An Alteration of the Draft ((a)(2))
2. The warrantor may use the following defenses:
   a) The Indorsement is effective under § 3-404 or § 3-405.

or b) The Drawer is precluded from asserting that his signature is unauthorized or that the Draft was altered (under § 3-406 and § 4-406).

(d) **Payment Warranties:**

1. Scope: Section 3-417(d) applies if:
   (i) A dishonored Draft is presented for Payment to *either*:
      a. The Drawer
      or b. An Indorser.
   or (ii) Any other Instrument is presented for Payment to a party obligated to pay the Instrument.
   and (iii) Payment is Received.
2. **Warranties**
   (1) The Person obtaining Payment (and a prior transferor of the Instrument) warrants to the Person making Payment that the warrantor is (or was at the time the Draft was transferred):
      a) A Person Entitled to Enforce the Instrument
      or b) A Person authorized to obtain Payment on behalf of a Person Entitled to Enforce the Instrument.
   (2) The Person making Payment may recover the following from *any* warrantor for breach of warranty:

   The amount paid
   \+ **Expenses and loss of interest** (resulting from Breach of Warranty)

(e) **Notice and Disclaimer:**

1. The Warranties in (a) and (d) cannot be disclaimed for Checks.
2. If the claimant does not notify the warrantor of a claim for breach within 30 days after the claimant has *reason to know* of the breach and the identity of the warrantor, the liability of the warrantor under (b) and (d) is discharged of any amount of damages he incurs from the delay (i.e., deductions for failure to mitigate).

(f) **Cause of Action:** A cause of action for Breach of Warranty (under this section) accrues when the claimant has *reason to know of the breach.*[14]

---

[14] Under former Article 3, the warrantor had to be the owner of the Check, and not a "Person Entitled to Indorse Check."

§ 4-208: Presentment Warranties:[15]

(a) **Presentment Warranties:**

I. Presentment warranties are made to the Drawee by the following Persons:
   - (i) The Person obtaining Payment or Acceptance (at the time of Presentment) if:
     - a) An Unaccepted Draft (as defined in § 4-104) is presented to the Drawee for Payment or Acceptance
     - and b) The Drawee Pays or Accepts the Draft (as defined in § 4-104) in Good Faith
   - (ii) A previous transferor of the Draft (at the time the previous transferor made its transfer) if:
     - a) An Unaccepted Draft (as defined in § 4-104) is presented to the Drawee for Payment or Acceptance
     - and b) The Drawee Pays or Accepts the Draft (as defined in § 4-104) in Good Faith

II. Presentment Warranties include:
   - (1) **Good Title:** The warrantor is (or was at the time the warrantor transferred the Draft) either:
     - a) A Person Entitled to Enforce the Draft (see § 3-301).
     - or b) A Person authorized to obtain Payment or Acceptance of the Draft (on behalf of a Person Entitled to Enforce the Draft).
   - and (2) **No Alteration:** The Draft has not been altered.
   - and (3) **Authorized Signature:** The warrantor has no knowledge that the signature (of the purported Drawer) is unauthorized.

Revised Article 3 (2002) adds:

- and (4) **Remote Consumer Item:** With respect to a Remotely Created Consumer Item, that the person on whose account the Item is drawn authorized the issuance of the Item in the amount for which the Item is drawn.

(b) **Recovery:**

1) Payment: If the Drawee paid for the Draft it may recover from the warrantor:
   - a) Damages for breach of warranty — equal to:

The Amount Paid by the Drawee

– **The Amount the Drawee received** (or is entitled to receive) **as Payment from the Drawer because of Payment**

[15] This section is almost identical to § 3-417's Presentment Warranty section.

plus b) Compensation for expenses and loss of interest (resulting from the breach)

2) **Acceptance:** If the Drawee Accepted the Draft, then the following rules apply:
   (i) The Acceptor may use "breach of warranty" as a defense not to pay the Draft (or to fulfill any of his other obligations under the Draft).
   and (ii) If the Acceptor already paid he may recover the amounts specified above for breach of warranty damages.
3) The Drawee's right to recover these damages is not affected by the Drawee's lack of *ordinary care* in making Payment.

(c) **Warrantor's Defenses:**

1) The warrantor may defend a claim for breach of warranty by proving that:
   a) The Indorsement is effective under § 3-304 ("Impostors; Fictions Payees") or § 3-405 ("Employer's Responsibility for Employee's Fraudulent Indorsements")
   or b) The Drawer is precluded from asserting a claim under
      1) § 3-406 (Contributory negligence)
      or 2) § 4-406 (Contributory negligence)
2) These defenses may be used only if the Drawee asserts a claim for Breach of Warranty (as per (a)) for the following breaches:
   a) Unauthorized Indorsement of the Draft
   b) Alteration of the Draft

(d) **Warranty for Dishonored Drafts:**

1. The warranties in this subsection are made by the Person obtaining Payment and any prior transferor of the Item if:
   a. *Either:*
      (i) A dishonored Draft is presented for Payment to the Drawer or an Indorser
      or (ii) Any other Item is presented for Payment to a party obligated to pay it
   b. The Item is paid in Good Faith
2. Dishonored Draft warranty:
   The warrantor warrants that he is (or was at the time the warrantor transferred the Draft) either:
   A) A Person Entitled to Enforce the Draft (see § 3-301)
   or B) A Person authorized to obtain Payment or Acceptance of the Draft (on behalf of a Person Entitled to Enforce the Draft)
3. **Recovery:**
   a) The Person making Payment may recover for breach of warranty from *any warrantor.*

b) Recovery Amount =

The Amount Paid
\+ **Expenses and loss of interest** (resulting from the breach)

(e) **Limitations:**

1. Non-waivability for Checks: The warranties in (a) and (d) cannot be disclaimed with respect to Checks.
2. Time Limit: The claimant must give notice of a claim within 30 Days after the claimant has *reason to know* both
   a) The Identity of the warrantor
   and b) That the breach occurred.
3. If the notice is given after the 30-Day time limit, the warrantor is discharged *to the extent* of any loss caused by the delay of notice.

(f) **Accrual of Action:**

A cause of action for breach of warranty begins to accrue when the claimant has *reason to know* of the breach.

C. LIABILITY OF PARTIES:

1. The Maker/Issuer of a Note or Cashier's Check: (§ 3-412)

This section applies only to Promissory Notes and Cashier's Checks ***(for Checks, see "DRAWER" below)***

OVERVIEW

General Obligations:

- The Maker is responsible for paying the amount on the Instrument.
- The Maker's liability arises only if it *Signs* the Instrument
- If the Maker negligently leaves parts of the Instrument blank, it is bound to any terms later filled in (§ 3-412(ii)) (Note: this applies only to Notes and Drafts drawn by the Drawer (including Cashier's Checks)).
- **Maker's Obligation Owed to:**
  - a) Any Indorsers who paid the instrument under an Indorser's liability (§ 3-415).
  - and b) Any Person Entitled to Enforce the Instrument (under § 3-301)
- **Defenses Available:** § 3-305 defenses are available to the Maker/Issuer (only "real defenses" if an HDC takes it).

Warranties Made—none

Relevant Section: § 3-412

§ 3-412: Obligation of Issuer:

a) This section applies only to:

1. Notes

and 2. Cashier's Checks

and 3. Other Drafts drawn on the Drawer (i.e., Teller/Bank Checks)

b) **Applicable Terms of Payment:** The Issuer of the above drafts is obliged to pay the Instrument according to the terms of the Draft at the time it was:

(i) Issued, or if it was not issued, when the Holder first took possession

or (ii) Completed (to the extent stated in § 3-115 and § 3-407)—if the Issuer Signed an Incomplete Instrument

c) This obligation is owed to:

i) A Person Entitled to Enforce the Instrument

and ii) An *Indorser* who paid the Instrument (under § 3-415)

2. *The Drawer of a Check or Draft: (§ 3-414)*

OVERVIEW

General Obligations:

- The Drawer will always be liable on a Check unless:
    - 1) He signs *"without recourse"* (§ 3-414)
    - or 2) The Payor Bank (i.e., Drawee) is insolvent as a result of a delay in Presentment (§ 3-414(f))
    - or 3) He doesn't sign the Instrument (§ 3-401)
    - or 4) The Draft is changed/altered (§ 3-410) (to the extent of the Alteration).
- The Drawer will not be primarily responsible to pay a Check directly to the Payee *until* the Bank first Dishonors the Check (§ 3-414(b)).
- **Obligations are Owed to** the Payee and all subsequent Indorsers.
- **Defenses Available:** § 3-305 defenses are available to the Drawer (only "Real Defenses" if an HDC takes it).

Warranties Made — none

Extent of Liability — The Drawer's contractual obligation to tender Payment will be discharged upon the Payor Bank's Acceptance or Payment of the Check (§ 3-414(c); see also § 3-409 to determine when Acceptance occurs).

Relevant Sections: § 3-414, § 3-401, § 3-410

§ 3-414: Obligation of Drawer:

(a) **Scope:** This section does not apply to:

1. Cashier's Checks

or 2. Other Drafts drawn on the Drawer

(b) **Obligation to Pay for Dishonored Draft** (uncertified)

1) If an Unaccepted Draft is dishonored, the Drawer is obliged to pay the Draft, according to its terms at the time it was:

(i) *Either:*

a) Issued — if the Draft was issued

or b) First possessed by a Holder — if the Draft was not issued

or (ii) Completed (to the extent stated in § 3-115 and § 3-407) — if the Drawer Signed an Incomplete Instrument

2) This obligation is owed to:

i) A Person Entitled to Enforce the Draft

and ii) An *Indorser* who paid the Draft (under § 3-415)

(c) **Discharge of Drawer:** If a Draft is Accepted by a Bank, the Drawer is discharged (regardless of when or by whom acceptance was obtained).

(d) **Dishonored Draft Accepted by a Non-Bank:** The Drawer has the same obligation (to pay the Draft) as an Indorser (under § 3-415(a) and (c)) if:

1) The Draft is accepted by a non-Bank.
and 2) It is dishonored by the Acceptor.

(e) **Disclaimer of Liability:**

1. The Drawer will not be liable under (b) if:
   a) The Draft *either:*
      1) States that it is drawn *"without recourse"*
      or 2) Otherwise disclaims the Drawer's liability (to pay the Draft)
   and b) The Draft is not a Check
2. A disclaimer of the liability under (b) is not effective if the Draft is a Check.

(f) **Discharge of Obligation:**

1. The Drawer may discharge its obligation to pay a Check by assigning its rights against the Drawee (with respect to the funds) to the Person Entitled to Enforce the Check.
2. The Drawer may do this only *to the extent* the Drawer is deprived of funds, when:
   (i) *Either:*
      a) A Check is not presented for Payment within 30 Days after its date
      or b) A Check is not given to a Depositary Bank for collection within 30 Days after its date[16]
   and (ii) The Drawee suspends payments after the 30 Day period expires (without paying the Check)
   and (iii) Because of the *suspension of payments,* the Drawer is deprived of funds maintained with the Drawee to cover the Payment of the Check (e.g., Bank is insolvent)
3. Limitation: The amount that may be discharged is limited to the amount of funds the Drawer is deprived of.

§ 3-401: Signature:

(a) **Liability on an Instrument:**

A Person will be liable on an Instrument only if:

(i) The Person has *Signed* the Instrument.
or (ii) A Representative has Signed it for the Person (and such signature is binding on the represented Person under § 3-402).

[16] Former 3-503 did not specify a time period; it merely prescribed a reasonable time standard, which was presumed to be less than 30 days in most courts.

(b) **Method of Signature:**

A signature may be made by:

(i) Any of the following means:
  a) Manually
  or b) By use of a machine or device

and (ii) The use of:
  a. A name (including a trade or assumed name)
  or b. Any of the following if they are *executed or adopted* by a Person with a *present intention to authenticate a writing*:
    1) Word
    or 2) Mark
    or 3) Symbol

§ 3-410: Acceptance Varying Draft:

(a) **Differing Terms:** If the Terms of a Drawee's Acceptance are different from the terms of the Draft (as presented):

1) The holder may refuse the Acceptance of the Draft.
2) The holder may treat the Draft as dishonored.
3) The Drawee may then cancel the Acceptance.

(b) **Place of Payment:** The terms of a Draft are not considered different if the Acceptance indicates Payment at a particular Bank or place in the U.S., *unless* the Acceptance states that the Draft can *only* be paid at that particular Bank or place.

(c) **Holder's Assent to Varying Terms:** If the Holder agrees to an Acceptance which varies the terms of a Draft, then the obligation of each Drawer and Indorser who does not expressly assent to the Acceptance is *discharged*.

3. *The Indorser:*

OVERVIEW

General Obligations:
- The Indorser Promises to pay the amount of the Instrument to any *Subsequent Indorser* (or Person Entitled to Enforce the Instrument) only after it has been Dishonored (§ 3-415).
- The Indorser may limit his liability by "*qualifying*" or *restricting* his Indorsement (example: signing "*without recourse*").
- **Obligations are Owed to:** subsequent Indorsers/Holders who paid the Instrument or are entitled to enforce it.
- **Defenses available:** Section 3-305 defenses are available to the Indorser (only "Real Defenses" if an HDC takes it).
- **Rights to Recourse Against Prior Parties:**
  - The Drawer: If an Indorser is sued for the value of an Instrument, he may sue the Drawer for the value of the Instrument (§ 3-414).
  - Previous Indorsers: An Indorser may also hold any *previous* Indorsers liable for the value of the Instrument. (But note: it may not sue Indorsers who Indorsed the Instrument *after* he did (§ 3-415)).

Warranties Made:
1) Transfer Warranties
2) Presentment Warranties—if the Instrument is a Draft and is paid or accepted by the Payor Bank.

Extent of Liability: The Indorser will be liable for the face Value of the Instrument up to 30 days after he Indorsed the Instrument.

Relevant Section: § 3-415

§ 3-415: Obligation of Indorser:

(a) **Obligation to Pay for Dishonored Draft:**

1) If an Instrument is dishonored, an Indorser is obliged to pay the amount due on the Instrument, according to the its terms at the time it was:
   - (i) Indorsed
   - or (ii) Completed (to the extent stated in § 3-115 and § 3-407), if the Indorser Indorsed an Incomplete Instrument
2) This obligation is owed to:
   - i) A Person Entitled to Enforce the Instrument
   - or ii) A *subsequent Indorser* who paid the Instrument (under this section)

3) This subsection is subject to subsections (b), (c), (d), (e), and Section 3-419(d).

(b) **Disclaimer of Liability:** The Indorser is not liable under (a) if the Indorsement *either:*

1) States that it is made *"without recourse"*
or 2) Otherwise disclaims the Indorser's liability (to pay the Instrument).

(c) **Discharge Without Notice of dishonor:**

The Indorser's liability (under (a)) will be *discharged* if:

1) Notice of dishonor is required (as per § 3-503)
and 2) Such notice is not given to an Indorser.

(d) **Discharge by Acceptance:**

The Indorser will be discharged of liability (under (a)) if a Bank accepts a Draft after an Indorsement is made.

(e) **Discharge for Checks:**

The liability (under (a)) of the Indorser will be discharged if:
a) The Draft Indorsed is a Check.
and b) *Either*:
1) The Check is not presented for Payment within 30 days after Indorsement.
or 2) The Check is not given to a Depositary Bank for collection within 30 days after Indorsement.[17]

[17] Under former 3-502 discharge occurred after a reasonable time passed of Indorsement; most courts presumed this to be about 7 days.

4. The Drawee/Acceptor: (Including Payor Bank)

OVERVIEW

<u>General Obligations:</u>
- The Drawee has <u>no</u> liability on a Draft until she Signs ("accepts") it (the fact that her name appears on the Draft as Drawee does not hold the Payor Bank liable to pay the Check to the Holder).
- The Drawee has only a <u>contractual duty</u> to the Drawer to pay the Payee (or other subsequent holder) upon demand, and will be liable for wrongful Dishonor and for not stopping Payment (pursuant to a valid Stop Payment Order), under its contract with the Drawer.
- Once the Drawee (i.e., Payor Bank) *Indorses* the Instrument it becomes an *<u>Acceptor</u>* and is subject to obligations under § 3-413 (i.e., it is obligated to pay the amount on the Instrument).

Obligations are Owed to: The Drawer, if it is a Customer (as per § 4-103(a)(5)).

Defenses Available: The Drawee will not be responsible for not paying an Item if:
- A valid reason for dishonor exists (see "DISHONOR" above)
- The Item is not Properly payable
- A Stop Payment Order is in effect

<u>**Warranties made:**</u> None.

Relevant Section: § 3-413

§ 3-413: Obligation of Acceptor:

(a) **Applicable Terms of Payment:**

1. The Acceptor of a Draft must pay the Draft, according to its terms at the time the Draft was:
   - (i) <u>Accepted</u> — even if the Acceptance states that the Draft is payable *"as originally drawn"* (or has equivalent terms)
   - or (ii) <u>As Varied</u> — if the Acceptance varies the terms of the Draft (see § 3-410)
   - or (iii) <u>As Completed</u> (to the extent stated in § 3-115 and § 3-407) — if the Draft was accepted while incomplete
2. <u>This obligation is owed to:</u>
   - i) The Drawer or a Person Entitled to Enforce the Draft
   - or ii) An *Indorser* who paid the Draft (under § 3-414 or § 3-415)

(b) **Exceptions**

1) Amount Stated: The Acceptor must pay the amount so stated on the Draft if the Acceptance of the Draft (or certification of a Check) specifically states the amount Accepted or Certified.
2) Holder in Due Course: The Acceptor must pay the amount of the Instrument at the time it was taken by an HDC if:
   - (i) The Certification or Acceptance does not state an amount.
   - and (ii) The amount of the Instrument is subsequently raised.
   - and (iii) The Instrument is then negotiated to an HDC.

D. FORGERY:

OVERVIEW

Forged signatures of a Drawer do not make a Note or Draft void.

Liability:

- The Person whose signature is forged on the Instrument will not be liable (i.e., the Bank can't charge its Customer's Account if a Check is forged), *unless* the Customer does not catch the forgery in time (§ 4-406)).
- The forger will be liable as if the Instrument were his own.
- Indorsers will be liable on forged Instruments for 30 Days after they Indorse it (§ 3-415). They will also be liable for breach of warranty (under § 3-416, and, if they knew of the forgery, also under § 3-417).

Burden of Proof: The Customer (i.e., owner of the Instrument) has the burden of proving that someone forged his signature.

Recovery: The Payor may recover for payments made on forged Instruments by asserting its rights under:

1. Transfer Warranties (§ 3-416; § 4-207)
2. Presentment Warranties (§ 3-417; § 4-208)
3. Indorser's Liabilities/Warranties (§ 3-415; § 4-207)

Forgeries of an Employee:

- Employers are generally liable for forgeries made by an Employee (§ 3-405)
- Employers are responsible to inspect monthly statements (or get a person not writing the Instruments to look at the statement to make sure that no employee is stealing or forging Instruments).

When Forgery Defense Doesn't Work:

1) **Issuance to an Imposter:** If the Issuer signs the Instrument and gives it to someone purporting to be someone else (example: Joe writes out a Check to Marlee, Inc. and gives it to Ike, who he mistakenly thinks is the President of Marlee (since Ike tells Joe that Marlee, Inc., took over DeeDee, Inc., to whom Joe owes Money). Ike then Indorses the Check to Susan. If Susan is an HDC, she may enforce the Check) (see § 3-404(a)-(b)).
2) **Fictitious Payee:** When an *authorized signer* writes a Check out to a phony or unauthorized Payee (example: a thief opens an account in the name of a phony person and deposits the money in that account) the Drawer may be liable since he trusted the Person he authorized to sign his Checks (§ 3-404(b)):[18]
   a) *Forged Signature* (of Drawer) — the Bank cannot charge the Drawer's Account if the signature is forged.
   b) *Forged Indorsement* — the Bank can charge Drawer's Account if the Indorsement is forged.

[18] Under former Article 3, if a Representative signs on behalf of a Drawer with the intention that the Payee receive the Check, a Bank may charge its customer's account (the rationale being that since the Payee is fictitious, the Check becomes like a Bearer Instrument, allowing anyone to validly Indorse it) (see former 3-405).

The Payor Bank does not bear the loss when the Indorsement is made by the wrongdoer in the name of the named Payee (§ 3-405(b)).

Relevant Sections: § 3-403, § 3-404, § 3-405

§ 3-403: Unauthorized Signature:

(a) **Unauthorized Signature Ineffective:** An Unauthorized signature is **ineffective** unless:

1) Otherwise provided in Article 3 or 4
2) The signature is effective to impose liability upon the signer in favor of a Person who in **Good Faith**:
   a) Takes it for Value
   or b) Pays the Instrument
3) **"Ratification":** The Unauthorized signature may be retroactively adopted by the Person whose name is Signed.
   - Ratification may be found from conduct or express statements.

(b) **Multi-Person Signatures:**

If an organization requires more than one signature to constitute the organization's authorized signature, the signature is deemed unauthorized if *any* of the required signatures are absent.

(c) **Liability:** Civil or criminal liability for persons making Unauthorized signatures is not affected by any provision of this Article which makes the Unauthorized signature effective for the purposes of this Article.

§ 3-404: Impostors; Fictitious Payees:

(a) **Impostor's Indorsement Effective:**

1) An Indorsement of an Instrument by any Person in the name of the Payee is *effective*, as if it were the Payee, in favor of a Person who:
   a) Pays the Instrument
   or b) Takes it for Value or Collection
2) This rule applies if an Impostor (by use of mail or otherwise)
   a) Induces the Issuer of an Instrument to Issue the Instrument to *either:*
      1) The Impostor himself
      or 2) A Person acting in concert with the impostor
   and b) Causes the Issuer to do so by impersonating *either* the:
      1) Payee of the Instrument
      2) A Person authorized to act for the payee

(b) **Unintended or Fictitious Payee:**

A. **Scope**—These rules apply if:
  (i) A Person whose intent determines to whom an Instrument is payable (see §3-110(a) or (b)) does not intend the Person identified as payee to have any interest in the Instrument.
  or (ii) The Person identified as payee is a fictitious Person.

B. Rules of Unintended or Fictitious Payee (These apply until the instrument is negotiated by special Indorsement):
  (1) Any Person in possession of the Instrument is considered its holder.
  (2) An Indorsement (made by anyone) in the name of the payee stated in the Instrument is effective as the Payee's Indorsement in favor of a Person who, in **Good Faith:**
    a) Pays the Instrument
    or b) Takes it for Value or Collection.

(c) **Intended Payee:** An Indorsement is made in the name of a Payee (under (a) and (b)) if:

  (i) It is made in a name *substantially similar* to that of the Payee.
  or (ii) The Instrument is deposited in a Depositary Bank Account in a name *substantially similar* to that of the Payee (whether or not Indorsed).

(d) **Failure to Use Ordinary Care**

1) A Person paying or taking for Value or collection an Instrument (to which (a) or (b) applies) will be liable on the Instrument if:
  a) He fails to use Ordinary Care when paying or taking the Instrument for Value or collection.
  and b) His failure to use Ordinary Care *substantially contributes* to the loss resulting from Payment of the Instrument.
  and c) A Person suffers damages as a result.
2) Such Person will be liable only to the extent of the amount lost as a result of the failure to use Ordinary Care.

§3-405: Employer's Responsibility for Fraudulent Indorsement by Employee:

(a) **Definitions**—the following definitions apply to this section:

(1) **"Employee"**—includes an independent contractor and Employee of an independent contractor retained by the employer

(2) **"Fraudulent Indorsement"**—

(i) For Instruments payable to employer—a forged Indorsement purporting to be that of the employer

or (ii) For Instruments where employer is Issuer—a forged Indorsement purporting to be that of the Person identified as the payee

(3) **"Responsibility"**

a) "Responsibility" includes the authority to:

(i) Sign or Indorse instruments on behalf of the employer

or (ii) Process instruments received by the employer for

a) Bookkeeping purposes

or b) Deposit to an Account

or c) Other disposition

or (iii) Prepare or process instruments for Issue in the employer's name

or (iv) Supply information determining the names or addresses of the payees of instruments (which were to be issued by the employer)

or (v) Control disposition of instruments to be issued in the employer's name

or (vi) Act otherwise with respect to instruments in a responsible capacity

b) *"Responsibility"* does not include authority that merely allows an employee to have access to instruments or blank/incomplete Instrument forms that are being stored, transported, or are part of incoming or outgoing mail, or have similar access.

(b) **Rights and Liabilities**:

1) A Fraudulent Indorsement will be effective (as the Indorsement of the Person to whom the Instrument is payable) as against a Person who in **Good Faith** pays the Instrument or takes it for Value or Collection if:

a) The Employer entrusted the employee with a "responsibility" specified in (3).

or b) The responsible employee (or someone working with such employee) makes a Fraudulent Indorsement.

or c) The Indorsement is made in the name of the Person to whom the Instrument is payable.

2) Failure to Use Due Care:

a) If the Person paying or taking for Value or collection the Instrument fails to use Ordinary Care in paying or taking the Instrument for Value or collection, he will be liable to anyone suffering as a result if it *substantially contributes* to the loss resulting from the fraud.

b) Such Person will be liable only for the amount lost as a result of its failure to use Ordinary Care.

(c) **"Made in the Name of the Payee"** A forged Indorsement made under (b) will be considered to have been made in the name of the Person to whom the Instrument is payable if:

(i) It is made in a name *substantially similar* to the name of that Person.

or (ii) The Instrument is deposited in a Depositary Bank account in a name *substantially similar* to the name of that Person (whether or not Indorsed).

E. ALTERATION: (§ 3-406; § 3-407)

OVERVIEW

The Drawer may be held liable if the Alteration resulted from his negligence (example: if the Drawer leaves room on the Draft for someone to add zeros).

An altered Instrument is still valid, *up to its original amount.*

Altered Certified Checks: A certifying Bank is protected against an HDC only if the certification states the amount of the Check at the time of certification (§ 3-413(b)).

Relevant Section: § 3-413(b)

§ 3-413(b): Obligation of Acceptor:

* * *

(b) **Exceptions**

1) Amount Stated: The Acceptor must pay the amount so stated on the Draft if the Acceptance of the Draft (or certification of a Check) specifically states the amount Accepted or Certified.
2) Holder in Due Course: The Acceptor must pay the amount of the Instrument at the time it was taken by an HDC if:
    - (i) The Certification or Acceptance does not state an amount.
    - and (ii) The amount of the Instrument is subsequently raised.
    - and (iii) The Instrument is then negotiated to an HDC.

F. STOLEN INSTRUMENTS: (§ 3-309)

OVERVIEW

A Bank will generally be liable if it Pays a stolen Instrument.

- The owner of the Instrument (i.e., the Payee or Holder) may bring an action in *Conversion* against the bank (§ 3-420).
- The Drawer may sue the Bank to have its account recredited for paying the stolen Instrument, since the stolen Instrument was not "properly payable" (§ 3-420).

Instrument Stolen from Payee:

- The Payee has a right to get a new Instrument from the Drawer/Indorser (§ 3-309).
- Since the underlying contract was already suspended upon receipt of the original Instrument, the Payee cannot sue the Drawer for breach of Contract if the Drawer refuses to Issue another Instrument.

Instrument Stolen from Drawer:

- The Drawer cannot sue for Conversion if an Instrument was stolen from his possession, since the unsigned Instrument (unsigned by Drawer) is a mere piece of paper (with no property rights).
- Once a Bank pays Money for the paper, the Drawer may sue both the thief and the Bank.

G. CONVERSION:

OVERVIEW

Conversion is the civil cause of action for stealing.

Revised Article 3 is not specific about how conversion arises. It simply refers to *common law* claims of conversion.[19]

- If the Bank does not obey restrictions, it is considered to be "*converting*" from the Signor or Indorser. Valid restrictions that the Bank must obey include:
  1. *Restrictions on further transfer* (example: "for deposit only") (§ 3-206(c))
  2. *Conditional Indorsements* — only applicable between the parties making the condition; all subsequent Indorsers take free of the condition.

Examples of cases where the Payor will be liable for conversion: (see also Liability Chart in Appendix)

- Bank takes an Instrument bearing a forged Indorsement.
- Bank pays an Instrument containing only one Indorsement, when it is payable to Multiple Payees jointly, not in the alternative.
- Bank pays an Instrument that was stolen from the Payee.

Relevant Sections: § 3-420, § 3-206

§ 3-420: Conversion of an Instrument:

(a) **Grounds for Conversion**

1) The law applicable to conversion of personal property also applies to instruments (i.e., common law and other statutes).
2) An Instrument is also converted if:
   a) A transferee takes it, without Negotiation, from a Person not Entitled to Enforce the Instrument (i.e., a forgery or missing Indorsement).
   or b) A Bank makes or obtains Payment for a Person not Entitled to Enforce the Instrument or receive Payment.
3) An action for conversion of an Instrument may not be brought by:
   (i) The Issuer or Acceptor of the Instrument

[19] Under former Article 3, the UCC listed four ways conversion may arise (see former 3-419):

1) Failure to Return a Draft when it is presented for acceptance
2) Failure to Pay or Return an Instrument
3) Failure to obey terms of a Restrictive Indorsement
4) Payment on a Forged Indorsement

or (ii) A Payee or Indorsee who did not receive delivery of the Instrument either:
1. Directly
or 2. Through delivery to an agent or a co-payee

(b) **Amount of Liability**

1. The amount of liability in (a) is *presumed* to be the *amount payable on the Instrument.*
2. Recovery may not exceed the amount of the plaintiff's interest in the Instrument.

(c) **Representative's Liability:**[20]

A Representative (other than a Depositary Bank) will be liable only for the amount of any proceeds not paid out to a Person not entitled to enforce the Instrument, if:

1) The Representative dealt with the Instrument or its proceeds in **Good Faith.**
and 2) The Representative dealt with an Instrument on behalf of someone not entitled to enforce an Instrument.
and 3) The Representative is not a Depositary Bank.

§ 3-206: Restrictive Indorsement:

(a) **Indorsement Prohibiting Further Transfer or Negotiation**:

An Indorsement **cannot** prevent further transfer or Negotiation of an Instrument by:

a) Limiting Payment to a particular Person
or b) Specifically prohibiting further transfer or Negotiation (e.g., "Pay to Mary Smith only")

(b) **Indorsement Stating a Condition:**

1. An Indorsement stating a condition to Payment to the Indorsee does not affect the rights of the Indorsee.
2. The Person paying the Instrument (or taking it for Value or collection) may disregard the condition. No rights or liabilities will be affected by disregarding it.

[20] Former § 3-419 only allowed a Depositary Bank to sue under its capacity as a Depositary Bank, and not a trustee.

(c) **Indorsements for Deposit:**

A. Scope: This subsection applies to instruments with the following Indorsements:

(i) Those described in § 4-201(b)

(ii) *"For deposit,"* or *"For collection,"* (or other words indicating a purpose to collect Payment for a particular Account) (in blank or to a particular Bank)

B. The following rules apply to the Indorsements described above:

(1) *A Person* (other than a Bank) who purchases such an Indorsed Instrument will have **converted** it, *unless:*

a. The Indorser receives the amount paid for the Instrument.

or b. The amount paid for the Instrument is applied consistently with the Indorsement.

(2) *A Depositary Bank* that purchases the Instrument or takes it for collection will **convert** it *unless:*

a. The Indorser receives the amount paid by the Bank for the Instrument.

or b. The amount paid for the Instrument is applied consistently with the Indorsement.

(3) *A Payor Bank*

a. The Payor Bank **converts** the Instrument if it:

1. Is also the Depositary Bank.

or 2. Takes the Instrument for immediate Payment over the counter (from a Person other than a Collecting Bank).

b. The Payor Bank will not be liable for conversion if:

1. The Indorser receives the amount paid for the Instrument.

or 2. The amount paid for the Instrument is applied consistently with the Indorsement.

(4) Except as otherwise provided in (3), a Payor Bank or Intermediary Bank may disregard the Indorsement, and is not liable if the proceeds are not received by the Indorser or applied consistently with the Indorsement.

(d) **Indorsements to Trustee/Fiduciary**

i) **Scope**:

1) The Following rules apply if an Instrument has an Indorsement containing words indicating that Payment is to be made to an agent, trustee, or other fiduciary, *for the benefit of the Indorser or another Person.*

2) The following rules do not apply to Indorsements made for deposit (under § 3-206(c)).

ii) **Rules Regarding Indorsements to Fiduciaries:**

(1) A Person receiving an Instrument which indicates that Payment is to be made to an agent may pay the Indorsee of the Instrument, without worrying that the Indorsee has breached a fiduciary duty to the Indorser, if:

a) The Person is *either:*

1. Purchasing the Instrument

or 2. Taking the Instrument from the Indorsee *for collection or Payment*

and b) There is no notice of a breach of fiduciary duty (as per § 3-307)

(2) Notice

a) A subsequent transferee or Person paying such an Instrument will not be deemed to have notice unless it knows that the fiduciary dealt with the Instrument or its proceeds in breach of fiduciary duties (see § 3-307).

(e) The above restrictions do not prevent a Person from becoming an HDC unless the Person is a *converter* (under (c)) or has notice or knowledge of a breach of fiduciary duty (as stated in(d)).

(f) **Defense to Payment:**

The obligor has a defense in an action to enforce Payment of an Instrument if Payment would violate a valid Restrictive Indorsement (under this section).

H. CONTRIBUTORY & COMPARATIVE NEGLIGENCE:[21]

OVERVIEW

Negligence of the Drawer is a defense the Payor Bank may use when the Drawer is partially at fault (§ 3-406; § 4-406).

- *Contributory Negligence* allows the bank to absolve itself of all liability (§ 3-406(a)).
- *Comparative Negligence* allows the bank to deduct the percentage of liability to which Drawer was at fault, but will not allow the bank to totally absolve itself of liability (§ 3-406(b)).

Drawer's Negligence:

- Duty to Look at Statements (§ 4-406)
  Drawer will not be able to recover the Check amount if she did not find mistakes in her Bank statements within one year (§ 4-406).[22]
- Invalid Checks in a Scheme — Drawer is responsible for any Checks paid as part of a "scheme" (group of Checks) that were paid 30 Days after the statement was received (§ 4-406).
- Forgeries by Employees — It is not safe to entrust all functions of Checking to one employee; thus, the Drawer may be liable (see also § 3-404; § 3-405).
- Leaving blank Checks or embossing machines unsecured is not, in itself, "*substantial*" enough to constitute negligence.

"Proximate Cause": Negligence of a Person must be the proximate cause of the forgery/wrong.

"Substantial Contribution" is a factual determination, and is required when asserting Contributory or Comparative negligence as a defense.

Reasonable Commercial Standards: Acceptable means of care for Good Faith purposes is required.

Relevant Sections: § 3-406, § 4-406

§ 3-406: Negligence Contributing to Forged Signature or Alteration of an Instrument:[23]

(a) **Preclusion from Defense:**

A Person will be precluded from asserting a defense of Alteration or forgery if:

1) The Person failed to use *Ordinary Care* (see § 3-103(7)).

---

[21] Under former Articles 3 and 4 there was no comparative negligence.

[22] Under former Article 4 there is no specific time frame to examine statements (see former 4-406).

[23] Former 3-406 does not provide for Comparative Negligence.

and 2) Failure to use the Ordinary Care *substantially contributed* to the Alteration or Forgery.

and 3) Such defense is asserted against a Person who, in **Good Faith:**

a) Pays the Instrument.

or b) Takes it for Value or collection.

(b) **Person Asserting Preclusion also Negligent:**

1) Loss will be allocated between the Person precluded from making the defense (in (a)) and the Person asserting the preclusion if:

a) The Person asserting the preclusion in (a) also failed to exercise Ordinary Care in paying or taking the Instrument.

b) That failure *substantially contributes* to loss.

2) The loss will be allocated to the extent each party's failure to use Ordinary Care contributed to the loss.

(c) **Burden of Proof** ("BOP"):

1) Under (a), the BOP that Ordinary Care was not used rests on the Person asserting the preclusion.

2) Under (b), the BOP that Ordinary Care was not used is on the Person precluded from using the defenses.

§ 4-406: Customer's Duty to Discover and Report Unauthorized Signature or Alteration:

(a) **Statement of Account**

If a Bank that has paid a Check or other Item sends its Customer a statement of account showing Payment of the Item, it must *either:*

1) Return the Item or make it available to the Customer.

2) Provide information in the statement, sufficient to allow the Customer to *reasonably* identify the Item paid. (If the Item is described by number, amount and date of Payment, sufficient information is provided; no need to return the Item, absent an agreement otherwise.)

(b) **Items Not Returned**

1) If the Items are not returned to the Customer, the Person retaining them shall *either:*

a) Retain the items for at least <u>7 years after receipt of the Items</u>

or b) Retain legible copies of the Items for at least <u>7 years</u> after receipt of the Items (if they have been destroyed)

2) Upon request by a Customer, a Bank must provide the Item paid (if destroyed it must send a copy) within a *reasonable* time after the request.

(c) **Customer's Duty**

1) If a Bank sends such a statement of Account, the Customer has a <u>duty to examine</u> it with *reasonable promptness*, and must check to see if a paid Item was Unauthorized due to *either*:
   a) An Unauthorized signature (e.g., forgery or agent acting outside the scope of authority).
   or b) Alteration.
2) The Customer must *promptly* notify the Bank of any Unauthorized payment if he should have *reasonably discovered it* based on the statement or Items provided.

(d) **Preclusion of Customer's Claims**

(1) A Customer is precluded from asserting the <u>Alteration</u> or the Customer's <u>Unauthorized signature</u> (against the Bank) if the Bank proves:
   a) The Customer *should reasonably have discovered* the Unauthorized Payment and did not notify the Bank.
   and b) It suffered a loss as a result of the Customer's failure.
(2) <u>Checks in a Scheme</u>: A Customer is precluded from asserting the <u>Alteration</u> or the Customer's <u>Unauthorized signature</u> (against the Bank) if the Bank proves:
   a) The Customer *should reasonably have discovered* the Unauthorized Payment and did not notify the Bank.
   and b) The Bank subsequently pays other items of the Customer that have Unauthorized signatures or Alterations by the same wrongdoer.
   and c) Such Payments occurred after the Customer had been given a *reasonable* time, not more than <u>30 days</u>, in which to examine the Items or statement and notify the Bank of the first Item.

(e) **Allocation of Loss**

1) Loss will be allocated between the Customer precluded from making the claims (under (d)) and the Bank asserting the preclusion if:
   a) The Customer proves that the Bank failed to exercise *Ordinary Care* in paying the Item (see § 4-104(c) and § 3-103(a)(7)).
   and b) That failure *substantially contributed* to the loss.

2) The loss will be allocated according to the amount each party's failure contributed to the loss (under subsection (d) for the Customer and Ordinary Care for the Bank).
3) If the Customer proves that the Bank did not pay the Item in *Good Faith* (see § 3-103(a)(4)) then the Customer is not precluded under (d).

(f) **Absolute Time Limit:**

1) Regardless of the care or lack of care of the Customer or the Bank, in order to assert any defense that a signature was Unauthorized or an Item was altered, the Customer must discover and report the problem within 1 year after the Statement or Items are made available to the Customer (according to § 4-406 (a)).
2) If the Customer is precluded under this subsection, the Payor Bank may not recover for Breach of Warranty under § 4-208 (with respect to the Unauthorized signature/Alteration to which the preclusion applies)(i.e., the Payor Bank may not choose to recredit the Drawer's Account and pass the loss to the Collecting Banks on the theory of breach of warranty).

VII. CHECKS AND BANKING

A. CHECKS:

1) Parties to the Check Transaction: (§ 4-105)

OVERVIEW

It is very important to know the "players" involved in the Check Transaction because the transaction involves many parties, each with different obligations and liabilities.

- Drawer — the Person writing the Check
- Drawee — (a.k.a. the Payor) the Person primarily responsible for paying the Check (usually the Payor Bank)
- Payee — the Person Entitled to Enforce the Check (a.k.a. Holder) (as per § 3-301)
- Indorser — the Person indorsing the Check (not the Drawer)
- Indorsee — the new Payee after the Instrument has been Indorsed
- Depositary Bank — the Bank where Payee deposits the Check (i.e., Payee's Bank)
- Collecting Bank — all Banks handling the Check (including Depositary Bank and forwarding banks), *except* for the Payor Bank
- Forwarding Bank/Clearinghouse — middleman who sends Checks from a Depositary Bank to the Payor Bank.
- Payor Bank — the Drawee/Bank paying the Check (i.e., Drawer's Bank; The Payor Bank is the Bank Ordered to pay the Check)
- Presenting Bank — the Bank presenting the Check to the Payor Bank

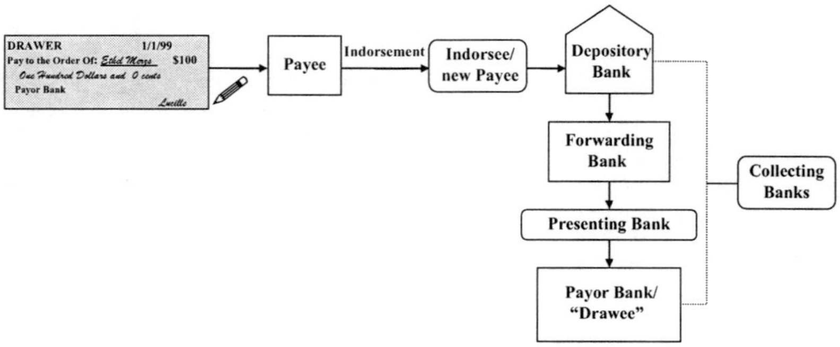

Relevant Section: § 4-105

§ 4-105: Definitions:

The following definitions apply for purposes of this Article:

(1) **"Bank"** — A Person engaged in the business of banking, including:

a. Savings Banks

and b. Savings and Loan Associations
and c. Credit Unions
and d. Trust Companies

(2) **"Depositary Bank"**—The first Bank to take an Item (even if it is also the Payor Bank), *unless* the Item is presented for immediate Payment over the counter.

(3) **"Payor Bank"**—A Bank that is the Drawee of a Draft

(4) **"Intermediary Bank"**—A Bank to which an Item is transferred in the course of collection (except the Depositary or Payor Bank)

(5) **"Collecting Bank"**—A Bank handling an Item for collection (except the Payor Bank)

(6) **"Presenting Bank"**—A Bank presenting an Item to the Payor Bank (a Presenting Bank cannot also be the Payor Bank)

2) Checks as Payment:

OVERVIEW

A Check is an acceptable substitute for Cash if it is given in the *Ordinary Course of Business* (§ 2-511(2)). Such payment is conditional and is defeated if the check is dishonored.

Dishonored Checks:

- An obligation to pay under a contract will not be discharged upon tender of a Negotiable Instrument.
- The obligation will be *Suspended* when the Instrument is tendered. The Instrument is considered a *conditional Payment.*
- The contractual obligation to pay will be "revived," however, if the Check is not honored (§ 3-310(b)).[24]
  - If a Contract is paid with a Certified Check, Cashier's Check, or Teller's Check, the contract will be immediately discharged (as if paid with cash) (§ 3-310(a)(1)), to the extent of the check amount.
  - If a Contract is paid with a Check it is *suspended* (§ 3-310); the obligation under the contract will be discharged once the Check is *Paid/Accepted* by the Bank.
  - A *Suspended* obligation cannot be the basis for a cause of action until the Check is dishonored (§ 3-310(b)(1)).

Delivery of a Cashier's Check in exchange for another Check is considered a final settlement (since the Bank Accepted the Check when it Signed the Cashier's Check).

Relevant Sections: § 3-310

§ 3-310: Effectiveness of Instruments as Payment:

(a) **Effectiveness of Certified/Bank Checks**

1. Unless otherwise agreed, any of the following Checks may be used to pay off an obligation, and shall discharge the obligation as if Money had been paid:
    a. Certified Check
    b. Cashier's Check
    c. Teller's Check

[24] Under former Article 3 the contractual obligation to pay is *discharged* upon tender of the Instrument. Thus, the Payee could not sue the Drawer or Indorser for contract damages *"off of the Instrument"* (i.e., for not paying the contract) if the Instrument is eventually dishonored (since the contract is automatically Discharged upon tender of the Check) (see former 3-802).

2. Discharge of an obligation does not affect the obligor's liability as Indorser of the Instrument.

(b) **Effectiveness of Notes and Uncertified Checks**

i) Unless otherwise agreed, if any of the following Instruments are used to pay off an obligation, the obligation will be *"Suspended"* in the amount of the Instrument (to the same extent the obligation would be discharged if paid off with Money):
  a) Note
  b) Uncertified Check

ii) This rule is subject to (a) above.

iii) Rules for Notes and Uncertified Checks:
  (1) Uncertified Checks—
    a. The obligation will continue to be "suspended" until:
      1) The Check is dishonored (in which case the obligation will be revived).
      or 2) The Check is Certified (in which case the obligation will be discharged as per (a)).
      or 3) The Check is Paid (in which case the obligation will be discharged as per (a)).
    b. Payment or certification of the Check results in discharge of the obligation in the amount of the Check.
  (2) Notes—
    a. The obligation will continue to be "suspended" until:
      1) The Note is dishonored (in which case the obligation will be revived).
      or 2) The Note is Paid.
    b. Payment of the Note results in discharge of the obligation in the amount of the Payment.
  (3) Dishonor of Check or Note:
    a. **Obligee Entitled to Enforce**—If the obligee of the obligation (for which the Instrument was taken) is the Person Entitled to Enforce the Instrument, upon dishonor he may enforce either:
      1) The Instrument
      or 2) The obligation (may sue on the underlying obligation, most likely an action in contract)
    b. **Instrument of a Third Party**—If an Instrument of a Third Person is Indorsed over to the obligee in Payment of the obligation, the obligee will be discharged; the discharge of the obligor on the

Instrument also discharges the underlying obligation (but the instrument may still be enforced against the third person Maker or Drawer) (e.g., Buyer delivers to seller an uncertified personal Check of X payable to the Order of buyer in Payment of the price of goods, and buyer Indorses the Check over to seller).

c. This rule (§ 3-310(b)(3)) is subject to (4) (below).

(4) Dishonor of Check or Note:

a. **Non-Obligee Entitled to Enforce**—If the Person Entitled to Enforce the instrument is not the obligee, the obligee may not enforce the "*suspended*" part of the obligation (i.e., the amount reflected in the Instrument).

b. **Obligee Without Possession of the Instrument**—If the obligee is the Person Entitled to Enforce the Instrument but no longer has possession of it (i.e., it was stolen, lost, or destroyed), then the following rules apply:

1. He may not enforce the "*suspended*" part of the obligation (i.e., the amount reflected in the Instrument).
2. The obligee's rights against the obligor are limited to enforcement of the Instrument, to such extent.

(c) **Other Instruments:**

1. The effect of an Instrument being used to pay for an obligation is:
   (i) That stated in § 3-310(a)—if the Bank is liable for the Instrument as Maker or Acceptor
   (ii) That stated in § 3-310(b)—in all other cases
2. This subsection applies only to instruments not included in § 3-310(a) or (b).

B. BANKS:

1. *The Bank's Role:*

OVERVIEW

Banks act like agents when cashing Checks (i.e., the Depositary Bank merely delivers the Check to its owner, whose Bank (the Payor Bank) gives the Payee's Bank (the Depositary Bank) the Money, who then gives it to the Payee).

Bank's Acceptance: A Bank will become liable for the amount of a Check only if it **Accepts** the Check by signing it (as per § 3-409(c) — by signing the check, the bank agrees to become liable on the instrument).

- A Bank has an opportunity to *delay* Acceptance under the "*Midnight Deadline Rule*" (described below). It is allowed to give its customers a ***Provisional Settlement***, which is a temporary credit to their Account, pending the lack of a timely notice of Dishonor. The Payor Bank has until its "*Midnight Deadline*" to decide whether the Check is *Properly Payable* or if it should be Dishonored (see "MIDNIGHT DEADLINE" below).
- The Bank is deemed to have Accepted a Check when it:
  1. Certifies the Check

  or **2.** Cashes the Check (i.e., pays the Check upon Presentment)

  or **3.** Neglects to send a Notice of Dishonor before its Midnight Deadline

2. Check Cashing:

OVERVIEW

Since cashing a Check upon Presentment is considered immediate Acceptance, it is risky for a Bank to "cash" a Check on the spot; if the Payor Bank Dishonors the Check, the Depositary Bank (which cashed the Check) would be responsible for paying it (§ 3-409).

In Order to avoid this liability and still give its Customers cash when they deposit their Checks, a Depositary Bank normally does the following:

- Gives the Payee a Loan (for the face amount of the Check)
- Takes the Check as *collateral* for the loan (see § 4-211)
  - If the Check is honored, the Depositary Bank will use the Proceeds of the Check to "re-pay" the "loan."
  - If the Check is Dishonored, the Depositary Bank can enforce its loan against the Payee; the collateral, however, is now worthless (since the Check has been Dishonored).
  - If there is an Insufficient amount of money to cover the "loan," the Bank will create an "**overdraft**" in its Customer's Account.

3. Overdrafts:

OVERVIEW

When an Overdraft occurs, the Drawee Bank has the option to pay the Instrument and will have a right to recover the overdraft amount from the Drawer.

The Overdraft may be paid off with money received from Checks deposited *simultaneously* or *subsequently* (see discussion below).

Right to Setoff: The Bank may also "Set off" the overdraft amount from any Money the Payee has in the Depositary Bank.

Note: § 4-210 and § 4-211 automatically create a Security Agreement for the Checks, so a separate Security Agreement is not necessary.

Special Overdraft Rules:

- The Bank may never take a Security Interest in an Account balance before a Check is deposited.
- All Checks delivered together, or subsequently, may be used as collateral for a bad Check.
- Thus, as deposited Checks get cashed, their money may be used to "pay off the loan."
- **Formula:** Bank's recoverable setoff amount is:

  $ Overdraft Amount
  − **$ Opening Balance**
  + **$ Subsequently paid Checks**

"Regulation CC": *Deadline for Payment*

- Regulation CC was created by the FDIC and supersedes the UCC.
- Regulation CC requires Depositary Banks to give customers their money within a certain amount of time (see Regulation CC, 12 CFR 229.10):
  - 2 Banking Days — if the Payor Bank and Depositary Bank are within the same Federal Reserve District
  - 4 Banking Days — if Payor Bank and the Depositary Bank are in a different Federal Reserve District
  - Next Banking Day — for all cash deposits, electronic payments, most government checks, and U.S. Postal Service Money Orders

Relevant Sections: § 3-409(a), § 4-210, § 4-211

§ 3-409(a): Acceptance of Draft and Certified Checks:

(a) **"Acceptance"** — occurs when the Drawee signs a Draft in agreement that it be paid upon presentation.

1) Signature Rules:
   a) The Drawee's signature alone is enough to convey Acceptance.
   b) Acceptance must be written on the Draft.
2) Effective Date:
   a) When notification of Acceptance (pursuant to instructions) is given
   or b) When the Accepted Draft is delivered—*for the purpose of giving rights on the Acceptance to any Person*
3) Acceptance may be made at any time.

§4-210: Security Interest of Collecting Bank in Items:

(a) A Collecting Bank has an S/I in an Item and any accompanying documents (or the proceeds of either) if:

   (1) Credit given for an Item deposited into an Account has been withdrawn or applied, to the extent that credit has actually been applied/withdrawn.
   or (2) The Bank has given credit available for withdrawal as of right for an Item, the Collecting Bank has an S/I to the extent credit is given (regardless of whether or not the credit is drawn upon or there is a right to charge back).
   or (3) The Bank makes an advance on or against the Item.

(b) Credit given for several Items received at one time:

   1. If credit given for several Items received at one time (or pursuant to a single agreement) is either withdrawn or applied, the S/I remains on all the items and accompanying documents (or their proceeds).
   2. **Credits first given are first withdrawn** for purposes of this section ("first in, first out" rule).

(c) **The Bank's Security Interest:**

   i) When a Collecting Bank receives *final settlement* for an Item, the settlement is considered a realization of the S/I (in the Item, documents, and proceeds).
   ii) As long as the Bank does not receive final settlement (or give up possession of the Item, documents, or proceeds for purposes other than collection) an S/I will continue to the extent not paid.

iii) The Bank's security interest ("S/I") will be subject to Article 9, except that:

(1) No security agreement is necessary to make the S/I enforceable (see § 9-404)).

and (2) No filing is required to perfect the S/I.

and (3) The S/I has priority over conflicting (perfected) S/Is in the Item, accompanying documents, or their proceeds.

§ 4-211: When Bank Gives Value for Purposes of Holder in Due Course:

- For purposes of determining a Bank's status as Holder in Due Course:

A Bank gives Value *to the extent* it has a security interest (as per § 4-210) in an Item (assuming the Bank complies with the other requirements of § 3-302 ("Holder in Due Course")).

C. BANKS AS HOLDERS IN DUE COURSE: (SEE ALSO "HOLDER IN DUE COURSE")

1) Bank as Holder—Special Indorsement Rules:

OVERVIEW

The UCC is very lenient when it comes to making a Bank an HDC.

Indorsement is usually needed for someone to be a Holder of an Identified Instrument, but under § 4-205 a Depositary Bank may become an HDC even without an Indorsement.

- If the Bank is a *Depositary Bank* taking a Check for collection (i.e., the Bank where the Payee deposits the Check (the "Depositary Bank") is also the "Payor Bank")), the Bank does not need an Indorsement (§ 4-205).
- If the Bank is the Payor Bank (i.e., the Bank responsible to pay the Check as Drawee), the Bank must Indorse the Check itself (in place of the Payee who forgot to Indorse it) if there is no Indorsement on it by the Payee.

Banks may require that the Indorser sign both her legal name and her name as it appears on the Check (as per § 3-204(d)).

- It is very important for a Bank to pay attention to the name of the Indorser, so as not to deposit Check money into the wrong account.
- Many people scam banks by indorsing a company/partnership Check and attempting to deposit it into their personal accounts.

Restrictive Indorsements: (§ 3-206) (see "INDORSEMENTS")

Relevant Section: § 4-205

§ 4-205: Depositary Bank as Holder of Unindorsed Item:

- **Scope:** The following rule applies if a Customer delivers an Item to a Depositary Bank for collection:

  (1) **Depositary Bank as Holder:**

  a. Lack of Indorsement irrelevant: The Depositary Bank becomes a Holder at the time it receives the Item for collection if the Customer was a holder of the Item (at the time of delivery), *regardless* of whether the Customer Indorses the Item.

b. Bank as Holder in Due Course: The Bank is an HDC if it satisfies the other requirements of § 3-302.

(2) **Depositary Bank's Warranty:**

a. The Depositary Bank warrants that the amount of the Item was paid to the Customer (or deposited in the Customer's Account).

b. The Depositary Bank makes this warranty to:

1. Collecting Banks.

and 2. The Payor Bank (or other Payor).

and 3. The Drawer.

2) Bank Taking in Due Course:

a) Value by a Bank:

OVERVIEW

The Bank is only an HDC to the extent that it gives Value (i.e., The Bank may charge back only the amount it had at risk) (§ 3-302(d); § 3-303(a)(1)).

- A **Promise to Pay** is considered Value only to the extent that it is performed (§ 3-303(a)(1)) (i.e., the Money was actually extended).
- The Bank must have *actually* given Value for the N/I to be an HDC (as per § 3-303(a)(1)); (see also § 3-302(d)) (i.e., if the Bank gave the Payee only $40,000 for a $60,000 N/I and Promised to pay the remaining $20,000 later, the Bank is an HDC only up to the $40,000 Value it actually gave).
- If the Instrument is purchased at a discount (i.e., purchased for less than the face value of the Instrument) and is only *partially paid*, the "value given" must be prorated (under § 3-302(d)) according to the following formula:

(Face Value of the N/I) **Money Already Paid**
Discounted price of N/I

- When Banks take a Security Interest in Checks, they are considered to have given Value. (§ 4-210) (Thus, when banks advance cash for a Check under § 4-211, they are considered to have given Value in the amount of the advance.)

Determining how much Value was given:

- Problems usually arise with *provisional settlements* (see "PROVISIONAL SETTLEMENTS" below) because it becomes difficult to determine how much Money was extended.
- Factors to Consider:
  - Look at how much the Customer had a right to withdraw (see Regulation CC rules, determining when the Customer has a right to withdraw Money from its Account, since it is at this point that the Bank is deemed to have given Value).
  - Look to see if the Customer actually made a withdrawal.
  - Look to see if the Bank gave the Customer an advance on a Check.

Relevant Sections: § 3-303, § 4-210, § 4-211

§ 3-303: Value and Consideration:

(a) **"Value"** — An Instrument is issued or transferred for **Value** if:

(1) It is issued or transferred for a *Promise of performance* (only to the extent the Promise has been performed).

or (2) A transferee acquires an S/I or other lien on the Instrument (other than a judicial lien).

or (3) It is issued or transferred as Payment or security of a pre-existing ("antecedent") claim (against any Person), whether or not the claim was due.

or (4) It is issued or transferred in exchange for an N/I.

or (5) It is issued or transferred in exchange for an irrevocable obligation to a third party by the Person taking the Instrument.

(b) **"Consideration"**—any consideration sufficient to support a simple contract.

1. The Drawer/Maker has a defense if the Instrument is issued without consideration.
2. If an Instrument is issued for a *Promise of performance*, the Maker/Drawer has a defense *to the extent* the Promise has not been performed (and is due).
3. If an Instrument is issued for Value (as stated in (a)), it will also be considered issued for consideration.

§4-210: Security Interest of Collecting Bank in Items:

(a) A Collecting Bank has an S/I in an Item and any accompanying documents (or the proceeds of either) if:

(1) Credit given for an Item deposited into an Account has been withdrawn or applied, to the extent that credit has actually been applied/withdrawn.

or (2) The Bank has given credit available for withdrawal as of right for an Item, the Collecting Bank has an S/I to the extent credit is given (regardless of whether or not the credit is drawn upon or there is a right to charge back).

or (3) The Bank makes an advance on or against the Item.

(b) Credit given for several Items received at one time:

1. If credit given for several Items received at one time (or pursuant to a single agreement) is either withdrawn or applied, the S/I remains on all the Items and accompanying documents (or their proceeds).
2. **Credits first given are first withdrawn** for purposes of this section ("first in, first out" rule).

(c) **The Bank's Security Interest:**

i) When a Collecting Bank receives *final settlement* for an Item, the settlement is considered a realization of the S/I (in the Item, documents, and proceeds).

ii) As long as the Bank does not receive final settlement (or give up possession of the Item, documents, or proceeds for purposes other than Collection) an S/I will continue to the extent not paid.
iii) The Bank's Security Interest ("S/I") will be subject to Article 9, except that:
    (1) No security agreement is necessary to make the S/I enforceable (see § 9-404)).
    and (2) No filing is required to perfect the S/I.
    and (3) The S/I has priority over conflicting (perfected) S/Is in the Item, accompanying documents, or their proceeds.

§ 4-211: When Bank Gives Value for Purposes of Holder in Due Course:

- <u>For purposes of determining a Bank's status as Holder in Due Course:</u>

A Bank gives Value *<u>to the extent</u>* it has a security interest (as per § 4-210) in an Item (assuming the Bank complies with the other requirements of § 3-302 ("Holder in Due Course")).

b) *Bank's Good Faith:*

OVERVIEW

A Bank's standard of Good Faith requires *both* (§ 3-103(a)(4)):
1. Honesty in Fact
and 2. Reasonable Commercial Standard

Note: *Lack of Ordinary Care* is not necessarily lack of Good Faith.

A Bank may not contract away its duty of Good Faith and Ordinary Care.

Relevant Sections: § 3-103(a)(4), § 4-103(a)

§ 3-103(a)(4): Definitions:

(a) The following definitions apply to Article 3:

* * *

(4) **"Good Faith"**—Requires both:
a) Honesty in Fact
and b) The Observance of *Reasonable Commercial Standards of Fair Dealing*

Revised § 3-103(a)(4): Definitions:

(4) **"Drawee"**—A Person Ordered in a Draft to make Payment (e.g., Bank) ((a)(2) in the pre-2002 UCC)

§ 4-103(a): Variation by Agreement:

(a) **Non-Waivable Responsibilities**

1. This Article's provisions may be varied by agreement of the parties.
2. **Exception:** Parties to such an agreement may not do the following:
   a) Disclaim the Bank's responsibility for
      1) Lack of Good Faith
      or 2) Failure to exercise *Ordinary Care*
   b) Limit the measure of damages for lack of Good Faith or failure to use Ordinary Care.
3. Parties may agree upon the *standards* by which the Bank's responsibility will be measured, as long as they are not *"manifestly unreasonable."*

c) Bank's Notice of Claims or Defenses:

OVERVIEW

Notice of Adverse Claims or Defenses includes the following:

1. **Overdue/"Stale" Instruments** are deemed to be Notice of a claim or defense (§ 3-304)
   - A Check is deemed "stale "after 90 Days (§ 3-304(a)(2)).[25]
   - An Instrument that is not a Check is deemed "stale" after an *unreasonably long* time has passed since the date of the Instrument (under the circumstances of the particular case (see § 3-304(a)(3)).
2. Any suspicious-looking Instrument is deemed to give notice of a claim or defense on that Instrument.
3. Instruments that are irregular or incomplete are deemed to give notice of a defense or claim (§ 3-302(a)(1)).
4. Notice of a defense described in § 3-305(a).
5. Notice of a claim described in § 3-306.
6. Instruments bearing apparent evidence of forgery or alteration.

Relevant Section: § 3-302(a)(1)

§ 3-302(a)(1): Holder in Due Course:

(a) A Holder is a **Holder in Due Course** (subject to § 3-302(c) and § 3-106(d)) if:

(1) The Instrument looks authentic — the Instrument when issued or negotiated to the Holder:

a. Does not bear apparent evidence of forgery or Alteration

or b. Is not otherwise so irregular or incomplete as to call into question its authenticity

[25] Under former Article 3, a Check is deemed stale after a *"reasonable time"* (usually 30 days) (see former 3-304).

3) Bank's Special Responsibilities to Its Customers: (See also Appendix Liability Chart)

OVERVIEW

Contractual Obligations: The Bank's duties to its Customers are primarily contractual duties. Thus, even if the Bank never accepts a Check (by signing it (§ 3-409)), the Bank may still be liable to a Customer under its contractual obligations to pay it (i.e., if the Bank refuses to Accept a Check, it will not be liable for the Value of the Check, since there was no Acceptance (as per § 3-409); however, a Bank will be liable for wrongfully Dishonoring the Check, since it has a contractual obligation with its Customer to pay Checks that are *properly payable* (§ 4-402); a bank may also be liable for damages resulting from ignoring a timely stop payment Order (§ 4-403)).

Contracts with Customer:

- A Bank and its Customer may "*contract out*" of any Bank duties specified in Article 4, except for the Bank's Duties of Good Faith and Ordinary Care (§ 4-103(a); § 4-103(e)).
- The Bank may not contract out of its obligations under *The Expedited Funds Availability Act* (12 USC § 4001) and Regulation CC (12 CFR § 229).

The "*Properly Payable*" Rule:

- Only when Checks are *"properly payable"* may a Bank charge its Customer's Account (otherwise the Bank will be liable on the Check) (§ 4-401(a)).
- Banks should not pay Checks that are not *"properly payable"* (§ 4-401(a)); if they do, they will have no right to recourse from the Drawer of the Check (i.e., the Bank will bear the loss for paying the Check since the Bank cannot charge the Drawer for it).

When Checks are Not *"Properly Payable"* (§ 4-401):

1) **Dishonor**—Checks that are Dishonored are not *properly payable.*
2) **Stop Payment Orders** ("SPO")—a Check subject to a *timely* SPO is ordinarily not *properly payable* (see SPOs).
3) **Forged Signature**—checks with a forged signature of the Drawer are not *properly payable* (§ 4-401 Off. Comm. 1).
4) **Forged Indorsements**—Checks with forged Indorsements are not *properly payable* (§ 4-401 Off. Comm. 1).
5) **Overdue Checks**—"*Stale*" Checks (as per § 3-304) are not *properly payable.*
6) **Alterations**—Altered Checks are *partially properly payable.* The Bank may charge the Drawer only for the *original amount* of the Check (§ 4-401(d)(1)).
7) **Post-dated Checks**—Post-dated Checks are ordinarily *properly payable* unless the Customer has given the Bank notice of the post-dating (in accordance with § 4-401(c)).[26]

---

[26] Under former Article 4, a post-dated check would not be properly payable if the Payor Bank paid it before its stated date.

8) **Improper Presenter**—A Check is *properly payable* only to a "Holder." The Bank must pay only a Holder "*Entitled to Enforce the Instrument*" (§ 4-401(a)—as "authorized by its Customer").
9) **Overdrafts** in an account do not prevent a Check from being properly payable (see § 4-401 Off. Comm. 1; see also "OVERDRAFTS," "DISHONOR," and "WRONGFUL DISHONOR" below).
   - If an overdraft occurs, the Bank has no obligation to pay the Draft, yet it *may* pay it and "*overcharge*" its Customer's Account (thereby entitling it to Payment).
   - Note: The Bank is responsible for any overdraft problems caused by wrongful charge of the Drawer's Account on a Check that is not *"properly payable."*

Other Responsibilities of a Bank:
1) **Special Duty of Ordinary Care and Good Faith**: The Bank has a duty to act with Ordinary Care and Good Faith when dealing with Instruments of its customers (§ 4-202(a)); these duties are not waivable (§ 4-103(a)).
2) **Timely Payment**: A Depositary Bank has a responsibility to make funds available to its Customer within 1–4 days (as per Regulation CC, 12 CFR § 229.10).
3) **Misencoding Checks**: The Bank cannot charge its Customer for an encoding mistake (§ 4-209; § 4-401).
4) **Certifying Checks**: A Bank has no obligation to Certify a Check. Its refusal to certify a Check is not considered to be a dishonor (§ 3-409(d)). (See also "DISHONOR" below.)
5) **Wrongful Dishonor**: A Bank will be held liable for any *actual damages* that arise from wrongfully dishonoring a customer's Check (§ 4-402) (see "DISHONOR" and chart of liability in appendix).
6) **Notice of Dishonor**: The Bank has a duty to give its Customer a *timely* notice of dishonor (as per Regulation CC, 12 CFR § 229.33) if it does not pay a Check.
7) **Obeying Stop Payment Orders**: A Bank will be held liable for damages if it ignores a *timely* Stop Payment Order by its Customer (see "STOP PAYMENT ORDERS" and chart on liability).
   - The Customer has the burden of establishing the amount of loss resulting from payment (§ 4-403).
8) **Bank Transfers**: The Bank will not be liable for the consequences of bad wire transfers (see UCC Article 4A).

Relevant Sections: § 4-103, § 3-409, § 4-401, § 4-209

§ 4-103: Variation by Agreement:

(a) **Non-Waivable Responsibilities**

1. This Article's provisions may be varied by agreement of the parties.

2. **Exception:** Parties to such an agreement may not do the following:
    a) Disclaim the Bank's responsibility for
        1) Lack of Good Faith
        or 2) Failure to exercise *ordinary care*
    b) Limit the measure of damages for lack of Good Faith or failure to use Ordinary Care.
3. Parties may agree upon the *standards* by which the Bank's responsibility will be measured, as long as they are not *"manifestly unreasonable."*

(b) **Other Regulations:** The following have the same effect as agreements under subsection (a) (whether or not specifically assented to by all parties interested in the items handled):

1. Federal Reserve regulations and operating circulars

and 2. Clearinghouse rules

and 3. Other similar official rules

(c) **Ordinary Care:**

1. Action or non-action will be considered exercised with *ordinary care* if it is approved by *either:*
    a. Article 4
    or b. Federal Reserve regulations or operating circulars
2. Action or non-action will be considered prima facie exercised with *ordinary care* if it is consistent with:
    a. Clearinghouse rules and the like
    or b. A general banking usage (not inconsistent with Article 4)

(d) **Other Procedures:** The specification or approval of certain procedures by this Article is not considered disapproval of other procedures that may be reasonable under the circumstances.

(e) **Damages:**

1) Damages for failure to exercise ordinary care in handling an Item =

$ Amount of Item
+ Any other proximate damages resulting from Bad Faith
– Amount that could not have been realized by the exercise of Ordinary Care

§ 3-409: Acceptance of Draft and Certified Checks:

(a) **"Acceptance"**—occurs when the Drawee signs a Draft in agreement that it be paid upon presentation.

1) Signature Rules:
    a) The Drawee's signature alone is enough to convey Acceptance.
    b) Acceptance must be written on the Draft.
2) Effective Date:
    a) When notification of Acceptance (pursuant to instructions) is given.
    or b) When the Accepted Draft is delivered—*for the purpose of giving rights on the Acceptance to any Person.*
3) Acceptance may be made at any time.

(b) **Acceptance of a Draft**: A Draft may be accepted, *even though* it:

a) Is not Signed by the Drawer
or b) Is otherwise incomplete
or c) Is overdue
or d) Has been dishonored

(c) **Undated Drafts:** The holder may complete the Acceptance by supplying a date in Good Faith if:

1) A Draft is payable at a fixed period after sight.
and 2) The Acceptor fails to date the Acceptance.

(d) **"Certified Checks"**

1) A Certified Check is a Check accepted by the Bank on which it is drawn.
2) Acceptance of Certified Checks—may be made by:
    a) Signing the Check (as indicated in § 3-409(a) above)
    or b) Writing on the Check an indication that it is *Certified*
3) The Drawee of a Check does not have to certify the Check.
4) A refusal to certify is not *dishonor* of the Check.

§ 4-401: When Bank May Charge Customer's Account:

(a) **Charging Customer's Account**

1. A Bank may charge the Customer's Account for an Item that is *properly payable* from the Account, even if the charge creates an overdraft.
2. An Item is "properly payable" if:
    a) It is authorized by the Customer.
    and b) It is in accordance with any agreement between the Customer and the Bank.

(b) **When Customer Not Liable**

The Customer is not liable for the overdraft if:

1. The Customer did not sign the Item.

and 2. The Customer did not benefit from the proceeds of the Item.

(c) **Post-dated Checks**

1. A Bank may charge the Customer's Account for an otherwise *properly payable* Check even though the Check is post-dated.
2. If the Customer gives the Bank *reasonable* notice of the post-dating, the Bank may not charge the Account before the Check date.
3. Requirements for Customer's Notice:
   a) Must describe the Check with *reasonable certainty.*
   b) Must be received within a *reasonable time and manner* before the Bank takes action as described in § 4-303.
   c) Notice will be effective for the period stated in § 4-403(b) for stop payment orders.
4. Bank's liability for charging post-dated Checks before date: If a Bank charges the Customer's Account for a post-dated Check before the date in the notice, then the Bank is liable for any damages for the loss resulting from the early charge, including damages for dishonor of subsequent items (under § 4-402).

(d) **Terms of Charge:**

i) A Bank may charge the Customer's Account if:

   1) The Bank makes **Payment**

   and 2) Payment is made to the **Holder**

   and 3) Payment is made in **Good Faith**

ii) The Bank may charge the indicated Account of its Customer according to:

   (1) Altered Item—the Original terms of the Altered Item

   (2) Completed Item—the terms of the Completed Item unless the Bank *has knowledge* that the completion was improper. (Note: It is okay if the Bank knows that the Item was completed.)

§ 4-209: Encoding and Retention Warranties:

(a) **Warranty for Encoding an Item:**

1. Encoder liable—A Person who encodes information on an Item (after it was issued) warrants to any subsequent Collecting Bank (and to the Payor Bank or other Payor) that the information is correctly encoded.

2. Depositary Bank also liable—If the Customer of a Depositary Bank encodes an Item, that Depositary Bank also makes the warranty.

(b) **Warranty for Retaining an Item:**

1. Retainer Liable—If a Person undertakes to retain an Item under an electronic Presentment agreement (§4-110), he warrants to any subsequent Collecting Bank (and to the Payor Bank or other Payor) that retention and Presentment of the Item comply with the agreement.
2. Depositary Bank also liable—If the Customer of a Depositary Bank undertakes to retain an Item, that Depositary Bank also makes the warranty.

(c) **Availability of Damages:**[27]

1. Limitation on damages available for breach of the above warranties: Damages are limited to an amount equal to:

   The loss suffered as a result of the breach
   + Expenses incurred as a result of the breach
   + Loss of interest incurred as a result of the breach
2. A Person may collect damages if:
   a) The Warranties were made to him under this section.
   and b) A warranty was breached.
   and c) He took the Item in Good Faith.

---

[27] Under the former Article 4, one could sue only under §4-202's Breach of Due Care. The revised §4-209's actions were not available.

4) Bank's Rights and Defenses:

OVERVIEW

1) **Bank's Right to Setoff:** The Bank has a right to set off any Money from a deposited Check for any outstanding debt a Customer owes the Bank (e.g., overdrafts).
2) **Right of Subrogation:** If the Payor Bank wrongfully pays the Payee, it will be liable for the Check amount, yet it will have a *right of subrogation* (i.e., it will be able to *"step into the shoes"* of any party involved with the Instrument (i.e., Drawer, HDC, Payee) in order to sue the wrongful party for the Check amount) (§ 4-407).
3) **Bank's Enforcement of Warranties:** The Bank may resort to transfer and presentment warranties under certain circumstances (see "WARRANTIES") (§ 4-207).
4) **Comparative Negligence:** If a Bank wrongfully made Payment, it may assert that the Customer was contributorily negligent and recover Money to the extent of the Customer's negligence (§ 3-406; § 4-406) (see "COMPARATIVE & CONTRIBUTORY NEGLIGENCE" below).
5) **Right to Restitution:** The Payor Bank may resort to restitution remedies (as per § 3-418: "payment by mistake," which is equivalent to court claims of restitution (§ 3-418(b)).
6) **Indorser's Liability:** If a Bank pays a Check by mistake, it can use § 3-415 to hold the Indorser liable for the Check (up to 30 Days from when it Indorsed the Check)—unless the Indorser indorsed the check "*without recourse*" (§ 3-415).
7) **Right to Charge-back:** The Payor Bank has a right to charge back the Customer's Account for overdrafting (§ 4-401(a)) (example: when the Bank pays a Check with insufficient funds in the Drawer's account) even if the Bank did not use Ordinary Care (§ 4-214(d)(2)).

Relevant Sections: § 4-407, § 4-406, § 3-418

§ 4-407: Payor Bank's Right to Subrogation on Improper Payment:

a) The Payor Bank will obtain **subrogation rights** if a Payor Bank has paid an Item *either:*

   1) After the Drawer or Maker had placed a stop payment Order on the Item

   or 2) After the Drawer or Maker's Account had been closed

   or 3) Under circumstances otherwise giving the Drawer or Maker a basis for objection

b) The Payor obtains subrogation rights only to prevent unjust enrichment and only *to the extent necessary* to prevent loss to the Bank because of paying the Item.

c) **Payor Bank's subrogated Rights** — The Payor Bank is subrogated to the Rights of:

(1) Any HDC on the Item, against the Drawer or Maker
and (2) The Payee (or any other Holder of the Item) against the Drawer or Maker *either:*
a) On the Item
or b) Under the transaction from which the Item arose
and (3) The Drawer or Maker against the Payee (or any other Holder of the Item) with respect to the transaction from which the Item arose

§ 4-406: Customer's Duty to Discover and Report Unauthorized Signature or Alteration:

(a) **Statement of Account**

If a Bank that has paid a Check or other Item sends its Customer a statement of account showing Payment of the Item, it must *either:*

1) Return the Item or make it available to the Customer.
2) Provide information in the statement, sufficient to allow the Customer to *reasonably* identify the Item paid. (If the Item is described by number, amount, and date of Payment, sufficient information is provided; no need to return the Item, absent an agreement otherwise.)

(b) **Items Not Returned**

1) If the Items are not returned to the Customer, the Person retaining them shall *either:*
a) Retain the items for at least <u>7 years after receipt of the Items</u>
or b) Retain legible copies of the Items for at least <u>7 years</u> after receipt of the Items (if they have been destroyed)
2) Upon request by a Customer, a Bank must provide the Item paid (if destroyed it must send a copy) within a *reasonable* time after the request.

(c) **Customer's Duty**

1) If a Bank sends such a statement of Account, the Customer has a <u>duty to examine</u> it with *reasonable promptness*, and must check to see if a paid Item was Unauthorized due to *either*:
a) An Unauthorized signature (e.g., forgery or agent acting outside the scope of authority)
or b) Alteration

2) The Customer must *promptly* notify the Bank of any Unauthorized payment if he should have *reasonably discovered it* based on the statement or Items provided.

(d) **Preclusion of Customer's Claims**

(1) A Customer is precluded from asserting the Alteration or the Customer's Unauthorized signature (against the Bank) if the Bank proves:

a) The Customer *should reasonably have discovered* the Unauthorized Payment and did not notify the Bank.

and b) It suffered a loss as a result of the Customer's failure.

(2) Checks in a Scheme: A Customer is precluded from asserting the Alteration or the Customer's Unauthorized signature (against the Bank) if the Bank proves:

a) The Customer *should reasonably have discovered* the unauthorized Payment and did not notify the Bank.

and b) The Bank subsequently pays other items of the Customer that have Unauthorized signatures or Alterations by the same wrongdoer.

and c) Such Payments occurred after the Customer had been given a *reasonable* time, not more than 30 days, in which to examine the Items or statement and notify the Bank of the first Item.

(e) **Allocation of Loss**

1) Loss will be allocated between the Customer precluded from making the claims (under (d)) and the Bank asserting the preclusion if:

a) The Customer proves that the Bank failed to exercise *Ordinary Care* in paying the Item (see § 4-104(c) and § 3-103(a)(7)).

and b) That failure *substantially contributed* to the loss.

2) The loss will be allocated according to the amount each party's failure contributed to the loss (under subsection (d) for the Customer and Ordinary Care for the Bank).

3) If the Customer proves that the Bank did not pay the Item in *Good Faith* (see § 3-103(a)(4)) then the Customer is not precluded under (d).

(f) **Absolute Time Limit:**

1) Regardless of the care or lack of care of the Customer or the Bank, in order to assert any defense that a signature was Unauthorized or an Item was altered, the Customer must discover and report the problem within 1 year after the

Statement or Items are made available to the Customer (according to § 4-406 (a)).

2) If the Customer is precluded under this subsection, the Payor Bank may not recover for Breach of Warranty under § 4-208 (with respect to the Unauthorized signature/Alteration to which the preclusion applies) (i.e., the Payor Bank may not choose to recredit the Drawer's Account and pass the loss to the Collecting Banks on the theory of breach of warranty).

§ 3-418: Payment or Acceptance by Mistake:

(a) **Drawee's Right to Revoke or Recover:**

1) Power to Recover: The Drawee may recover the amount of the Draft from the Person who received Payment if the Drawee:
    a) Pays the Draft.
    and b) Acted on the mistaken belief that:
        (i) Payment of the Draft had not been stopped (pursuant to § 4-403).
        or (ii) The drawer's signature on the Draft was authorized.
2) Power to Revoke: If the Drawee Accepts the Draft (instead of paying for it), and the above conditions are met, he may revoke Acceptance.
3) These rights are not affected by the Drawee's failure to exercise Ordinary Care in paying or accepting the Draft.
4) This subsection is subject to (c) below.

(b) **Person Paying or Accepting Party's Rights:**

1. If an Instrument was Accepted or Paid by *mistake*, the Person Paying or Accepting may (to the extent permitted by the law governing mistake and restitution, i.e., common law and other statutes):
    (i) Recover Payment from the Person who received Payment (i.e., restitution)
    or (ii) Revoke Acceptance.[28]
2. Section 3-418(b) applies only to cases not covered by (a).
3. This subsection is subject to (c) below.

[28] This provision was not part of former Article 3.

(c) **Defenses:**

1. Remedies in (a) and (b) may not be asserted against a Person who:[29]
   - a. Took the Instrument:
     - 1. In Good Faith
     - and 2. For Value
   - or b. Changed his position:
     - 1. In Good Faith
     - 2. In Reliance on the Payment or Acceptance (example: taking Money out of Bank Account)
2. This subsection does not limit remedies provided by § 3-417 or § 4-407.

(d) **Effect of Revocation or Recovery:**

1. This section applies if:
   - a) An Instrument is Paid or Accepted by mistake
   - and b) The Payor or Acceptor either:
     - 1. Recovers Payment (under (a) or (b))
     - or 2. Revokes Acceptance (under (a) or (b)).
2. Effect of Revocation or Recovery: If the above conditions are fulfilled, then:
   - a) The Instrument is deemed not to have been Paid or Accepted.
   - and b) The Instrument is treated as dishonored.
   - and c) The Person from whom Payment is recovered obtains the same rights as a Person Entitled to Enforce the dishonored Instrument.
3. Even though a Payor Bank may have paid an Item under § 4-215, it may have a right to recover the Payment under § 3-418.

[29] Former Article 3 limited these defenses to HDCs.

D. THE COLLECTION PROCESS: FOR DRAFTS, INCLUDING CHECKS:

1) *Presentment:*

OVERVIEW

Presentment is a "Demand" for *Payment* or *Acceptance* of an Instrument. Presentment is made by the Payee or subsequent Holder (i.e., Person Entitled to Enforce the Instrument) to *either:*

- The Drawee or Acceptor for drafts

or
- The Maker for other instruments

Presentment must be made in a timely manner, within:

- 30 days after the Instrument is Indorsed

or
- 90 days after the Drawer signs it (§ 3-414(f); § 3-415(e))[30]

When a Check is Negotiated to the Depositary Bank:
The Depositary Bank normally makes a "settlement" ("provisional settlement") for the amount of the Check to its Customer.

The Bank has three Methods of Settling a Check:

1) Provisional settlement: The Depositary Bank may take the Check and *delay Acceptance* of the Check by giving the Payee a "*provisional settlement*" (i.e., the Depositary Bank credits its customer's account, with the ability to deduct the credit if the Check later bounces).

or 2) Final settlement: The Depositary Bank may Accept the Item on the spot and credit its customer's Account as a final settlement or by Certifying the Item. A Depositary Bank ordinarily will not do this, since it will be liable on the Check if the Payor Bank dishonors the Check.

or 3) Payment: The Depositary Bank can pay for the Check on the spot (i.e., "cash the Check"). Most banks will not do this, since Payment constitutes a "final settlement." Thus, if the Check is later dishonored, the Bank would be liable for the amount of the Check. (As discussed below, most banks give the Payee a "loan" in the amount of the Check, which is secured by the Check itself.)

[30] Former Article 3 is not specific on this Issue. A Check is presumed to be overdue (i.e., "stale") 30 days after Drawer's signature, and 7 days after Indorsement for purposes of holding the Indorser liable (and the Drawer, if the Bank is insolvent) (see former 3-503(2)).

When a Check is presented to the Payor Bank:

- According to the UCC, the Payor Bank may give the Presenting Bank a provisional settlement for the Check it presents to the Payor Bank for settlement. This provisional settlement will automatically become a final settlement if the Payor Bank does not send the Presenting Bank (i.e., the Depositary or Forwarding Bank) a notice of dishonor by its Midnight Deadline (§ 4-301) (see § 3-502 Off. Comm.).
- **Dishonor:** The Payor Bank may recover this settlement if it returns the Check or gives a notice of dishonor by its Midnight Deadline (§ 4-104).
- If the Bank does not send such a notice or return the Check by its Midnight Deadline, the provisional settlement will become a **final settlement**, and the Payment on the Check will become final (§ 4-215).
- **Effect of Regulation CC:**
  - When dealing with Checks (as opposed to other drafts or non-Check items), Regulation CC supersedes the UCC. According to Regulation CC, a Payor Bank cannot make a provisional settlement to a Collecting Bank. In fact, all settlements between banks are final.
  - The only settlement that may be provisional is between the Depositary Bank and its Customer (see Regulation CC, 12 CFR § 229.36).

Relevant Sections: § 3-501, § 4-108, § 4-212

§ 3-501: Presentment:

(a) "**Presentment**" — Presentment occurs when a creditor (a "Person Entitled to Enforce an Instrument") (or his Representative) makes a demand to either:

(i) One of the following, to Pay the Instrument:
a) The Drawee
or b) A Party obliged to pay the Instrument
or c) The Bank in the case of a Note or Accepted Draft payable at a Bank

or (ii) The Drawee to Accept a Draft

(b) Presentment Rules

(1) **Place and Manner of Presentment:**
a) Presentment may be made:
1) At the place designated in the Instrument.
and 2) By any *commercially reasonable means* (including an oral, written, or electronic communication).
b) Presentment must be made at the place of Payment designated in the Instrument if it is payable at a Bank in the U.S.
c) Presentment is effective when the demand (for Payment or Acceptance) is received by the Person being presented with the Instrument.

d) If there are two or more Makers, Acceptors, Drawees, or other payors, demand is effective if made to any one of them.

(2) **Requirements Upon Demand**—The Person making Presentment must, upon demand:
   (i) Physically exhibit the Instrument (unless agreed otherwise, as with an electronic Presentment)
   and (ii) Give reasonable identification and reasonable evidence of authority to present (if the presentor is a Representative)
   and (iii) *Either*:
      a) Sign a Receipt for any Payment made (on the Instrument)
      or b) Surrender the Instrument—if full Payment is made

(3) **Action Upon Presentment Which Will Not Constitute Dishonoring**
The party to whom Presentment is made may do the following without dishonoring an Instrument:
   (i) Return the Instrument—for lack of a necessary Indorsement
   or (ii) Refuse Payment or Acceptance—for failure of the Presentment to comply with:
      a) The terms of the Instrument
      or b) An agreement of the parties
      or c) Other applicable law

(4) **"Cut-Off Hour" for Receipt of Instruments:**
The party to whom Presentment is made may treat the Presentment as if it occurred on the next business day if:
   a) That party has established a "cut-off" hour (no earlier than 2:00 P.M.) for the receipt and processing of Instruments presented for Payment or Acceptance.
   and b) Presentment is made after the cut-off hour.

5) **Section 3-501(b) is subject to:**
   a) Article 4
   and b) Agreement of the Parties
   and c) Clearinghouse rules and the like

§4-108: Time of Receipt of Items:

(a) **Cut-Off hour:**

1. A Bank may fix an hour after 2:00 P.M. as a cut-off hour for purposes of:
   a) Handling Money and Items
   b) Making entries on its books

2. The cut-off hour has been allowed in order to allow banks time to:
    a) Process items
    and b) Prove balances
    and c) Make the necessary entries on its books (to determine its position for the day)

(b) **Deferral of Receipt:**

An Item or deposit of Money may be treated as being received at the opening of the next Banking Day if it is received *after*:

1. The cut-off hour
or 2. The close of the Banking Day

§ 4-212: Presentment:

(a) **Presentment by Notice:**

1. If an Item is not payable by, through, or at a Bank, then (unless otherwise instructed) a Collecting Bank may "present" the Item by sending a ***written***[31] notice indicating that the Bank is holding the Item for Acceptance or Payment.
2. Notice Requirements:
    a) Must be in writing
    b) Must be sent to the party to Accept or Pay
    c) Must be sent in time to be received by the time Presentment is due
3. Honoring Party's Request: The Bank must honor any request of the party to Accept or Pay (under § 3-501) by the close of the next Banking Day following the day it receives the request.

(b) The Presenting Bank may treat an Item as dishonored and charge any Drawer (or Indorser) by sending notice of the facts, if:

1. Presentment is made by notice.
and 2. Payment, Acceptance, or Request for Compliance (with a requirement under § 3-501) is not received by:
    a) **Demand Items:** 3 Banking days after notice was sent (at the close of business on the third day).
    or b) **Other Items:** The close of the business day after maturity.

[31] Revised Article 3 (2002) changes the requirement of a "Writing" to a "Record."

2) Settlement:

a) The Midnight Deadline Rule: (§ 4-104)

OVERVIEW

The *Midnight Deadline* is the midnight of the day *after* a Check is Presented for Payment to the **Payor Bank**

- The Midnight Deadline runs from the time the Payor Bank gets the Check to when the Payor Bank must decide whether to pay or dishonor a Check.
- The Midnight Deadline also applies to Depositary and Collecting Banks with regard to the time that they must *forward* Checks and Dishonor notices by the Midnight Deadline after they are received.
- Note: The UCC counts *Banking Days* (usually ending at 2:00 P.M.) (Therefore, if a Check is deposited on Tuesday at 12:00 P.M., the Midnight Deadline is Thursday at 12:00 A.M. (Wednesday night); if the Check is deposited at 4:00 P.M. on Tuesday, the Midnight Deadline is Friday at 12:00 A.M. (Thursday night)).

Upon Presentment: Since Presentment begins the Midnight Deadline countdown, it is important to determine when it actually occurred.

The **Payor Bank** must send a notice of dishonor by its Midnight Deadline in order not to be held liable for paying the Check (see Regulation CC exception for Checks below).

If the Payor Bank sends a notice of dishonor to a **Collecting Bank**, the Collecting Bank has an obligation to *forward* the notice by its *Midnight Deadline*. **(Note: Collecting Banks' Provisional Settlements are not subject to the Midnight Deadline Rule. The only effect the Midnight Deadline Rule has on these banks is that they are obligated to *forward* a notice of dishonor by the Midnight Deadline).**

"Regulation CC"

- When dealing with Checks (as opposed to other drafts or non-Check Items) Regulation CC supersedes Article 4.
- Regulation CC requires banks to give customers their Money within a certain amount of time (Regulation CC, 12 CFR § 229.10):
  - 2 Banking Days if the Payor Bank and Depositary Bank are within the same Federal Reserve district.
  - 4 Banking Days if the Payor Bank and Depositary Bank are in different Federal Reserve districts.
  - 1 Banking Day for cash deposits, electronic payments, most government checks, and U.S. Postal Service money orders.
- Extension — Regulation CC allows the Midnight Deadline to be extended under certain circumstances, including when a notice of dishonor is sent by expeditious means, but still arrived late (Regulation CC 12 CFR § 229.30(d)). Otherwise, if the Payor Bank does not act by its Midnight Deadline it will be held liable for the Check (§ 4-302(9)).

Relevant Sections: § 4-104(a)(10), § 4-213

§ 4-104(a)(10): Definitions:

(a) The following definitions apply to Article 4, unless the context requires otherwise:

* * *

(10) **"Midnight Deadline"**— for a Bank is the *later* of:
a. Midnight on the next Banking Day after it receives the relevant Item or notice
or b. Midnight on the next Banking Day from which the time for taking action begins to run

§ 4-213: Settlement by Bank:

(a) **Time and Medium:**

i) The time and medium of settlement may be prescribed by:
a) Federal Reserve regulations or circulars
and b) Clearinghouse rules and the like
and c) Agreement

ii) Default Rule: If there are no such prescriptions of time or medium, the following shall apply:

(1) **Medium of Settlement:**
a) Cash
or b) Credit to an Account (in a Federal Reserve Bank) of or specified by the Person receiving the settlement

(2) **Time:**

(i) When the settlement is sent or delivered— for settlements tendered by
a) **Cash**
or b) **Cashier's Check**
or c) **Teller's Check**

(ii) When credit is made— for settlements tendered by **credit in a Federal Reserve Bank** Account

(iii) *Either*:
a) When a credit or debit is made— for settlements tendered by a **credit** or **debit to an Account** in a Bank
b) When Authority is sent or delivered— for settlements tendered by **authority to charge an Account**

(iv) When Payment is made to the Person receiving the settlement— for tender made by **Funds Transfer** (under § 4A-406(a))

(b) **Other Mediums of Settlement:** Settlement occurs when it is accepted by the Person receiving the settlement, if the settlement is not by a medium or time authorized by (a).

(c) **Finality for Cashier's or Teller's Check:**

(1) Settlement is final when the Check is finally paid if:
a) Settlement is made by Cashier's Check or Teller's Check
and b) The Person receiving the settlement Presents or forwards the Check for collection *before* the Midnight Deadline (of the Person receiving Payment) (see § 4-104(10)).

(2) Settlement is final at the *Midnight Deadline* (of the Person receiving Payment) if:
a) Settlement is made by Cashier's Check or Teller's Check.
and b) The Person receiving the settlement fails to Present or forward the Check for collection *before* the Midnight Deadline (see § 4-104(10)).

(d) **Finality for Authority to Charge Account**:

Settlement is final when the Account charged has available funds to cover the amount of the Item, if:

1. There is an agreement that permits the Bank giving settlement to give an authority to charge an Account as settlement.

and 2. Settlement is made by giving authority to charge the Account of the Bank making settlement in the Bank receiving settlement (and the Bank accepts the authority).

b) The Provisional Settlement:

OVERVIEW

As mentioned above, the Depositary Bank may delay final settlement on a Check by giving its Customer a "*provisional settlement.*"

If the Bank did not breach its duty of care, it may revoke its provisional settlement if the Payor Bank dishonors the Check.

- When dealing with Checks, **Regulation CC** applies, allowing only the Depositary Bank to make a provisional settlement (See Regulation CC 12 CFR § 229.36 and see also "PRESENTMENT," above). According to Regulation CC, the Payor Bank can make a final settlement only to its Presenting Bank.
- When dealing with other drafts, each Collecting Bank and the Payor Bank may give its Presenting Bank a "*provisional settlement.*"

The Payor Bank's "*provisional settlement*" becomes permanent by its *Midnight Deadline* (if it is not dishonored before then).

"*Charge-Back*"—If dishonor occurs, the provisional settlement may be revoked (this is known as "charge-back") (§ 4-214).

- Even if the Depositor (Customer) took cash as a provisional settlement (or wrote a Check against the deposit), the Bank may debit the Customer's Account or hold the Customer liable for the overdraft amount (the Bank usually recovers the money from Checks subsequently deposited into the account the Customer maintains with the Depositary Bank) (§ 4-210).
- Notice of Charge-back: The Bank **must** send notice to the Customer if it charges back the customer's account (§ 4-214(a)) (If the Bank neglects to send a notice it will be liable for damages such as subsequent overdrafts).

"Check Cashing"—Check Cashing is usually done by giving the Customer an advance from the provisional settlement and taking a security interest, using the Check as collateral for the cash advanced (§ 4-210) (see "CHECK CASHING" above).

In Between the time the Check is presented for Payment and the time the Payor Bank makes a Final Settlement, the Payor Bank may dishonor the Check.

The Bank is not liable for Unaccepted Checks or Checks with stop payment orders (§ 3-408).

Relevant Sections: § 4-214, § 4-215, § 4-302

§ 4-214: Provisional Settlement:

(a) **Bank's Power to Charge Back:**

1. Options available: If a Collecting Bank makes a *provisional settlement* for a Check (i.e., advances its Customer Money for an Item

(see §4-104(12) and §4-213) or credits a Customer's Account), and that Check is later dishonored or suspended, resulting in the Bank's failure to receive a final settlement, the Bank may:

a) Revoke the settlement it gave

or b) Charge back the Customer's Account for the amount of credit given

or c) Obtain a refund from its Customer

2. The Bank must *either:*

a) Return the Item (i.e., Check)

or b) Send the Customer a notification of the facts

3. **Time Limit:**

a) To avoid liability, the Bank must send the notification or return the Item:

1) By its Midnight Deadline

or 2) Within a *reasonable time* after it learns the facts

b) If the Bank misses the above deadline, it may still revoke, charge back the credit, or obtain a refund from the Customer, but it will be liable for any loss *caused by the delay.*

4. Termination of options: These options will terminate if and when a settlement for the Item received by the Bank is or becomes final.

(b) **Returning Items**—An Item is returned by a Collecting Bank when it is sent or delivered to:

1. The Bank's Customer

or 2. The transferor

or 3. Pursuant to instructions

(Note: This subsection does not apply to Checks—see Regulation CC)

(c) If a Depositary Bank is also a Payor, it may:

1. Charge back the amount of an Item to its Customer's Account

or 2. Obtain a refund (in accordance with §4-301)

(d) **The Right to Charge Back is not affected by:**

(1) Previous use of a credit given for the Item

or (2) Any Bank's failure to use Ordinary Care (although a Bank failing to use Ordinary Care remains liable; see §4-103(e) for measure of damages)

(e) **Failure to Charge Back:** A failure to charge back or claim a refund from the Customer does not affect other rights of the Bank against its Customer (or any other party). (Note: These might include warranty causes of action or enforcement of the Instrument.)

(f) **Determining Foreign Exchange Rate:**

If the Bank advanced dollars for an Item payable in foreign currency, the dollar amount of the charge-back or refund is calculated using the

Bank-offered spot rate for the foreign currency on the day that the Person entitled to the charge-back or refund learns that it will not receive Payment in ordinary course (unless otherwise fixed by the parties).

§ 4-215: Finality and Availability of Items:

(a) **Finality of an Item:** An Item is considered *finally paid* by the Payor Bank once it has *either:*

(1) Paid the Item in Cash

or (2) Settled for the Item, *without* having a right to revoke the settlement under:

a) Statute

or b) Clearinghouse rule

or c) Agreement

or (3) Made a **provisional settlement** (as per § 4-214) and failed to revoke the settlement in the time and manner permitted by:

a) Statute

or b) Clearinghouse rule

or c) Agreement

(b) **Finality of Provisional Settlement:**

If provisional settlement for an Item does not become final, the Item is not finally paid.

(c) **Finality of Provisional Payments Between Banks:**

Provisional settlements become final (i.e., "firms-up") upon final Payment of an Item by the *Payor Bank* if:

1. The Provisional settlement for the Item (between the Presenting and Paying banks) is made *either*:
   a) Through a Clearinghouse
   b) By debits and credits in an Account between the banks

and 2. Provisional debits or credits for the Item are entered in Accounts between *either:*

a. The Presenting and Payor Banks

or b. The Presenting Bank and successive prior Collecting Banks in a series

(d) **Responsibility to Customer for Final Settlements:**

1) If a Collecting Bank receives settlement for an Item (which is or becomes final), the Bank is accountable to its Customer for the amount of the Item.
2) If the Bank previously gave its Customer a provisional credit for the Item in an Account, the Bank's receipt of final settlement for the Item makes the provisional credit final ("firms up" the provisional credit).

(e) **Availability of Provisional Settlements and Items — Bank's Time Limit:**

I. This subsection is subject to:
   (i) Any applicable law stating a time for availability of funds (Checks, for example, are controlled by Regulation CC or similar applicable state law)
   and (ii) Any right of the Bank to apply the credit to an obligation of the Customer (right of setoff, such as a credit card balance owed to the Bank)

II. When a Bank credits a Customer's Account for an Item, the Customer will have a right to withdraw those funds, when the following conditions are met:
   (1) **Provisional settlements:** If the Bank received a Provisional settlement for the Item, the credit becomes available when:
      a) The settlement becomes final.
      and b) The Bank has had a *reasonable time* to receive return of the Item (this could depend on the distance the Item has to travel, the number of banks through which it has to pass, and other pertinent facts).
      and c) The Item has not been received within that time.
   (2) **The Bank is Both the Depositary and Payor Bank** — In this case, if the Item is finally paid, the credit becomes available 2 Banking Days after the Bank receives the Item (at the opening of the second Banking Day).

(f) **Availability of Money Deposits:**
   1. A deposit of Money becomes available for withdrawal, as of right, at the opening of the next Banking Day after the Bank receives the deposit.
   2. This subsection is subject to:
      a) Any applicable law stating a time for availability of funds (example: Regulation CC).
      b) Any right of a Bank to apply a deposit to an obligation of the depositor.

§ 4-302: Payor Bank's Responsibility:

(a) **Bank's Liability:** If an Item is presented to and received by a Payor Bank, the Bank is accountable for the amount of:

   (1) **A Demand Item Other than a Documentary Draft** (whether properly payable or not) if:
      a. The Payor Bank retains the Item beyond the Midnight Deadline (of the Banking Day of receipt without settling) and it is not also the Depositary Bank.

or b. The Payor Bank does not pay or return the Item (under § 4-301) until after the Midnight Deadline (regardless of whether it is also the Depositary Bank).

or c. The Payor Bank does not send notice of dishonor until after the Midnight Deadline (regardless of whether it is also the Depositary Bank).

or (2) **Any Other Properly Payable Item**—*unless*:

a. The Bank Accepts or Pays the Item within the time allowed for Acceptance or Payment (of that Item).

or b. The Bank Returns the Item and its accompanying documents within the time allowed for Acceptance or Payment (of that Item).

(b) **Exceptions to Liability of Payor Bank to Pay:**

The liability in (a) is subject to defenses based on:

1. Breach of Presentment warranty (under § 4-208)

or 2. Proof that the Person seeking enforcement of the liability either Presented or transferred the Item in order to defraud the Payor Bank

c) *Dishonor:*

1. Time of Dishonor

OVERVIEW

Dishonor occurs when the Drawee/Payor Bank returns a Presented Item by its *Midnight Deadline* either:

1. Without paying or Accepting the Check

or 2. Without any of the reasons specified in § 3-501(b)(3) (i.e., improper Indorsement or failure to comply with the terms of the Instrument)

Time for Dishonor:

- The Drawee has to **Accept** or **Pay** the Draft within a certain amount of time; this time varies according to the Instrument.
  1. **Time Drafts** (see § 3-502(b)(3),(4))
  2. **Drafts Payable on Demand** (usually not Checks)—(see § 3-502(b)(2))
  3. **Checks** (except those presented for Immediate Payment) (§ 3-502(b)(1))—Dishonor occurs according to Articles 3 and 4, and Regulation CC (i.e., as detailed above)
  4. **Other Non-Check Drafts:** Dishonor occurs according to Articles 3 and 4 (Regulation CC applies only to Checks).
- **Banker's Exception to Delay Payment for Checks**:
  - When dealing with Checks presented to a Bank, § 3-502(b)(1) directs a person to Article 4, which discusses the *Midnight Deadline* rule.
  - Banks can delay Payment or Acceptance until their Midnight Deadline if, instead of paying the Holder, they give him a *provisional settlement* (which need not be finalized until the Midnight Deadline).
- **Exceptions to the Dishonor Deadline:**
  1) A Bank may be excused if it tries to send a Notice or return the Check with *due diligence* (§ 4-108).
  2) Regulation CC Exception—If a Bank returns a Check using a more expeditious method of delivery, it will be excused for missing its Midnight Deadline (Regulation CC 12 CFR § 229.30).
  3) Clearing-House Rules Exception—If a Check is redeposited after being dishonored, the Bank will not be liable to pay the Check even if it sends notice of dishonor after its Midnight Deadline.

Relevant Section: § 3-502

§ 3-502: Dishonor:

(a) **Rules Governing Dishonor of a <u>Note:</u>**

(1) <u>Notes Payable on Demand</u> — A Note is considered dishonored when:
a) Presentment is duly made to the Maker.
and b) The Note is not paid on the day of Presentment.
(2) <u>Notes Not Payable on Demand</u> —
a) This section applies to Notes not Payable on Demand if:
1. They are payable at or through a Bank.
or 2. The terms of the Note require Presentment.
b) The Note will be considered dishonored if:
1. Presentment is duly made.
and 2. The Note is not paid by the *<u>later</u>* of:
a) The day it becomes payable.
or b) The day of Presentment.
(3) <u>Other Notes Not Payable on Demand</u> — The Note is dishonored if it is not paid on the day it becomes payable.

(b) **Rules Governing Dishonor of an Unaccepted <u>Draft</u>** (other than a Documentary Draft):

(1) <u>Check Presented for Payment at a Later Date</u> — A Check is dishonored when:
a) The Check is duly presented for Payment to the Payor Bank.
and b) The Check is not presented for immediate Payment over the counter.
and c) The Payor Bank *either*:
1. Returns the Check in a timely fashion.
or 2. Sends a timely notice of dishonor or non-payment (under § 4-301 or § 4-302).
or 3. Becomes accountable for the amount of the Check under § 4-302 (Late Return).
(2) <u>Draft Payable on Demand</u> —
a) This section applies to drafts:
1. Payable on Demand
and 2. Not falling under (1) above (This section covers demand drafts (other than Checks) and Checks presented for immediate Payment (official comment))
b) The Draft will be considered dishonored if:
1. The Draft is duly presented to the Drawee for Payment.
and 2. The Draft is not paid on the day of Presentment.

(3) Time Draft Payable at a Specified Date (stated in the Draft) — the Draft will be considered dishonored if:

(i) **Draft Presented for Payment:**

a) The Draft is duly presented for Payment to the Drawee.

and b) Payment is not made by the *later* of:

1. The day of Presentment.
2. The day the Draft becomes payable.

or (ii) **Draft Presented for Acceptance:**

a) The Draft is duly presented for Acceptance before the Draft becomes payable.

and b) The Draft is not accepted on the day of Presentment.

(4) Time Draft Payable on Elapse of a Period of Time After Sight or Acceptance — the Draft is dishonored if:

a) The Draft is duly presented for Acceptance.

and b) The Draft is not accepted on the day of Presentment.

(c) **Rules Governing Dishonor of an Unaccepted Documentary Draft** (e.g., drafts under a Letter of Credit): The rules in § 3-502(2),(3), and (4) apply to Unaccepted Documentary Drafts *except* that Payment or Acceptance may be delayed until the end of the third business day after Payment or Acceptance would otherwise be required (under § 3-502(2),(3),(4)) without the Draft being considered dishonored.

(d) **Rules Governing Dishonor of an Accepted Draft:**

(1) Draft Payable on Demand — the Draft will be considered dishonored if:

a. The Draft is duly presented to the Acceptor for Payment.

and b. The Draft is not paid on the day of Presentment.

(2) Draft Not Payable on Demand — the Draft will be considered dishonored if:

a. The Draft is duly presented for Payment to the Acceptor.

and b. Payment is not made by the *later* of:

i) The day of Presentment.

or ii) The day the Draft becomes payable.

(e) **Dishonor Without Presentment:**

Dishonor may occur without Presentment if:

1. Presentment is otherwise required for dishonor (under § 3-502).

and 2. Presentment is excused (under § 3-504).

and 3. The Instrument is not duly Accepted or Paid.

(f) **Consent to Late Acceptance:**

A Draft will not be considered dishonored from the time of Acceptance if:

a) Dishonor occurred because the Draft was not timely accepted (under 3-502(b)(3)(ii) or (4)).
b) The Person entitled to demand Acceptance consents to a late Acceptance.

2. Notice of Dishonor

OVERVIEW

Notice Requirement for Dishonor (§ 3-503)
- A Draft can be dishonored only if the Payor Bank either:
  1) Sends a *notice of dishonor* by its Midnight Deadline
  or 2) Returns the Check by its Midnight deadline
- Liability on dishonored Checks:
  - Notice or return is necessary to make the *Indorser* and *Drawer* liable on the dishonored Check (since, according to § 3-415 and § 3-414 they become liable only upon dishonor. Note: Although the Drawer is always liable on its Check, the Payee can't go to the Drawer for Payment until the Check is first dishonored by the Drawee/Payor Bank).
  - The Payor Bank will be liable to pay the Check if it doesn't return the Check or send a notice of dishonor by its Midnight Deadline (§ 4-302(a)(1)).
  - The Collecting Banks (including the Depositary Bank) will be liable to Pay the Check if they do not forward the returned Check or notice of dishonor by their Midnight Deadlines.
- The Notice requirement may be waived (§ 3-504(b)).

When Dishonor Does Not Occur: Dishonor does not occur if (§ 3-409(d)):
1) A Bank refuses to Certify a Check (§ 3-409(d))
or 2) An Instrument is returned for lack of necessary Indorsement (§ 3-501(3))
or 3) Payment/Acceptance is refused because the presenter failed to comply with terms of its Bank agreement (§ 3-501(3)(ii))
or 4) The Check was returned because the Draft was not timely accepted (i.e., it was "stale" (§ 3-502(f))) and the Person entitled to demand Acceptance consents to a late Acceptance (§ 3-502(f)).

Relevant Sections: § 3-503, § 3-504, § 3-505, § 4-108

§ 3-503: Notice of Dishonor:

(a) **When Indorser and Drawer Obligated:** The obligation of an Indorser (under § 3-415(a)) and a Drawer (under § 3-414(d)) may not be enforced *unless*:

(i) The Indorser or Drawer is given Notice of Dishonor (complying with § 3-503) of the Instrument.

or (ii) Notice of Dishonor is excused (under § 3-504(b)).

(b) **Requirements for Notice:**

1. By Whom Given—Notice of Dishonor may be given by any Person.
2. Method of Notice—Notice of Dishonor may be given by any *commercially reasonable* means (including oral, written, or electronic communication).
3. Contents of Notice—Notice will be sufficient if it:
    a) *Reasonably identifies* the Instrument
    and b) Indicates that the Instrument has been dishonored or that it has not been Paid or Accepted
4. Return of Instrument as Notice—Return of an Instrument given to a Bank for collection is sufficient notice.

(c) **Deadline for Notice:**

(i) Notice by Collecting Bank: If an Instrument is taken for collection by a Collecting Bank, Notice of Dishonor must be given by the Bank by midnight of the next Banking Day (i.e., The Bank's "Midnight Deadline") after the Bank received Notice of Dishonor from the Payor Bank.
(ii) Notice by Other Person: If an Instrument is taken for collection by a Collecting Bank, Notice of Dishonor may be given by any Person other than the Bank within 30 days from the date that Person received Notice of Dishonor.
(iii) Other Instruments: Notice of Dishonor must be given within 30 days after the date on which dishonor occurred.
(iv) This subsection is subject to § 3-504(c).

§ 3-504: Excused Presentment and Notice of Dishonor:

(a) **Presentment Excused**—Presentment is not needed for Payment or Acceptance if:

(i) The Person entitled to present the Instrument cannot make Presentment with *reasonable diligence.*
or (ii) The Maker or Acceptor *either:*
    1. Repudiated his obligation to pay the Instrument.
    or 2. Died.
    or 3. Is in insolvency proceedings.
or (iii) The Instrument's terms do not require Presentment to enforce the obligation of the Indorsers or the Drawer.
or (iv) The Drawer or Indorser (whose obligation is being enforced) *either:*
    1. Has waived the requirement of Presentment.

or 2. Otherwise has no reason to expect that the Instrument be Paid or Accepted.

or 3. Otherwise has no right to require that the Instrument be Paid or Accepted.

or (v) *Either:*

1. The Drawer instructed the Drawee not to pay or Accept the Draft.

or 2. The Drawee was not obligated to the Drawer to pay the Draft.

(b) **Notice of Dishonor Excused:**

1. A Notice of Dishonor is not required if:
   (i) The terms of the Instrument do not require notice to enforce the obligation of a party to pay the Instrument.
   or (ii) The party (whose obligation is being enforced) waived notice.
2. A waiver of Presentment is also a waiver of Notice of Dishonor.

(c) **Delay of Notice of Dishonor Excused:** Delay of Notice of Dishonor is excused if:

1. The delay was caused by circumstances beyond the control of the Person giving the notice.

and 2. The Person giving the notice exercised *reasonable diligence* after the cause of the delay ceased to operate.

§3-505: Evidence of Dishonor:

(a) **Admissible Evidence to Presume Dishonor:** The following evidence is admissible to create a presumption of Dishonor and a presumption that Notice of Dishonor was conferred:

(1) Protest Documents—any document which purports to be a Protest (must be in regular form, as provided in §3-505(b))

(2) Writing or Stamps—a purported writing or stamp of the Drawee, Payor Bank, or Presenting Bank, on the Instrument or accompanying the Instrument stating that Acceptance or Payment has been refused (unless the reasons for refusal of Payment/Acceptance are not consistent with dishonor)

(3) Books or Records—the Drawee, Payor Bank, or Collecting Bank may provide books or records which show dishonor, if the Books/Records were kept *in the ordinary course of business* (even if there is no evidence of who made the entry)

(b) **Protest:**

1. **"Protest"**—a protest is a certificate of dishonor made by *either*:
   a) A United States Counsel

or b) A United States Vice Counsel
or c) A Notary Public
or d) Another Person authorized to administer oaths by the law of the place where dishonor occurs.

2. The protest may be made upon providing information *satisfactory* to that Person.
3. Requirements of Protest—The Protest must:
   a) Identify the dishonored Instrument
   and b) Certify that *either*:
      i) Presentment has been made
      or ii) If Presentment was not made, the reason why it was not made
   and c) Certify that the Instrument has been dishonored by non-acceptance or nonpayment
4. The Protest may also certify that Notice of Dishonor has been given to some or all of the parties.

§ 4-108: Time of Receipt of Items:

(a) **Cut-Off hour:**

1. A Bank may fix an hour after 2:00 P.M. as a cut-off hour for purposes of:
   a) Handling Money and Items
   b) Making entries on its books
2. The cut-off hour has been allowed in order to allow banks time to:
   a) Process items
   and b) Prove balances
   and c) Make the necessary entries on its books (to determine its position for the day)

(b) **Deferral of Receipt:**

An Item or deposit of Money may be treated as being received at the opening of the next Banking Day if it is received *after*:

1. The cut-off hour
or 2. The close of the Banking Day

3. Valid Reasons for Dishonor

OVERVIEW

The following are acceptable reasons for a Bank to dishonor a Check:

1) *Dishonor for Overdrafts*—
   - Banks may dishonor a Check if their Customer has insufficient funds in its account.
   - The Bank may choose any Order it wants to pay Checks (if the Customer does not have enough Money in its Account to pay for all of them) (§ 4-303(b)).
2) *Dishonor by SPO*—The Bank must dishonor a check if instructed to do so by a Stop Payment Order (§ 4-402, see "STOP PAYMENT ORDERS" below).
3) *Stale Items*—A Bank may dishonor an Item if it is "stale" (§ 3-304).
4) *Dishonor of Check not Properly Payable*—This is a valid excuse for dishonor since banks may pay only "properly payable" Checks (as per § 4-401(a)).

Relevant Sections: § 4-303(b), § 4-402(a), § 4-401(a)

§ 4-303(b): Time Limit for Stop Payment Orders:

***

(b) Subject to subsection (a), items may be Accepted, Paid, Certified, or charged to the indicated Account of the Bank's Customer *in any order*.

§ 4-402(a): Bank's Liability for Wrongful Dishonor:

(a) **"Wrongful Dishonor"**

A Payor Bank will have **wrongfully dishonored** an Item if the Bank dishonors:

a) A *properly payable* Item

or b) An Item that would create an overdraft and the Bank had *agreed* to pay the overdraft

§ 4-401(a): When Bank May Charge Customer's Account:

(a) **Charging Customer's Account**

1. A Bank may charge the Customer's Account for an Item that is *properly payable* from the Account, even if the charge creates an overdraft.
2. An Item is "properly payable" if:
   a) It is authorized by the Customer.
   and b) It is in accordance with any agreement between the Customer and the Bank.

4. Wrongful Dishonor

OVERVIEW

Wrongful Dishonor:
- If the Bank wrongfully stops payment claiming insufficient funds, a "Customer" (usually the Drawer) may take action under § 4-402 (and may also sue under common law for libel if it can prove intent).
- **Liability is limited** to *actual damages* for Dishonoring Checks.

Liability for Wrongful Dishonor: (See also Liability Chart in appendix)
- To Drawer — If the Drawer is the Customer (as per § 4-104(a)(5)) the Payor Bank will be liable for damages incurred as a result of the wrongful dishonor (§ 4-402(b)).
- To Payee/Holder — The Payor Bank will not be liable to the Holder since the Payor Bank is not liable on an unaccepted Draft (§ 3-408), and the Check has not been accepted, but rather Dishonored (under § 3-409; § 3-502).
  - Note: The Payor Bank has not Signed the Check as per § 1-201(39) (see § 3-401 and § 3-409(a) (Signature needed for Acceptance).

Relevant Sections: § 4-104(a)(5), § 4-402

§ 4-104(a)(5): Definitions:

(a) The following definitions apply to Article 4, unless the context requires otherwise:

* * *

(5) **"Customer"** —
a. A Person who has an Account with a Bank
or b. A Person for whom the Bank has agreed to collect items, including a Bank that maintains an Account with another Bank

§ 4-402: Bank's Liability for Wrongful Dishonor:

(a) **"Wrongful Dishonor"**

A Payor Bank will have **wrongfully dishonored** an Item if the Bank dishonors:

a) A *properly payable* Item
or b) An Item that would create an overdraft and the Bank had *agreed* to pay the overdraft

(b) **Liability of Payor Bank**

1. A Payor Bank is liable to its Customer for damages *proximately caused* by the wrongful dishonor.
2. Limitation of Liability:
   a) Liability is limited to *actual damages proved.*
   b) Liability may include damages for:
      1) An arrest of the Customer.
      or 2) Prosecution of the Customer.
      or 3) Other consequential damages.
3. Whether damages were *"proximately caused"* by the wrongful dishonor is a question of fact (to be determined on a case-by-case basis).

(c) **Time of Determining Insufficiency of Account**

1. A Payor Bank may determine the Customer's Account balance (on which to base a decision not to Honor an Item) at any time between the time the Item is received by the Payor Bank and *either*:
   a) The time the Payor Bank returns the Item.
   or b) The time the Payor Bank gives notice (instead of return).
2. Only one determination need be made.
3. Redetermination: If the Bank decides to redetermine the Customer's Account balance (to determine sufficiency of funds), the later Account balance is the one used to determine whether an Item is wrongfully dishonored.

5. Dishonoring Cashier's or Certified Checks

OVERVIEW

Dishonor of Certified Checks (§ 3-411):

- The Drawer is not liable if a Bank Dishonors a Certified Check (§ 3-414(c)).[32]
- The Bank is liable for the *full amount* of a Certified Check as it appears on the date of Certification (§ 3-413(b)).
- **Effect of Dishonor on Drawer:** When a Bank Dishonors a Certified Check, the Holder cannot sue the Person giving the Check since:
  - The Contract being satisfied with the Certified Check is *discharged* when the Certified Check is presented to the Payee (§ 3-310(a)).
  - The Drawers and Indorsers of a Check that has subsequently been Certified are relieved of liability (under § 3-414(c) and § 3-415(d) for Indorsers, since a Certified Check is considered to be "Accepted" (§ 3-409), which under § 3-414 and § 3-415 relieves the Indorser and Drawer of liability).
- However, the Holder may enforce the Instrument against the Bank that Accepted (i.e., Certified) it, and may also get additional compensation for expenses, loss of interest, and consequential damages (subject to possible defenses of the Bank) (§ 3-411).

Relevant Sections: § 3-413(b), § 3-414(c), § 3-411, § 4-213(c)

§ 3-413(b): Obligation of Acceptor:

* * *

(b) **Exceptions**

1) Amount Stated: The Acceptor must pay the amount so stated on the Draft if the Acceptance of the Draft (or certification of a Check) specifically states the amount Accepted or Certified.
2) Holder in Due Course: The Acceptor must pay the amount of the Instrument at the time it was taken by an HDC if:
    - (i) The Certification or Acceptance does not state an amount.
    - and (ii) The amount of the Instrument is subsequently raised.
    - and (iii) The Instrument is then negotiated to an HDC.

[32] Note: A Bank does not have to certify a Check (§ 3-409(d)) and the Bank's refusal to certify a Check is not considered a dishonor (§ 3-409(d)).

§ 3-414(c): Obligation of Drawer:

* * *

(c) **Discharge of Drawer:** If a Draft is Accepted by a Bank, the Drawer is discharged (regardless of when or by whom acceptance was obtained).

§ 3-411: Refusal to Pay Cashier's, Teller's, or Certified Checks:

(a) **"Obligated Bank"**—*for this section*—means:

1. The Acceptor of a Certified Check

and 2. The Issuer of a Cashier's Check or Teller's Check (bought from the Issuer)

(b) **When Bank is Liable:**

1. An Obligated Bank will be liable to a Person entitled to Payment of a Check if it wrongfully:
   (i) Refuses to pay a Cashier's Check or Certified Check
   or (ii) Stops Payment of a Teller's Check
   or (iii) Refuses to pay a dishonored Teller's Check
2. A Person asserting the right to enforce the Check is entitled to:
   i) <u>Compensation</u>—for expenses and loss of interest *resulting from the nonpayment*
   and ii) <u>Consequential damages</u>—if the obligated Bank refuses to pay after receiving notice of particular circumstances giving rise to the damages.

(c) **When Bank is not Liable:** Expenses or consequential damages (under (b) above) are NOT recoverable if the Bank refuses to pay because:

(i) The Bank suspends Payments.

or (ii) The Obligated Bank asserts a claim or defense of the Bank that it has reasonable grounds to believe is available against the Person Entitled to Enforce the Instrument.

or (iii) The Obligated Bank has a reasonable doubt whether the Person demanding Payment is the Person Entitled to Enforce the Instrument.

or (iv) Payment is prohibited by law.

§ 4-213(c): Settlement by Bank:

* * *

(c) **Finality for Cashier's or Teller's Check:**

(1) Settlement is final when the Check is finally paid if:
    a) Settlement is made by Cashier's Check or Teller's Check.
and b) The Person receiving the settlement Presents or forwards the Check for collection *before* the Midnight Deadline (of the Person receiving Payment) (see § 4-104(10)).

(2) Settlement is final at the *Midnight Deadline* (of the Person receiving Payment) if:
    a) Settlement is made by Cashier's Check or Teller's Check.
and b) The Person receiving the settlement Fails to Present or forward the Check for collection *before* the Midnight Deadline (see § 4-104(10)).

d) Stop Payment Orders: ("SPOs")

OVERVIEW

If the Drawer has a contract claim against the Payee, he may attempt to stop payment on his check before the Payor Bank pays it (example: If a seller defrauds a buyer, the buyer has an "adverse claim" against the seller, and is, therefore, not liable on the Check he used to pay the seller. The seller is said to have "voidable title" to the Check).

The Customer must give its Bank a Stop Payment Order ("SPO") within a *"reasonable time"* in order to make the SPO effective (§ 4-403).

Reasonable Notice: The Drawer must give its Bank reasonable notice to Stop Payment on a Check:

- **Cut-Off hour** (§ 4-303): Banks may set a cut-off hour, after which they will not Honor SPOs.
- **Effectiveness** (§ 4-403):
  - *Oral* Notice—good for 14 Days (may be extended to 6 months by a written SPO within the 14-Day period)
  - *Written* Notice—good for 6 Months (may be renewed in writing for 6 more months).

Damages:

1) If the Bank does not respond to a valid stop payment order in time, it will be liable for any resulting *actual damages* (losses incurred as a result of a stop payment order) to its Customer.
2) The Customer has the burden of proving the actual damages incurred.
3) *Prima Facie* evidence of actual damage is that the Customer made the SPO within a reasonable time and that he lost money as a result of the Check being paid.

Payor Bank's Liability for Wrongful Payment: (see also Liability Chart in appendix)

- *To Drawer*—The Payor Bank will be responsible to pay the Drawer for:
  1. *Actual Damages* resulting from not stopping payment (§ 4-403: Bank cannot charge its Customer's Account for Checks not "properly payable" (§ 4-401)).
  2. Any subsequent damages resulting from the wrongful payment (example: loss from bounced checks if an overdraft occurs from wrongful payment (§ 4-403(c)), *unless* the SPO was made too late (§ 4-303(a))
     - Note: The Bank may Stop Payment even if the SPO was late; Payee has no right to force the Bank to pay the check since the Bank did not Accept the check (§ 4-409).
  3. **HDC Exception**—If the Holder was an HDC, there will probably be no damages if an SPO was not obeyed, since the Drawer would have to pay the HDC anyway. Damages may result if the Drawer has a defense that is good against an HDC (i.e., a "real defense"; see "DEFENSES").

- *To Depositary Bank*—If the Depositary Bank paid the Check, it may be compensated up to the Value given to its Customer (i.e., the Payee/Holder), and can claim Payment from *either:*
  1) The Payor Bank, (since they are HDCs)
  or 2) The Payee (under § 4-318: Payment by Mistake).

Waiver of Bank's Liability on SPOs: Waivers will be effective unless the SPO was not followed as a result of *lack of due care* (since § 4-103 doesn't allow a Bank to waive its duty of care).

Burden of Proof: The burden of establishing the fact and amount of loss resulting from Payment of an Item contrary to a stop payment order is on the Customer (§ 4-403).

Relevant Sections: § 4-403, § 4-303, § 4-402

§ 4-403: Customer's Right to Stop Payment:

(a) **The Stop Payment Order Process:**

1. A Customer (or anyone authorized to draw on the Account (if there is more than one Person)) may:
   a) Stop Payment of any Item drawn on its Account.
   or b) Close its Account.
2. Procedure:
   a) The Customer must order the Bank to stop payment or close the Account.
   b) The Customer must describe the Item or Account with *reasonable certainty.*
   c) The order and description must be received by the Bank at a time and in a manner that affords the Bank a *reasonable opportunity* to act on it before it takes an action described in § 4-303.
3. If more than one signature is required to draw on an Account, any of the signatories may stop Payment or close the Account.

(b) **Effectiveness of a Stop Payment Order:**

1. A Stop payment order ("SPO") will remain in effect for:
   a) ***Written*** SPO[33]—6 months
   b) Oral SPO—effective for 14 Days (unless confirmed in *writing* before the 14 days are over)
2. Renewal: An SPO may be renewed for additional 6-month periods with a ***writing*** to the Bank (while the SPO is still in effect)

[33] Revised Article 3 (2002) changes the requirement of a "Writing" to a "Record."

(c) **Burden of Proof; Damages:**

1. The Customer has the burden of establishing the fact and amount of loss resulting from the Payment of an Item (contrary to an SPO or order to close an Account).
2. The loss from Payment of an Item contrary to an SPO may include damages for dishonor of subsequent items (under § 4-402).

§ 4-303: Time Limit for Stop Payment Orders:

(a) **Time Limit:**

1. **Scope; "The Four Legals":** This section applies if a Payor Bank, while processing an Item presented for Payment, *either:*
    a. Receives Legal Notice: The Payor Bank receives knowledge or a legal notice affecting the Item (example: that the Drawer has filed a petition in bankruptcy; the Drawer made an assignment for the benefit of creditors).
    or b. Receives a stop payment order: The Payor Bank receives an Order of the Drawer stopping Payment on the Item.
    or c. Is Served Order of Attachment: The Payor Bank is served an attachment of the Drawer's Account ("legal process").
    or d. Exercises a Setoff: The Payor Bank exercises a right of setoff against the Drawer's Account.

(Note: These are sometimes called "**The Four Legals.**")

2. **Time Limit for Bank to Terminate, Suspend, or Modify:** If any one of the four events listed above takes place, and a reasonable time for the Bank to act on it expires (or the setoff is exercised), then:
    a. Such event has priority.
    and b. The knowledge, notice, stop payment order, legal process, or setoff is deemed too late to terminate, suspend, or modify the Bank's right or duty to:
        1) Pay the Item.
        or 2) Charge its Customer's Account for the Item.
3. The above time limit applies provided that the event plus a reasonable time to act on it occur after one of the following, whichever is earliest:
    (1) The Bank Accepts or Certifies the Item.
    (2) The Bank Pays the Item in Cash.
    (3) The Bank Settles for the Item without having a right to revoke the settlement (under a Clearinghouse rule, statute, or agreement) (example: the Bank Settles for an Item presented over the counter for immediate Payment by a

Cashier's Check or Teller's Check, which the Person agrees to take).

(4) The Bank becomes accountable for the amount of the Item (under § 4-302).

(5) For Checks:

a. A cutoff hour between 1 hour after the opening of the Banking Day after the Bank received the Check and the close of the next Banking Day passes.

b. If no cutoff hour is fixed, the close of the Banking Day after the day the Bank received the Check comes to a close.

(b) Subject to subsection (a), items may be Accepted, Paid, Certified, or charged to the indicated Account of the Bank's Customer *in any order*.

§ 4-402: Bank's Liability for Wrongful Dishonor:

(a) **"Wrongful Dishonor"**

A Payor Bank will have **wrongfully dishonored** an Item if the Bank Dishonors:

a) A *properly payable* Item

or b) An Item that would create an overdraft and the Bank had *agreed* to pay the overdraft

(b) **Liability of Payor Bank**

1. A Payor Bank is liable to its Customer for damages *proximately caused* by the wrongful dishonor.
2. Limitation of liability:
   a) Liability is limited to *actual damages proved.*
   b) Liability may include damages for:
      1) An arrest of the Customer.
      or 2) Prosecution of the Customer.
      or 3) Other consequential damages.
3. Whether damages were *"proximately caused"* by the wrongful dishonor is a question of fact (to be determined on a case-by-case basis).

(c) **Time of Determining Insufficiency of Account**

1. A Payor Bank may determine the Customer's Account balance (on which to base a decision not to Honor an Item) at any time

between the time the Item is received by the Payor Bank and *either*:

a) The time the Payor Bank returns the Item.

or b) The time the Payor Bank gives notice (instead of return).

2. Only one determination need be made.
3. Redetermination: If the Bank decides to redetermine the Customer's Account balance (to determine sufficiency of funds), the later Account balance is the one used to determine whether an Item is wrongfully dishonored.

3) The Final Settlement: (§ 4-215)

OVERVIEW

It is very important to determine when final settlement has occurred since a Bank cannot Dishonor a Check after final settlement has been made.

§ 3-418 applies after final settlement has been made, allowing recovery of Payment made by mistake. (Note: A Drawee Bank may not recover under "Payment by Mistake" if it pays a check and later discovers that there were insufficient funds or that the account was closed.)

When Final Settlement Occurs:

- The Payor Bank's "provisional settlement" becomes "final" by its Midnight Deadline (unless it is Dishonored before then) (but see Regulation CC extension exceptions as discussed above).[34]
- The Depositary Bank's "provisional settlement" will become "final" on the Payor Bank's Midnight Deadline *unless* the Depositary Bank receives a Notice of Dishonor to be forwarded to its Customer.
- Delivery of a Cashier's Check in exchange for another Check is considered to be a final settlement.
- Payment of cash for a Check by the Payor Bank is considered a final settlement. (Note: Banks usually do not cash Checks — they give the Payee a loan for the Check amount; see § 4-210 and the discussion above about "Cashing Checks.")

Recovery After Final Settlement: The Payor Bank may recover money after final settlement only if:

1. Mistake was involved (§ 3-418)

or **2.** Presentment Warranties were breached (§ 4-208 (see "WARRANTIES" below))

RECOVERY OF PAYMENTS MADE:

1) Right to Charge back: The Payor Bank has a right to charge back the Customer's account for overdrafting (§ 4-401(a)) (example: when the Bank pays a Check with insufficient funds in the Drawer's Account) even if the Bank did not use Ordinary Care (§ 4-214(d)(2)).
2) Right to Restitution: The Payor Bank may resort to restitution remedies (under § 3-418: "Payment by Mistake." This is equivalent to court claims of restitution (§ 3-418(b)).
3) Indorser's Liability: If a Bank pays a Check by mistake, it can hold the Indorser liable for the Check if a Transfer or Presentment warranty is breached (§ 3-418).
4) Rights of Subrogation (§ 4-407): If the Bank wrongfully paid the Payee, it can sue the Payee as if it were the Drawer (i.e., The Bank obtains the rights

---

[34] Under former Article 4, Payment is final only upon *"posting"*; this rule no longer applies under the Revised Article 4 (thus, the posting date is irrelevant).

and standing to sue the Drawer for any claims the Drawer has against the Payee).

Relevant Sections: § 3-418, § 4-301, § 4-302

§ 3-418: Payment or Acceptance by Mistake:

(a) **Drawee's Right to Revoke or Recover:**

1) Power to Recover: The Drawee may recover the amount of the Draft from the Person who received Payment if the Drawee:
   a) Pays the Draft.
   and b) Acted on the mistaken belief that:
      (i) Payment of the Draft had not been stopped (pursuant to § 4-403).
      or (ii) The drawer's signature on the Draft was authorized.
2) Power to Revoke: If the Drawee Accepts the Draft (instead of paying for it), and the above conditions are met, he may Revoke Acceptance.
3) These rights are not affected by the Drawee's failure to exercise Ordinary Care in paying or accepting the Draft.
4) This subsection is subject to (c) below.

(b) **Person Paying or Accepting Party's Rights:**

1. If an Instrument was Accepted or Paid by *mistake*, the Person Paying or Accepting may (to the extent permitted by the law governing mistake and restitution, i.e., common law and other statutes):
   (i) Recover Payment from the Person who received Payment (i.e., Restitution)
   or (ii) Revoke Acceptance.[35]
2. Section 3-418(b) applies only to cases not covered by (a).
3. This subsection is subject to (c) below.

(c) **Defenses:**

1. Remedies in (a) and (b) may not be asserted against a Person who:[36]
   a. Took the Instrument:
      1. In Good Faith
      and 2. For Value

---

[35] This provision was not part of former Article 3.
[36] Former Article 3 limited these defenses to HDCs.

or b. Changed his position:
1. In Good Faith
2. In Reliance on the Payment or Acceptance (example: taking Money out of Bank Account)

2. This subsection does not limit remedies provided by § 3-417 or § 4-407.

(d) **Effect of Revocation or Recovery:**

1. This section applies if:
   a) An Instrument is Paid or Accepted by mistake
   and b) The Payor or Acceptor either:
      1. Recovers Payment (under (a) or (b))
      or 2. Revokes Acceptance (under (a) or (b)).
2. Effect of revocation or recovery: If the above conditions are fulfilled, then:
   a) The Instrument is deemed not to have been Paid or Accepted.
   and b) The Instrument is treated as dishonored.
   and c) The Person from whom Payment is recovered obtains the same rights as a Person Entitled to Enforce the dishonored Instrument.
3. Even though a Payor Bank may have paid an Item under § 4-215, it may have a right to recover the Payment under § 3-418.

§ 4-301: Recovery and Return:

(a) **Revoking and Recovering Settlement:** A Payor Bank may revoke and recover a settlement if:

a) The Payor Bank tendered the settlement before midnight of the Banking Day of receipt of a demand Item (other than a Documentary Draft)
and b) The Demand Item was not Presented for immediate Payment (i.e., over the counter)
and c) Before its Midnight Deadline and before it has made Final Payment, the Bank
   (1) Returns the Item
   or (2) Sends a ***written*** notice[37] of dishonor or nonpayment if the Item is unavailable for return (example: when Presentment is made by a Presentment notice and the

[37] Revised Article 3 (2002) changes the requirement of a "Writing" to a "Record."

Item is retained by the Collecting Bank). (For Checks, Regulation CC governs method of giving notice.)

<u>*Revised Article 3 (2002) adds:*</u>

or (3) Returns an image of an Item, if the party to which the return is made has entered into an agreement to accept an image as a return of the Item, and the image is returned in accordance with that agreement.

(b) **Recovery and Revocation when Payor Bank is also Depositary Bank:**

1. <u>A Payor Bank may</u>:
    a) Return the Item
    and b) Send notice of dishonor
    and c) *Either*:
        1) Revoke any credit given
        or 2) Recover the amount of credit given
        or 3) Recover the amount withdrawn by its Customer
2. **Availability:** In order to take the above actions:
    a) A Demand Item must be received by a Payor Bank for credit on its books.
    b) The Payor Bank must act within the time limit and in the manner specified in (a).

(c) **Time Limit for Notice of Dishonor:**

Unless a previous notice of dishonor has been sent, an Item is dishonored when:

1) The Item is returned (for purposes of dishonor)
or 2) Notice is sent (in accordance with this section)

(d) **When an Item is Considered "Returned":**

(1) <u>Items Presented through a Clearinghouse:</u>
    a) When the Item is *delivered* to:
        1. The Presenting Bank
        or 2. The Last Collecting Bank
        or 3. The Clearinghouse
    or b) When the Item is *sent* (see § 1-201(38)) or *delivered* in accordance with Clearinghouse rules
(2) <u>All other Cases:</u> When the Item is *sent* (see § 1-201(38)) or *delivered*:
    a) To the Bank's Customer
    or b) To the transferor
    or c) Pursuant to instructions

§ 4-302: Payor Bank's Responsibility:

(a) **Bank's Liability:** If an Item is presented to and received by a Payor Bank, the Bank is accountable for the amount of:

(1) **A Demand Item Other than a Documentary Draft** (whether properly payable or not) if:

a. The Payor Bank retains the Item beyond the Midnight Deadline (of the Banking Day of receipt without settling) and it is not also the Depositary Bank.

or b. The Payor Bank does not pay or return the Item (under § 4-301) until after the Midnight Deadline (regardless of whether it is also the Depositary Bank).

or c. The Payor Bank does not send notice of dishonor until after the Midnight Deadline (regardless of whether it is also the Depositary Bank).

or (2) **Any Other Properly Payable Item** — *unless*:

a. The Bank Accepts or Pays the Item within the time allowed for Acceptance or Payment (of that Item).

or b. The Bank Returns the Item and its accompanying documents within the time allowed for Acceptance or Payment (of that Item).

(b) **Exceptions to Liability of Payor Bank to Pay:**

The liability in (a) is subject to defenses based on:

1. Breach of Presentment warranty (under § 4-208)

or 2. Proof that the Person seeking enforcement of the liability either Presented or transferred the Item in order to defraud the Payor Bank

VIII. DOCUMENTS OF TITLE AND LETTERS OF CREDIT:

A. DOCUMENTS OF TITLE:

OVERVIEW

Documents of Title ("DOTs") are used to "transform" property rights in goods to "paper," so people can transfer title to goods more easily (without having to transfer possession every time people want to transfer interests). Just like other Negotiable Instruments, they can be freely negotiated. The only difference is that they are often payable in goods and not money.

- Documents of title are considered *"Commodity Paper,"* while drafts and Notes are considered *"Money Paper"* (Another type of commercial paper is "*investment paper*," which represents securities under Article 8. Since it is beyond the scope of this book, "investment paper" will not be discussed further).

Documents of Title, such as Warehouse Receipts are often considered NEGOTIABLE.

- Documents of title will be considered Negotiable only if they meet the requirements of § 7-104 (i.e., they are made to *"Bearer" or "Order"* or run to a named Person or his assigns).

The rules governing the Negotiation of the Document of Title and the Negotiable Instrument are very similar.

Letters of Credit are another form of Commercial Paper. Letters of Credit combine Documents of Title and Negotiable Instruments law in one transaction.

Documents of Title are governed by Article 7 of the UCC. Letters of Credit are governed by Article 5 of the UCC and the Uniform Customs and Practices for Documentary Credits and Demand Guarantees ("The UCP").

Bills of Lading and Warehouse Receipts are the most common Documents of Title. A Letter of Credit is not considered a Document of Title.

Bill of Lading ("BOL")—A BOL is a document issued by a *Carrier* when it takes goods for shipment. The BOL is issued so that the seller does not lose title to goods while they are in transit (in the Carrier's possession).

Warehouse Receipt ("W/R")—A W/R is issued by a *bailee* (usually a warehouseman) when it takes goods for storage. The W/R is issued so that the seller does not lose title to goods while stored in the bailee's warehouse (and in the bailor's possession).

Payment and Acceptance (§ 2-310):

- In a document transaction, the buyer pays for the goods when the *documents* arrive (not when the goods arrive) (§ 2-512).

- **Payment is not Acceptance** (§ 2-512(2)): If goods are non-conforming, the buyer may reject them under § 2-601 and then sue for his money back (§ 2-711).
- The buyer, thus, loses his right to inspect the goods before Payment (§ 2-512) (he may protect himself by requiring a professional inspector's document).

Relevant Sections: § 2-514, § 7-104

§ 2-514: When Documents Deliverable on Acceptance; When on Payment:

1) Documents delivered upon Acceptance — Documents (against which a Draft is drawn) are to be delivered to the Drawee upon *Acceptance* of the Draft if:

   a) The Draft is payable more than 3 days after Presentment.

   and b) The Parties do not otherwise agree.

2) Documents delivered upon Payment — Documents (against which a Draft is drawn) are to be delivered to the Drawee upon *Payment* of the Draft if:

   a) The Draft is not payable more than 3 days after Presentment.

   or b) The Parties so agree.

§ 7-104: Negotiable and Non-Negotiable Documents of Title:

(1) **Requirements for Negotiability:** A Document of Title (including a Bill of Lading) will be considered Negotiable if:

   (a) The goods under the document are to be delivered *to Bearer or Order* of a named Person (according to the terms of the document).

   or (b) It *runs to a named Person or assigns*, where recognized in Overseas trade.

(2) **Non-Negotiable Documents:**

   1. Any other Document not fulfilling the requirements of § 7-104(1) will be considered non-negotiable.
   2. A Bill of Lading will not be made Negotiable by simply stating that the goods are consigned to a named Person, providing that the goods are to be delivered only against a written Order Signed by the named Person.

B. HOLDER BY DUE NEGOTIATION: ("HDN")

OVERVIEW

Documents of Title can be Negotiated in a manner similar to Negotiable Instruments. In fact, just as Article 3 gives the Holder in Due Course protection with respect to a Negotiable Instrument, Article 7 affords protection to a Holder by Due Negotiation.

Requirements to be Classified as a Holder by Due Negotiation ("HDN") (§ 7-501):

1. **Holder:** The HDN must be a Holder (under § 1-201(20))

and 2. **Due Negotiation:** The DOT must be *"Duly Negotiated"* to the Holder:

a) Negotiation: The Holder must take the Document of Title by *Negotiation* (as per § 7-501(1)).

and b) Purchase: The Holder must take by *Purchase* (as per § 1-201(32)).

and c) New Value: The Holder must have taken the DOT for *New Value* (as per § 1-201(44)). It cannot receive the DOT in settlement or Payment for a previous monetary obligation (i.e., an "antecedent debt").

and d) Regular Course of Business Financing: Both parties must be *Merchants* (as defined in § 2-104(1); see § 7-501 Official Comment 1).

and e) Good Faith: The Holder must have demonstrated *Honesty in Fact* and observance of *Reasonable Commercial Standards* (as per § 2-103 (stricter standard of Good Faith required since both parties must be merchants)).

Rights of the HDN (§ 7-502; § 7-503):

- The Holder by Due Negotiation (under § 7-501) will usually take priority in the goods, even against someone in possession of the goods.

Possession of Goods v. Possession of DOT (§ 7-503):

- Situations occasionally arise when an unscrupulous warehouseman will Issue a DOT to someone and then sell the goods to another person.
- **Document of Title Priority:** In such a situation, the Person holding the Document of Title will take priority over the Person in Possession of the goods *unless* the Person with the DOT:

1. Was issued the DOT after the goods had been sold.

or 2. Put the Goods into the Stream of Commerce: By entrusting goods to a Merchant (Note: a personal shipper, i.e., one directly employed by the Merchant would not qualify under this exception, since the Code's reference to "to ship" or "to store" refers only to someone who is a professional shipper/Warehouseman who issues a BOL/DOT (see § 2-403(3)).

or 3. Acquiesced to the goods in procurement: (example: The buyer leaves the goods in the seller's warehouse after he bought them.)

Forgery: If signatures on a DOT are not legitimate, the DOT will not be valid, even to an HDN (§ 7-504 (no forgery); (§ 7-501(1)) (Indorsement to negotiate); see § 1-201(39) for definition of "Signed").

Regular Course of Business:

- DOT's require Negotiation in the *"Regular Course of Business"* (i.e., between merchants) (§ 7-501; § 7-504 Off. Comm.).
- Regular Course of Business v. Ordinary Course of Business
  - *Ordinary Course* — Sold by a merchant (someone in the business of selling such goods).
  - *Regular Course* — Both parties are merchants or professionals.

Warranties upon Negotiation of Document of Title (§ 7-507):

The transferor of a DOT makes the following Warranties:

1) The transferor has a legal right to transfer the goods represented by the DOT.
2) The Documents are genuine.
3) The transferor has no knowledge of any act that would impair the validity or worth of the document.

Relevant Sections: § 7-501, § 7-502, § 7-503

§ 7-501: Due Negotiation:

(1) **Manner of Negotiation:**

a) Named Person: A *Negotiable* Document of Title "running" to the Order of a named Person can be Negotiated only if:

1) Indorsement — The identified Person in the document Indorses it.

and 2) Delivery — The document is delivered into the possession of the holder.

b) Bearer: If the Instrument is Indorsed in blank (i.e., "to Bearer" or with a "Blank Indorsement"), it can be Negotiated by *delivery* alone.

(2) **Delivery as Negotiation**:

(a) A Negotiable Document of Title may also be Negotiated by Delivery alone if it "runs" to Bearer (by its original terms).

(b) A Document of Title will be considered as if it had been negotiated if it is delivered to the *identified Person.*

(3) Special Indorsement: If a Negotiable DOT has been Indorsed to an identified Person, the special Indorsee must Indorse and Deliver it to negotiate it.

(4) **"Due Negotiation"**: Requirements for a Negotiable Document of Title to be *"duly negotiated"*:

a) It is Negotiated (in the manner stated above in this section) to a **Holder** (as per § 1-201(20))

and b) The Holder takes by ***Purchase*** (as per § 1-201(32))

and c) It is Purchased:

1. In **Good Faith** (as per § 1-201(19))

and 2. **Without any notice** of another Person's claims or defenses against the document

and 3. For **Value** (as per § 1-201(44))

and 4. In the *regular course of business or financing* (i.e., from a merchant)

and d) The negotiation does not involve receiving the document in settlement or Payment of a Money obligation

(5) **Non-Negotiable Documents:** Indorsement of a non-negotiable Document neither makes it Negotiable nor adds to the transferee's rights.

(6) **Naming Person to Notify upon Arrival:** The naming of a Person (in a Negotiable DOT) to be notified when goods (represented by the DOT) arrive does not:

a) Limit the negotiability of the bill

or b) Constitute notice to a Purchaser of the bill that the named Person has any interest in the goods

§ 7-502: Rights Acquired by Due Negotiation:

(1) **Rights by Due Negotiation:** A Person acquires the following rights if a Negotiable Document has been *Duly Negotiated* to him (subject to § 7-205 and § 2-703):

(a) Title to the Documents

and (b) Title to the goods

and (c) All rights accruing under the law of agency and estoppel (including rights to goods delivered to the bailee after the document was issued)

and (d) *Either:*

1. The direct obligation of the *Issuer* to hold or deliver the Goods according to the terms of the Document free of any defense or claim by the Issuer (except those arising under the terms of the Document or under Article 7)

or 2. Delivery Orders: The bailee's obligation accrues only when:
   a) The bailee accepts its obligation.
   and b) The obligation acquired by the Holder is that the Issuer (and any Indorser) will procure the Acceptance of the bailee.

(2) **Title and Rights** (subject to § 7-503):

a) Title and rights acquired by negotiation will not be defeated by:
   1) Any stoppage of goods (represented by the document)
   or 2) Surrender of the goods by the bailee
b) Title and rights acquired by negotiation will not be impaired, even if:
   1. Negotiation (or any prior negotiation) constituted a breach of duty
   or 2. Any Person has been deprived of possession of the document by:
      a) Misrepresentation
      or b) Fraud
      or c) Accident
      or d) Mistake
      or e) Duress
      or f) Loss
      or g) Theft
      or h) Conversion
   or 3. A Previous sale (or other transfer of the goods or document) has been made to a third Person

§ 7-503: Defeated Documents of Title:

(1) Interests before Issuance: A DOT confers no right in goods against a Person who:

(a) Didn't deliver or entrust such goods (or DOT covering them) to a merchant (as per § 2-403)
and (b) Didn't acquiesce title in the procurement by the bailor (or his nominee) of any DOT
and (c) Had a legal or perfected S/I in the goods *before* the Document was issued

(2) Unaccepted delivery orders:

a) Title to goods based upon an *unaccepted delivery order* is subject to the rights of anyone to whom a negotiable Warehouse Receipt or BOL (covering such goods) has been *duly negotiated*.

b) Such a title may be defeated under § 7-504 to the same extent as the rights of the Issuer or a transferee from the Issuer.

(3) BOL issued to a freight forwarder

a) Title to goods based on a BOL issued to a freight forwarder is subject to the rights of anyone to whom a bill issued to the freight forwarder is *duly negotiated.*

b) Delivery by the carrier (in accordance with Part 4 of Article 7) pursuant to its own BOL discharges the carrier's obligation to deliver.

C. BILLS OF LADING:

OVERVIEW

"Bill of Lading" ("BOL") — A BOL is a document issued by a *carrier* who takes the goods for shipment. The BOL is issued so that the seller does not lose title to the goods while they are in transit (i.e., in the carrier's possession).

The BOL Transaction:

- If the BOL is *Negotiable:*
  - The carrier will Issue the seller a Bill of Lading, to *"seller's Order."*
  - Subsequently, the seller will Indorse the BOL and *negotiate* it to the buyer (and send it ahead of the goods).
  - In Order to get the goods, the buyer must present the BOL upon delivery.
    - Problems:
      - Seller is not assured Payment.
      - Seller may not be able to send the BOL to buyer before the goods arrive.
      - The buyer cannot inspect goods before accepting them from the Carrier (§ 2-323).

The Sight Draft Transaction:

- The sight draft transaction tries to alleviate the above-mentioned problems.
- Procedure:
  - The seller will *draw* a "Draft" (example: a Check) against the buyer (this way, seller writes a "Check" out to himself, ordering the buyer (instead of seller's Bank) to pay seller):
    - Parties to the Draft:
      - Drawer (usually the seller)
      - Payee (usually the seller)
      - Drawee/Payor (usually the buyer)

Since the seller is the Drawer, the buyer (as Payor) is only liable to pay the seller by the terms of the contract (and until the buyer signs the Draft he is not liable by the terms of the Draft, as specified in Articles 3 and 4).

The seller Indorses the *Negotiable BOL* and the Draft (making it a "sight draft").

The seller sends the documents to the buyer through the Banking Channels:

- The seller gives his Bank the sight draft and the Negotiable BOL.
- The seller's Bank gives the sight draft and BOL to the buyer's Bank.
- Buyer's Bank tenders the BOL to the buyer upon Acceptance of the Draft (i.e., buyer Indorses the Draft, binding himself to pay it under Article 3 and 4).
- Once the carrier arrives with the goods the buyer exchanges the BOL with the carrier for the goods.
- The seller enforces the accepted Draft against the buyer.

Payment and Acceptance of the Underlying Goods (§ 2-310):

- In a document transaction the buyer pays for the goods when the *documents* arrive (not when the goods arrive) (§ 2-512; § 2-507).
- The buyer, therefore, loses his right to inspect the goods before Payment (he may protect himself by requiring a professional inspector's document) (§ 2-512; § 2-513(3)).
- **Payment is Not Acceptance of Goods**: Buyer may reject goods under § 2-601 and then sue for his money back (even after it has paid for the goods) (§ 2-512(2)).

Dishonor:

- A sight draft is considered *dishonored* if it is not paid within 3 days after Due Presentment (under § 3-502(c) and § 3-502(b)(2)).

Due Presentment:

- Due Presentment may be made orally, electronically, in writing, or in any other *commercially reasonable manner* (§ 3-501(a)(1)).
- Presentment is effective when a demand for Payment is *received* by the Drawer (i.e., the Buyer).
- Presentment—A Collecting Bank (a Bank that takes the seller's Draft for collection purposes) presents the Draft by sending the Drawee (the buyer) a notice that the Bank is holding the Draft for Payment (§ 4-212(a)).
- Presenting Bank—A Presenting Bank (the Bank enforcing the Check directly against the buyer or buyer's Bank) has the additional duty of informing the seller of dishonor (§ 4-503); if the Presenting Bank accepts Personal Checks as Payment for the Draft, it will be liable if the Check is dishonored.[38]

Problem with the sight draft transaction:

Under a sight draft transaction, the buyer only has to *Accept* the Draft (by signing it) before the Bank releases the Bill of Lading to the buyer; however, the buyer doesn't actually have to pay the Draft until seller enforces it; thus, there is still a risk that the buyer can "skip town" or go bankrupt and never pay it. The Letter of Credit transaction (detailed below) tries to eliminate this risk by holding a Bank responsible for Payment (since banks are presumed to be more reliable than others (see "LETTERS OF CREDIT" below)).

Relevant Section: § 2-323

§ 2-323: Bill of Lading:

(1) **Requirements of the Bill of Lading:**

a. The seller must obtain a Negotiable Bill of Lading (unless otherwise agreed) if:
   1. The contract involves an *overseas* shipment.

[38] This is the law under former 4-211(1)(d). Although Revised § 4-213 does not expressly say this, it would probably violate Revised § 4-202's Duty of Care requirement for Banks.

and 2. The terms are FOB (vessel), CIF, or C&F.

b. Contents of the Negotiable Bill of Lading:
   1. FOB—must state that goods have been loaded on board
   2. CIF or C&F—must state that the goods have been received for shipment

(2) **Multi-Part Documents**

i) When a Bill of Lading has been issued in a set of parts, only one part need be tendered *unless:*
   a) The agreement expressly requires that a full set be tendered.
   or b) *Both:*
      1. The buyer demands that a full set be tendered.
      and 2. The documents are not to be sent from abroad.

ii) The following rules apply even if the contract expressly requires a full set of documents to be tendered:
   (a) Due tender of a single part of the BOL is acceptable to cure improper delivery (as per § 2-508(1)).
   and (b) Documents sent from abroad: If the documents are sent from abroad, the Person tendering an incomplete set of documents may require still Payment upon furnishing an indemnity (which the buyer deems to have been made in Good Faith), even if the full set is demanded.

(3) **"Overseas"**—an "overseas" contract or shipment is one:

a) Involving shipment by water or air

and b) That is subject to commercial, financial, or shipping practices characteristic of *international deep water commerce*, either by usage of trade or agreement

D. LETTERS OF CREDIT:

OVERVIEW

The Letter of Credit Transaction:

- The Letter of Credit ("L/C") Transaction has become very popular in recent years, especially between geographically distant parties.
- The L/C transaction helps ensure that the seller will get paid upon delivery of the goods.
- The Letter of Credit is a document that requires the buyer's Bank to pay the seller (or seller's Bank) upon the occurrence of certain conditions. These conditions are usually nothing more than a *checklist* of documents that must be received in order for the buyer's Bank to release the funds to the seller.

Applicable Law: Letter of Credit transactions are usually governed by international treaties, banking laws, and the Uniform Customs and Practices for Documentary Credits and Demand Guarantees ("UCP"). Article 5 of the UCC briefly summarizes the rights and liabilities of the parties involved, yet subjects itself to any accepted statute or treaty governing Letters of Credit (§ 5-102(3)).

Procedure:

- The buyer's Bank makes a loan to the buyer before opening (i.e., creating) the L/C.
- The buyer's Bank opens an L/C with the seller's Bank (or seller), promising to pay the seller upon tender of the documents specified in the L/C.
- The seller's Bank usually "writes" the L/C and specifies the list of documents required by the buyer in Order for it to *"release"* (i.e., pay) the L/C. (These documents usually include a Bill of Lading, an invoice, applicable visas required for the goods to enter the country, and certificates of approval from an outside source.)

Once the buyer's Bank receives the appropriate documents it "releases" the Letter of Credit, and pays the seller.

Liabilities of the Parties:

- The Issuing Bank (buyer's Bank):
  - The Issuing Bank must pay the seller's Bank upon fulfillment of the L/C's conditions (§ 5-109).
  - The Issuing Bank has no obligation to interpret the Merchant's customary practices when determining whether the conditions of the L/C have been fulfilled (in Order to make the buyer pay) (§ 5-109(1)(c)).
  - According to the UCP, the Issuing Bank may pay the seller's Bank as long as all documents are *not inconsistent* with the L/C (though there is no need for them to be identical).
- The seller's Bank (§ 5-107)—A seller's Bank can have 2 levels of responsibility, depending on the L/C's terms:
  - A *Confirming Bank* is liable to pay the seller for an L/C once it approves the L/C, even if the Issuing Bank fails to pay. (The L/C must specify that

seller's Bank is a Confirming Bank, otherwise it will be presumed an Advising Bank (§ 2-325).)
- An *Advising Bank* is not liable to the seller; it just advises that the L/C's conditions are fulfilled and pays the seller once the Issuing Bank pays it.

- <u>The Buyer</u>:
  - Liable to the seller under its contract with the *seller* for the price of the goods.
  - Liable to reimburse the *Issuing Bank* for any loan made to pay the L/C to the seller's Bank (§ 5-114), once the Issuing Bank has actually paid the seller.

The Independence Doctrine:

- Although the terms of the L/C usually reflect the underlying contract between the buyer and seller, payment of the L/C is a totally *separate* obligation.
- ***The Letter of Credit is enforceable even if the contract between the buyer and seller is invalid or breached.***
- A Bank may not look at the validity of the documents or the underlying contract used to fulfill the L/C's conditions.
- **<u>Fraud Exception</u>** (§ 5-114(2)):
  - When Fraud is involved a party may obtain a court injunction to stop its Bank from paying the L/C.
  - <u>Fraud includes:</u>
    - Forgery

    and
    - Fraud in the transaction
  - <u>Fraud in Transaction</u>: Even if fraud exists in the transaction, the Bank may still be obligated to pay the Letter of Credit (§ 5-114(2)):
    - **Bank <u>Must</u> Pay** if the Person to whom the Bank owes the Money is a Holder in Due Course.
    - **Bank <u>May</u> Pay** if its Customer tells the Bank not to pay, even though there is no court order forbidding payment.
    - If there is an underlying Draft, the Bank can attempt to stop Payment according to the "stop payment order" rules (§ 4-303), but cannot stop payment once the Issuing Bank has accepted the Draft.

<u>Other Rules:</u>

- L/Cs are presumed *irrevocable* (§ 2-325(3)).
- L/Cs must be *seasonably provided*, or the buyer will be deemed to have repudiated his obligation to pay (§ 2-325(1)).
- Payment by L/C *"suspends"* the obligation to pay (under the contract) (§ 2-325(2)). Only upon dishonor of the L/C may the seller demand Payment directly from the buyer (§ 2-325(2)).

Relevant Sections: § 2-325, § 5-109, § 5-114

§ 2-325: Letter of Credit:

(1) Failure of a buyer to seasonably provide an agreed Letter of Credit is a breach of the contract for sale.

(2) **L/C as Payment:**

- a) The delivery of a proper L/C to the seller *suspends* the buyer's obligation to pay.
- b) If the L/C is dishonored, the seller may require Payment directly from buyer upon *seasonable notification*.

(3) Definitions:

- a) **"Letter of Credit"** (or "banker's credit")—means (unless otherwise agreed) an irrevocable credit issued by a financing agency of good repute.
- b) **"Confirmed Credit"**—means that the credit carries the direct obligation of a financing agency that does business in the seller's financial market.

§ 5-109: Issuer's Obligation to Its Customer:

(1) **Issuing Bank's Obligations**:

- i) An Issuer Bank's obligation to its customers include:
  - 1) Good Faith
  - 2) The Observance of any general banking customs/usage
- ii) The issuing Bank's obligations do not (unless otherwise agreed) include any liability or responsibility for:
  - (a) Performance of the underlying sales contract (or other transaction between the Customer and the Beneficiary)
  - (b) Any act or omission of any Person (other than itself) for loss or destruction of a:
    - 1. Draft
    - or 2. Demand
    - or 3. Document in transit
    - or 4. Document in the possession of others
  - (c) Knowing or complying with any customs or usage of any particular trade

(2) **Duty to Examine**:

1. An Issuer must examine the documents with care to determine whether they appear to comply with the terms of the Letter of Credit—*on their face* (see § 5-103).
2. The Issuing Bank assumes no liability or responsibility (unless otherwise agreed) for the genuineness, falsification, or

effect of any document that appears regular *on its face* when examined (see §5-114 for each party's duties, privileges, and responsibilities).

(3) A non-Bank Issuer is not bound by any banking usage (i.e., terms/customs of the trade) of which it does not know.

§5-114: Issuer's Duty to Honor; Right to Reimbursement:

(1) **Independent Significance:**

a) An Issuer must Honor a Draft or Demand for Payment if it complies with the terms of the L/C, regardless of whether the goods or documents conform to the underlying contract.
b) The Issuer is not excused from its duty to Honor such a Draft or demand if the L/C has a general term requiring *all* documents to be satisfactory to the Issuer (example: Bill of Lading, Inspection Certificate, Invoice).

(2) **When Bank Does Not Have To Honor L/C:**

i) The Bank may not have to Honor the L/C when documents appear on their face to comply with the terms of the L/C if:
  a) A required document does not conform to the warranties made on Negotiation or Transfer of
    1) A Document of Title (as per §7-507).
    or 2) A certified security (as per §8-306).
  or b) A required document is Forged or Fraudulent.
  or c) There is Fraud in the Transaction.
ii) In such cases, the following rules determine when the Issuing Bank may Honor or dishonor the L/C:
  (a) Holder in Due Course: An Issuer must Honor the Draft or demand for Payment if Honor is demanded by a Negotiating Bank or other Holder of the Draft who has become:
    1) A **Holder In Due Course** of a Draft (as per §3-302)
    or 2) A **Holder by Due Negotiation** of a Document (as per §7-502)
    or 3) A **Bona Fide Purchaser** of a Certified Security (as per §8-302)
  (b) All other cases:
    1. Court Order: A court order (from the appropriate jurisdiction) may enjoin the Issuing Bank from honoring such an L/C.

2. Customer's Notice: An Issuer acting in **Good Faith** *may* Honor the Draft or demand for Payment, even if its Customer notifies it of Fraud, Forgery, or other defects not apparent on the face of the documents without a court order.

(3) An Issuer which has duly honored a Draft or demand for Payment is entitled to:

a) *Immediate Reimbursement* of any Payment it made under the L/C (unless otherwise agreed)

and b) Have funds effectively available no later than the day *before* maturity of any Acceptance made under the L/C.

Part Two

E-Z RULES™ FOR NEGOTIABLE INSTRUMENTS

Part Two
CONTENTS

§1-201(4): "Bank":

Any person engaged in the business of banking.

§1-201(5): "Bearer":

The person in possession of an Instrument, Document of Title, or certificated security which is *either:*

a) Payable to Bearer

or b) Indorsed in blank

§1-201(6): "Bill of Lading":

1. **Definition:** A document evidencing the receipt of goods for shipment, including an airbill
2. A Bill of Lading ("BOL") may be issued by a person engaged in the business of *either:*

   a) Transporting goods

   or b) Forwarding goods
3. **"Airbill"**—a document which acts as a Bill of Lading for air transportation (The airbill is equivalent to a Bill of Lading which is used in marine or rail transportation), and includes:

   a) An air consignment note

   b) An air waybill

§1-201(7): "Branch":

Includes a separately incorporated foreign branch of a Bank.

§1-201(15): "Document of Title":

1. Documents of Title include the following:

   a) Bill of Lading

   b) Dock warrant

   c) Warehouse receipt

   d) Order for delivery of goods

e) Any other document which is:
   1) Considered to adequately evidence that the holder of the document has the right to receive, hold, and dispose of the document and the goods it covers
   or 2) Recognized as such in the *regular course of business or financing*

2. **Requirements**:

   a) The Document purports to cover goods in the bailee's possession
   and b) *Either*:
      1. Purports to be Issued by a bailee
      or 2. Is addressed to a bailee
   and c) The goods covered by the document are *either:*
      1. Identifiable
      or 2. A fungible portion of an identified mass

§1-201(19): "Good Faith":

"Good Faith" means honesty in fact in the conduct or transaction concerned (see also §3-103(a)(4) for Negotiable Instruments).

§1-203: Good Faith:

"Every contract or duty within this act imposes an obligation of Good Faith in its performance or enforcement."

§1-201(20): "Holder":

1. With Respect to a **Negotiable Instrument:**

   a) *Instruments Payable to "Bearer"* — the Holder is the Person in Possession of the Instrument.
   b) *Instruments Payable to an Identified Person* — the Holder is the Person identified in the Instrument.[1] (i.e., has possession)

2. With Respect to a **Document of Title:**

The Holder is the Person in Possession of the Document if the goods are deliverable to:

   a) The "Bearer"
   or b) The Order or the Person in possession of the Document

[1] Former Article 3 required that the Person be in possession of an Instrument drawn to Bearer.

§1-201(21): "Honor":

To "Honor" an Instrument is to *either*:

a) Pay it

or b) Accept to pay it, and eventually pay it

or c) Purchase or discount a Draft, if, where a credit so engages, it complies with the terms of the credit.

§1-201(24): "Money":

1. A medium of exchange authorized or adopted by a domestic or foreign government.
2. "Money" includes any monetary unit of account established by an intergovernmental organization or by agreement between two or more nations (example: The European ECU).

§1-201(30): "Person":

The term "Person" includes an individual or an organization

§1-201(32): "Purchase":

A "**Purchase**" is any *voluntary transaction* creating an interest in property, including a:

1. Sale (i.e., involving a buyer and seller)

or 2. Discount

or 3. Negotiation

or 4. Mortgage

or 5. Pledge (example: a security interest)

or 6. Lien

or 7. Issue or Reissue

or 8. Gift (donee)

§1-201(33): "Purchaser":

A **"Purchaser"** is a Person "who takes by *Purchase*" (example: a buyer, a secured party, etc. (as per §1-201(32))).

§ 1-201(35): "Representative":

The term "Representative" includes the following:

a) An agent

b) An officer of a corporation or association

c) A Trustee

d) An executor or administrator of an estate

e) Any other Person empowered to act for another

§ 1-201(39): "Signed":

Includes any symbol executed or adopted by someone *intending* to authenticate a writing.

§ 1-201(43): "Unauthorized":

1. An Unauthorized signature is made without actual, implied, or apparent authority.
2. A Forgery is a type of Unauthorized signature.

§ 1-201(44): Value:

(* Note: This definition does not apply to Article 3 or 4; see § 3-303 for definition ***)**

1) A Person is deemed to give **"Value"** if he acquires his rights *either:*

    (a) In return for *either:*
        1. A Binding Commitment to **extend credit** (example: Letter of Credit)
        or 2. An Extension of **immediately available credit**
    or (b) As Security for total or partial **satisfaction** of a pre-existing claim
    or (c) By accepting delivery pursuant to a pre-existing contract for Purchase
    or (d) In return for any "sufficient" consideration (as would support a simple contract)

2) **This definition does not apply to Articles 3 and 4;** refer to the following sections for the appropriate definition:

   a) § 3-303: Negotiable Instruments
   b) § 4-208; § 4-209: Bank Collections

§ 3-303(a): Value (applying to Articles 3 and 4):

An Instrument is issued or transferred for **Value** if:

(1) It is issued or transferred for a *Promise of performance* (only to the extent the Promise has been performed)

(2) The transferee acquires a security interest or other lien on the Instrument (other than a judicial lien)

(3) It is issued or transferred as Payment or security of a pre-existing ("antecedent") claim (against any Person), whether or not the claim was due

(4) It is issued or transferred in exchange for an N/I

(5) It is issued or transferred in exchange for an irrevocable obligation to a third party by the Person taking the Instrument.

§ 1-201(45): "Warehouse Receipt":

A receipt issued by a Person engaged in the business of storing goods for hire.

ARTICLE 3

PART 1:

General Provisions and Definitions

§3-101: Short Title:

"This Article may be cited as *Uniform Commercial Code—Negotiable Instruments.*"

§3-102: Subject Matter:

(a) **Scope**

1. This Article applies to Negotiable Instruments.
2. This Article does NOT apply to:
   a. Money
   b. Payment Orders (governed by Article 4A)
   c. Securities (governed by Article 8).

(b) **Subject to Articles 4 and 9:** If there is a conflict between this Article and Articles 4 or 9, Articles 4 and 9 govern.

(c) **Overriding Laws:** The following supersede any inconsistent provision of this Article (to the extent of the inconsistency):

1. Regulations of the Board of Governors of the Federal Reserve System
2. Operating Circulars issued by the Federal Reserve Banks.

§3-103: Definitions:

(a) The following definitions apply to Article 3:

(1) **"Acceptor"**—A Drawee who has *accepted* a Draft
(2) **"Drawee"**—A Person ordered in a Draft to make Payment (e.g., Bank)
(3) **"Drawer"**—The Person ordering Payment—either by *Signing* or being *identified* in a Draft
(4) **"Good Faith"**—Requires both:
a) Honesty in fact
and b) The observance of *reasonable commercial standards of fair dealing*

(5) **"Maker"**—A Person who *signs* or is *identified* in a Note as the Person undertaking to pay

(6) **"Order"**

a) An "Order" is a written instruction to pay Money.

b) To be effective, the Order must be *Signed* by the Person giving the Order.

c) The Order may be addressed to anyone (this includes the Person giving the instruction, one or more persons jointly, or in the alternative).

d) An authorization to pay, alone, will not be considered an Order unless the Person authorized to pay is actually *Ordered* to pay.

(7) **"Ordinary Care"**

a) A Person engaged in business—reasonable commercial standards (prevailing in the location and business that the Person is in).

b) A Bank—reasonable commercial standards do not require a Bank to examine an Instrument if:

a) Failure to examine does not violate the Bank's prescribed procedures.

and b) The Bank's procedures do not vary unreasonably from general banking usage (not disapproved by Articles 3 or 4).

and c) The Bank takes the Instrument by automated means for processing Collection or Payment.

(8) **"Party"**— a party to an Instrument

(9) **"Promise"**—

a) A Written undertaking to pay Money.

b) Must be *Signed* by the Person undertaking to pay.

c) An acknowledgment of an obligation, alone, is not a promise to pay; the Obligor must specifically *undertake* to pay the obligation.

(10) **"Prove [a fact]"**—to meet the burden of establishing a fact (as per §1-201(8))

(11) **"Remitter"**—A Person who purchases an Instrument from its Issuer, and the Instrument is payable to an identified Person (other than the Purchaser)

Revised §3-103(a): Definitions:

(1) **"Acceptor"**—A Drawee who has *accepted* a Draft

(2) **"Consumer Account"**—An account established by an individual primarily for personal, family, or household purposes

(3) **"Consumer Transaction"** — A transaction in which an *individual* incurs an obligation primarily for personal, family, or household purposes

(4) **"Drawee"** — A Person Ordered in a Draft to make Payment (e.g., Bank) ((a)(2) in the pre-2002 UCC)

(5) **"Drawer"** — The Person ordering Payment — either by *Signing* or being *identified* in a Draft

(6) **"Good Faith"** — Requires both:

a) Honesty in Fact
and b) The observance of *reasonable commercial standards of fair dealing*

(7) **"Maker"** — A Person who *signs* or is *identified* in a Note as the Person undertaking to pay

(8) **"Order"**

a) An "Order" is a written instruction to pay Money.
b) To be effective, the Order must be *Signed* by the Person giving the Order.
c) The Order may be addressed to anyone (this includes the Person giving the instruction, one or more persons jointly or in the alternative).
d) An authorization to pay, alone, will not be considered an Order unless the Person authorized to pay is actually *Ordered* to pay.

(9) **"Ordinary Care"**

a) A Person Engaged in Business — reasonable commercial standards (prevailing in the location and business that the Person is in).
b) A Bank — reasonable commercial standards do not require a Bank to examine an Instrument if:
  a) Failure to examine does not violate the Bank's prescribed procedures.
  and b) The Bank's procedures do not vary unreasonably from general banking usage (not disapproved by Articles 3 or 4).
  and c) The Bank takes the Instrument by automated means for processing collection or Payment.

(10) **"Party"** — a party to an Instrument

(11) **"Principal Obligor"** — the Accommodated Party (or any other party) to an instrument against whom a secondary obligor has recourse under this article

(12) **"Promise"** —

a) A Written undertaking to pay Money.
b) Must be *Signed* by the Person undertaking to pay.
c) An acknowledgment of an obligation, alone, is not a promise to pay; the Obligor must specifically *undertake* to pay the obligation.

(13) **"Prove [a fact]"**—to meet the burden of establishing a fact (as per § 1-201(8))

(14) **"Record"**—information that is inscribed on a tangible medium that is

a) Stored in an electronic or other medium
and b) Is retrievable in perceivable form

(15) **"Remitter"**—A Person who purchases an Instrument from its Issuer, and the Instrument is payable to an identified Person (other than the Purchaser)

(16) **"Remotely Created Consumer Item"**—An item which is

a) Drawn on a consumer account
and b) Is not created by the payor bank
and c) Does not bear a handwritten signature purporting to be the signature of the drawer

(17) **"Secondary Obligor"**—*includes:*

a) An Indorser or Accommodation Party
or b) A Drawer—having an obligation described in § 3-414(d)
or c) Any other party to the Instrument that has recourse against another party to the instrument (pursuant to § 3-116(b))

(b) Other definitions applying to this Article and the sections in which they appear are:

"**Acceptance**" Section 3-409
"**Accommodated Party**" Section 3-419
"**Accommodation Party**" Section 3-419
"**Alteration**" Section 3-407
"**Anomalous Indorsement**" Section 3-205
"**Blank Indorsement**" Section 3-205
"**Cashier's Check**" Section 3-104
"**Certificate of Deposit**" Section 3-104
"**Certified Check**" Section 3-409
"**Check**" Section 3-104
"**Consideration**" Section 3-303
"**Draft**" Section 3-104
"**Holder in Due Course**" Section 3-302
"**Incomplete Instrument**" Section 3-115

"**Indorsement**" Section 3-204
"**Indorser**" Section 3-204
"**Instrument**" Section 3-104
"**Issue**" Section 3-105
"**Issuer**" Section 3-105
"**Negotiable Instrument**" Section 3-104
"**Negotiation**" Section 3-201
"**Note**" Section 3-104
"**Payable at a Definite Time**" Section 3-108
"**Payable on Demand**" Section 3-108
"**Payable to Bearer**" Section 3-109
"**Payable to Order**" Section 3-109
"**Payment**" Section 3-602
"**Person Entitled to Enforce**" Section 3-301
"**Presentment**" Section 3-501
"**Reacquisition**" Section 3-207
"**Special Indorsement**" Section 3-205
"**Teller's Check**" Section 3-104
"**Transfer of Instrument**" Section 3-203
"**Traveler's Check**" Section 3-104
"**Value**" Section 3-303

(c) The following definitions in other Articles apply to this Article:

"**Bank**" Section 4-105
"**Banking day**" Section 4-104
"**Clearinghouse**" Section 4-104
"**Collecting Bank**" Section 4-105
"**Depositary Bank**" Section 4-105
"**Documentary Draft**" Section 4-104
"**Intermediary Bank**" Section 4-105
"**Item**" Section 4-104
"**Payor Bank**" Section 4-105
"**Suspends payments**" Section 4-104

(d) In addition, Article 1 contains general definitions and principles of construction and interpretation applicable throughout this Article.

§ 3-104: Negotiable Instrument:

(a) **Requirements of a Negotiable Instrument** (except as provided in (c) and (d)):

(1) Must be payable *"to Bearer"* or *"to Order"* either at the time it:
a) Is Issued
or b) First comes into Possession of a Holder

and (2) Must be Payable either *on demand* or *at a definite time*

and (3) Must <u>not</u> undertake or instruct the promisor (or Person Ordering Payment) to do *anything other than pay*, except that the promise may also include:
  - (i) An undertaking or power to give, maintain, or protect <u>collateral</u> to secure Payment
  - or (ii) An Authorization or power to the Holder to
    - a) Confess judgment on collateral
    - or b) "Realize on" collateral
    - or c) Dispose of collateral
  - or (iii) A Waiver of the benefit of any law intended for the advantage or protection of an obligor.

4) Must be an *<u>Unconditional Promise or Order</u>* to pay

5) Must Promise a *<u>fixed amount</u>*

6) Must Promise/Order to pay *<u>Money</u>* (with or without interest or other charges described in the Promise or Order)

(b) **"Instrument"** — refers to a Negotiable Instrument

(c) **Negotiable Instrument and Check**

An Order is a Negotiable Instrument and a Check if it:

1) Meets all the requirements of 3-104(a) (except for §3-104(a)(1) — where there is no need to say "Order" or "Bearer")

and 2) Otherwise falls within the definition of "<u>Check</u>" (as per 3-104(f)).

(d) **Promise or Order Not an N/I:** A Promise or Order is not an Instrument if:

1) <u>It is not a Check</u>.

and 2) It contains a *<u>conspicuous statement</u>* (however expressed) that either:
  - a) The Promise or Order is <u>not</u> Negotiable.
  - or b) The Promise or Order is <u>not</u> an Instrument governed by Article 3.

and 3) This statement appears on the Promise or Order *either* at the time:
  - a) It is issued.
  - or b) It first comes into possession of a holder.

(e) **Notes and Drafts:**

1) An Instrument is a "**<u>Note</u>**" if it is a *Promise.*

2) An Instrument is a "**<u>Draft</u>**" if it is an *Order* (example: a Check).

3) A Person may treat an Instrument as either a Draft or a Note if it falls within the definition of both.

(f) **"Checks"** —

1. A Check is:
   - (i) <u>A Draft</u> — other than a Documentary Draft (see §4-104), Payable on Demand and drawn on a Bank

or (ii) <u>A Cashier's Check</u>—or Teller's Check

2. An Instrument may be a Check even if it is referred to as something else on its face (example: the Check says it is a "Money Order").

(g) **"Cashier's Check"**—<u>A Draft</u> in which both the Drawer and the Drawee are the same Bank (or branches of the same Bank).

(h) **"Teller's Check"**—<u>A Draft</u> drawn by a Bank, either:

(i) On another Bank
or (ii) Payable at or through a Bank

(i) **"Traveler's Check"**—An Instrument that is:

(i) Payable on Demand
and (ii) Drawn on or payable at or through a Bank
and (iii) Designated by the term *"Traveler's Check"* (or by a substantially similar term)
and (iv) Requires a countersignature (by the Person whose specimen Signature appears on the Instrument) as a condition to Payment

(j) **"Certificate of Deposit"**—

1. A Certificate of Deposit is an Instrument containing an acknowledgment by a Bank that:
   a. A Sum of Money has been received by a Bank
   and b. The bank promises to repay that sum of Money
2. A Certificate of Deposit is a Note of the Bank

§3-105: Issue of Instrument:

(a) **"Issue"**—An Instrument is issued upon the <u>first</u> delivery of the Instrument by the Maker or Drawer (whether to a holder or non-holder) for the purpose of giving any Person rights on the Instrument

(b) **Unissued, Incomplete, and Conditional Instruments**

1) <u>Unissued Complete Instruments</u>:
   a. Binding on the Maker and Drawer
   b. *Defense:* Non-issuance
2) <u>Unissued Incomplete Instruments</u>
   a. Binding on the Maker and Drawer *if completed*
   b. *Defense:* Non-issuance
3) <u>Conditionally Issued Instruments</u>
   a. Binding on the Maker or Drawer
   b. *Defense:* Failure of the condition

4) Instruments Issued for a special purpose
   a. Binding on the Maker or Drawer
   b. *Defense:* — The special purpose to be fulfilled is a defense if not fulfilled

(c) **"Issuer"** — A Maker or Drawer of an Instrument (applies to Issued and Unissued Instruments)

§3-106: Unconditional Promise or Order:[2]

(a) **"Unconditional Promise or Order"**

1. Except as provided in this section, a Promise or Order is considered *Unconditional* (for purposes of §3-104(a)) unless it states:
   - (i) An express condition to Payment
   - or (ii) That the Promise or Order is *subject to* or *governed by* another **writing**
   - or (iii) That the *rights and obligations* of the Promise are stated in another **writing**
2. A reference to another **writing** does not, *itself*, make a Promise or Order conditional

(b) **Not Considered Conditional:** The following examples will not make a Promise or Order become conditional:

- (i) Referencing another **writing** stating rights with regard to:
  - a) Collateral
  - or b) Prepayment or acceleration of Payment
- or (ii) Limiting Payment to a particular fund or source (e.g., limiting a Check to Money in particular Bank Account)

(c) **Co-signatures Not Conditional:**

1. If, as a condition to Payment, a Promise or Order requires a *countersignature* by a Person whose sample signature appears on the Instrument, the Instrument will not be considered conditional (for purposes of §3-104(a)), *even if the Note requires the countersignature as a condition for Payment.*
2. Failure to countersign:
   - a) The failure of a Person (whose sample signature appears on the Note) to countersign an Instrument is a Defense to the Issuer's obligation to pay the Instrument.
   - b) Failure to countersign will not prevent a *transferee* of the Instrument from becoming a Holder of the Instrument.

[2] In states adopting Revised Articles 2, 3, and 4 (2002), the requirement for a writing is replaced with a requirement for a "record," which could include anything recorded in a tangible or electronic medium and retrievable in tangible form (as per §3-103(a)(14)).

(d) **Statements Allowing Issuer to Assert Defenses Not Conditional:**

1. A Promise or Order will not be made conditional (for the purposes of § 3-104(a)) if it:
   a) Contains a statement subjecting the rights of a holder or transferee to the Issuer's claims or defenses against the Original Payee

   and b) The statement was required by applicable statutory or administrative law

   and c) The statement was made at the time the Promise or Order either:
      i) Was first issued

      or ii) First came into possession of a holder
2. If an Instrument contains the above statement, there can never be a Holder in Due Course of that Instrument.

§ 3-107: Instrument Payable in Foreign Money:

Unless the Instrument otherwise provides, an Instrument that states a payable amount in foreign Money may be paid *either*:

a) In foreign Money

or b) In an equivalent dollar amount, to be calculated by using the current Bank-offered *spot rate:*

1. For the Purchase of dollars

and 2. At the place where Payment is actually made

and 3. On the day Payment of the Instrument is actually made

§ 3-108: Payable on Demand or at a Definite Time:

(a) **"Payable on Demand"** — An Instrument will be considered *"Payable on Demand"* if:

(i) It states that it is payable *either*:
   a. "On Demand"

   or b. "At Sight"

   or c. It otherwise indicates at the will of the Holder

or (ii) It does not state any time for Payment

(b) **"Payable at a Definite Time"**

1. An Instrument will be considered *"Payable at a Definite Time"* if:
   a. It is payable on the lapse of a <u>*definite period of time*</u> after Sight or Acceptance of the Promise or Order

   or b. At *either:*
      1. A <u>fixed date</u> (or dates)

      or 2. At a time *readily ascertainable* at the time the Promise or Order is Issued

2. Payment at the defined time may be subject to the rights of:
   (i) Prepayment
   or (ii) Acceleration
   or (iii) Extension at the option of the Holder
   or (iv) Extension to a further definite time *either*:
      a. At the Option of the Maker or Acceptor
      or b. Automatically upon the occurrence of a specified event

(c) **Payable upon Demand and Fixed Date**—If an Instrument is payable both upon a Fixed Date or upon Demand (made any time before the fixed date):

1. The Instrument will be considered *"Payable on Demand"* until the Fixed Date.
2. The Instrument will be considered *"Payable at a Definite Time"* on the fixed date if demand for Payment is not made before that date.

§3-109: Payable to Bearer or to Order:

(a) **Payable to Bearer:** A Promise or Order is Payable to Bearer if it:

(1) Indicates that:
   a) It is "Payable to Bearer"
   or b) It is "Payable to the Order of Bearer"
   or c) It otherwise indicates that the Person in possession of the Promise or Order is entitled to Payment

or (2) Does not state a Payee

or (3) Indicates that it is:
   a) "Payable to Cash"
   or b) "Payable to the Order of Cash"
   or c) It otherwise indicates that it is not payable to an identified Person

(b) **Not Payable to Bearer:**

1. A Promise or Order that is not Payable to Bearer is Payable to Order if it is payable *either*:
   (i) To the Order of an Identified Person (e.g., "To the order of John Doe")
   or (ii) To an Identified Person or Order (e.g., "To John Doe or order")
2. A Promise or Order that is not Payable to Order is payable to the identified Person.

(c) **Indorsement's Effect on to Whom Instrument Is Payable:**

1. An Instrument Payable to Bearer may become Payable to an Identified Person if it is *specially Indorsed* to the Identified Person (as per §3-205(a)).

2. An Instrument made Payable to an Identified Person may become Payable to Bearer if it is Indorsed "in Blank" (as per §3-205(b)).

§3-110: Identification of Person to Whom Instrument Is Payable:

(a) **Signer's Intent:**

1. The Person to whom an Instrument is payable is determined by the intent of the Person signing the Instrument as Issuer or on behalf of the Issuer (whether or not that Person is authorized).
2. The Instrument is payable to the Person intended by the signer, even if that Person is identified in the Instrument by another name (example: David Drawer, president of Corporation owes money to the cleaning lady, Joan Smith, who often goes by the nickname Jane Smith. An impostor, also named Jane Smith came to David to get the Check; since David never saw Jane, he gave it to the impostor. However, David Intended to make Payment to Jane Smith, the cleaning lady, and not Jane Smith, the thief. Thus, Jane Smith, the impostor, is not a holder. Since David Drawer's intent controls, the name appearing on the Instrument is intended to be for Jane the cleaning lady. It is not properly payable to Jane the impostor.).
3. If more than one Person signs the Instrument and they do not all intend for the same Person to be Payee, the Instrument will be payable to any of the persons intended by one or more of the signers.

(b) **Automated Signatures** (i.e., Check-writing machines)**:** The Payee will be determined by the intent of the Person supplying the name of the payee to the machine (whether or not authorized to do so).

(c) **Identification of Payee and Holder:**

i) Determining Payee: A Person to whom an Instrument is payable may be identified *in any way*, including:
   a) Name
   b) Identification number
   c) Account number
   d) Office (e.g., President, Treasurer)

ii) Determining Holder:
   (1) **Instruments Payable to a Person or Account:**
      a. *PAYABLE TO AN ACCOUNT* (if the Account is Identified only by an Account number): The Instrument is payable to the Person to whom the Account is payable.

b. *PAYABLE TO PERSON AND ACCOUNT NUMBER*: The Instrument will be Payable to the *Named Person,* whether or not that Person owns the specified Account.

(2) **Instruments Payable to a Representative:**

(i) *PAYABLE TO A TRUST, ESTATE, or TRUSTEE or REPRESENTATIVE of a trust or estate*: The Instrument is payable to the trustee, representative, or successor of either (whether or not the Beneficiary is named).

(ii) *PAYABLE TO AN AGENT OR REPRESENTATIVE OF IDENTIFIED PERSON*: The Instrument is Payable to the represented Person, or the representative and the representative's successor.

(iii) *PAYABLE TO A FUND OR ORGANIZATION that is not a legal entity*: The Instrument is Payable to a representative of the members of the fund/organization.

(iv) *PAYABLE TO AN OFFICE OR A PERSON DESCRIBED AS HOLDING AN OFFICE*: The Instrument is Payable to the named Person, the incumbent of the office, or a successor of the incumbent.

(d) **Payable to Two or More Persons**:

1. Payable to multiple Persons *alternatively* (e.g., Esther or Lauren): It is Payable to any of them (and may be negotiated, discharged, or enforced by any of them in possession).
2. Payable to multiple Persons jointly (e.g., Esther and Lauren): It is payable to all of them (and may be negotiated, discharged, or enforced only by all of them together).
3. Presumption of alternative payability: If the Instrument is not clear whether it is payable to multiple parties alternatively or jointly, it will be presumed alternatively.

§3-111: Place of Payment:

a. **Place Stated in the Instrument:** An Instrument is Payable at the Place of Payment stated in the Instrument.

b. **Address of Drawee or Maker in Instrument:** If no Place of Payment is stated, the Instrument is Payable at the address of the Drawee or Maker stated in the Instrument.

c. **Place of Business of Drawee or Maker:** If no address is stated, the place of Payment is the place of business of the Drawee or Maker.

d. **More Than One Place of Business:** If the Drawee or Maker has more than one place of business, the Person Entitled to Enforce the Instrument may choose any place of business of the Drawee or Maker.

e. **Residence of Drawee of Maker:** If the Drawee or Maker has no place of business, the place of Payment is the residence of the Drawee or Maker.

f. These rules are subject to Article 4 of the UCC.

§3-112: Interest:

(a) **Assumption of interest free Instrument:** Unless the Instrument provides otherwise,

(i) An Instrument is <u>not payable with interest</u>.

and (ii) If the Instrument provides for interest, it will be payable from the *date of the Instrument* (as per §3-113).

(b) **Terms of Interest:**

1. <u>Method of stating interest</u>: Interest may be stated in an Instrument as *either*:
   a. A *fixed* or *variable* amount of <u>Money</u>
   or b. A *fixed* or *variable* <u>rate</u> (or rates) <u>of Interest</u>
2. <u>Amount of interest</u>: the amount of interest on the Instrument may:
   a. Be stated or described in the Instrument in any manner
   or b. Refer to information not contained in the Instrument
3. <u>Interest rate not ascertainable</u>: If the interest rate is not ascertainable from its description in the Instrument, the interest rate shall be the *judgment rate* in effect:
   a. At the time interest first accrues
   and b. At the place of Payment

§3-113: Date of Instrument:

(a) **Dated Instruments:**

1. An Instrument may be <u>ante-dated</u> or <u>post-dated</u>.
2. The date stated will determine the time of Payment if the Instrument is payable at a fixed period after such date.
3. An Instrument Payable on Demand is not payable before the date of the Instrument (subject to §4-401(c)) (example: If the Instrument is post-dated, the Payee cannot demand Payment before the post-date)

(b) **Undated Instruments:** If an Instrument is not dated, the Date of the Instrument will be:

a) The Date it is <u>Issued</u>
or b) The Date it first comes into <u>Possession of a Holder</u> (if the Instrument is not Issued)

§3-114: Contradictory Terms of an Instrument:

If an Instrument contains contradictory terms:

a. Handwritten terms will prevail over typewritten and printed terms.

b. Typewritten terms will prevail over printed terms.

c. Words will prevail over numbers.

§3-115: Incomplete Instruments:

(a) **"Incomplete Instrument"**

1. An Incomplete Instrument is a *Signed writing* that:
   a. At the time of the signing, the contents show that the Instrument is incomplete
   and b. The Signer intended the Instrument to be completed by adding words or numbers
2. The Incomplete Instrument does not have to be issued by the signer.

(b) **Enforcing the Incomplete Instrument:**

1. If an Incomplete Instrument is a *Negotiable Instrument* (as per §3-104), it may be enforced:
   a) <u>According to its incomplete terms</u>—if it is not completed
   or b) <u>According to its filled-in terms</u>—if it is changed by completion
2. If the Incomplete Instrument is <u>not</u> initially Negotiable (as per §3-104), but, upon completion, the requirements of §3-104 are met (making it a Negotiable Instrument), then the Instrument may be enforced <u>according to its completed terms</u>.
3. This subsection is subject to §3-115(c) (below).

(c) **Alteration:** An Alteration (as per §3-407) will occur if words or numbers are added to the Instrument *without* the signer's authority.

(d) **Burden of Proof:** The burden of proving that an Alteration occurred is on the party asserting the lack of authority of the signer.

§3-116: Joint and Several Liability; Contribution:

(a) The following people will be *jointly and severally liable* in the capacity in which they sign (unless otherwise provided for in the Instrument), if they have the same liability on the Instrument as either:

1. Makers
or 2. Drawers
or 3. Acceptors
or 4. Indorsers who Indorse as joint payees
or 5. Anomalous Indorsers

(b) **Right to Contribution:** If a party having joint and several liability pays the Instrument, it will have a right to receive contribution (in accordance with applicable law) from any party having the *same* joint and several liability on the Instrument (subject to §3-419(e) and possible agreement of the affected parties).

(c) **Discharge:** Even if a party having joint and several liability is discharged by the Person Entitled to Enforce the Instrument, the right to Contribution from such discharged party by others having the *same* joint and several liability will not be affected.

Revised Article 3 (2002) eliminates this section §3-116(c)

§3-117: Other Agreements Affecting Instrument:

a) A Party's obligation to pay an Instrument may be modified, supplemented, or nullified by a separate agreement (e.g., security agreement, mortgage) of the obligor and the Person Entitled to Enforce the Instrument so long as:

1. The Instrument is Issued (or the obligation incurred) *in reliance* on the agreement.
or 2. The Instrument is Issued (or the obligation incurred) as *part of the same transaction* giving rise to the agreement. (Note: In this case the Instrument may not be a Negotiable Instrument—see §3-104 and §3-106.)

b) The agreement will be a valid defense to Payment of the Instrument to the extent the agreement modifies, supplements, or nullifies the obligation. (Note: This defense is not good against a subsequent Holder in Due Course of the Note that took it without notice of the agreement (See §3-117, Off. Comm. 1).)

c) This section is subject to applicable law regarding exclusion of proof of contemporaneous or previous agreements (parol evidence rule).

§3-118: Statute of Limitations:

(a) **Note Payable at a Definite Time**

1. An action to enforce a Note Payable at a Definite Time must be brought within 6 years after:
   a. The due date stated in the Note
   or b. The accelerated due date, if a due date is accelerated
2. This section is subject to §3-118(e) (below).

(b) **Demand**

1. If demand is made to the Maker of the *Note Payable on Demand*, an action to enforce the obligation to pay the Note must commence within 6 years after the demand is made.
2. If demand is not made—action is *barred* if:
   a) The principal has not been paid for a continuous 10 years.
   and b) The interest has not been paid for a continuous 10 years.
3. This section is subject to §3-118(d)-(e).

(c) **Unaccepted Drafts**

1. An action to enforce an obligation of a party to an unaccepted **Draft** must be commenced by the *earlier* of:
   a) 3 years after the dishonor of the Draft
   b) 10 years after the date of the Draft
2. This section is subject to §3-118(d).

(d) **Checks Which Are Bank Obligations:**

An action to enforce the following must be made within 3 years after demand for Payment is made to the Acceptor or Issuer:

1) Certified Check
2) Teller's Check
3) Cashier's Check
4) Traveler's Check

(e) **Certificates of Deposit:**

1. An action to enforce a Certificate of Deposit ("CD") must be made within 6 years after *demand* to the Maker (of the CD).
2. If the Instrument (CD) has a due date (and the Maker is not obligated to pay before that date), the 6-year period may not start before the due date.

(f) **Accepted Drafts**—Actions to enforce Accepted Drafts *other than Certified Checks* must be commenced as follows:

  (i) **Payable at a Definite Time:** Within 6 years after the due date (or date stated on the Draft/Acceptance), if the obligation of the Acceptor is Payable at a Definite Time.
  (ii) **Payable on Demand**: Within 6 years after the date of Acceptance

(g) **Other Causes of Action**

  1. The following actions must be commenced within 3 years after the cause of action accrues:
     (i) **Actions Based on Conversion,** including:
        a) Actions for conversion of an Instrument
        b) Actions for Money had and received
        c) Like actions based on conversion
     (ii) **Breach of Warranty**
     (iii) Actions to enforce an obligation, duty, or right arising under Article 3 (and not governed by this section)
  2. This section is subject to any other non-UCC law regarding claims for *indemnity* or *contribution*.

§3-119: Notice of Right to Defend Action:

a) In an action for breach of an obligation for which a third Person is answerable (pursuant to Article 3 or 4 of the UCC), the defendant may give the third Person **written** notice of the litigation.[3]

b) The third party may give similar notices to any other Person who is answerable.

c) The Person notified will be bound by any facts determined in the litigation (which are common to the defendant and the notified Person) if:

  1. The Person does not attend the litigation to defend himself (after seasonable receipt of notice)
  and 2. The Notice sent to him states that:
     (i) The Person notified may come in and defend
     and (ii) Failure to do so will bind the notified Person as to any determination of fact common to both actions (which may come up in subsequent litigation between the party giving notice and the Person notified).

[3] Revised Article 3 (2002) changes the requirement of a "Writing" to a "Record."

PART 2:

Negotiation, Transfer, and Indorsement

§3-201: Negotiation:

(a) **Negotiation** is the Transfer of Possession of an Instrument, *whether voluntary or involuntary,*

1. BY: A Person other than the Issuer
2. TO: A Person who thereby becomes a Holder

(example: Instrument is Payable to Bearer and it is stolen by thief or is found by finder; either thief or finder can become the Holder of the Instrument when possession is obtained)

(b) **Requirements for Negotiation:**

1. Instruments Payable to an Identifiable Person (except for Negotiation by Remitter):
   - Negotiation requires *both:*
     a. Transfer of Possession of the Instrument
     and b. Indorsement of the Instrument by the Holder (i.e., the Instrument cannot be forged)
2. Instruments Payable to Bearer: May be negotiated by Transfer of Possession alone

§3-202: Negotiation Subject to Rescission:

(a) Negotiation will be effective even if it is obtained:

(i) From an infant, a corporation exceeding its powers, or a person without capacity
or (ii) By fraud, duress, or mistake
or (iii) In breach of duty, or as part of an illegal transaction

(b) **Rescission:** Negotiation may be rescinded or may be subject to other remedies (to the extent permitted by other law), unless those remedies are asserted against a:

1. Subsequent Holder in Due Course
or 2. Good Faith Purchaser who
   a. Paid for the Instrument
   and b. In Good Faith
   and c. Without knowledge of facts that are a basis for rescission or other remedy.

§3-203: Transfer of Instruments; Rights Acquired by Transfer:

(a) **Time of Transfer** — An Instrument is transferred when it is delivered if:

1) The purpose of the delivery is to give the receiver the right to enforce the Instrument.

and 2) The Person delivering it is not the Issuer (i.e., Maker or Drawer (See §3-105)).

* (b) **Rights of the transferee** ("shelter provision") — The transferee will acquire the following rights by transfer (whether or not the Instrument is negotiated):

policy to promote business

1) Any rights of the transferor to enforce the Instrument
2) Any rights of the transferor as an HDC, *unless* the transferee engaged in fraud or illegality affecting the Instrument

(c) **Transfer Without Indorsement:**

1) A Transferee will have the right to obtain an *unqualified Indorsement* from the transferor if:
   a) The Instrument is transferred for Value, even if transferor did not Indorse the Instrument.
   and b) The parties don't otherwise agree.
2) In such a case the transferee does not become a Holder because the transferor did not Indorse it. (But note: The transferee can still have the rights of an HDC pursuant to §3-203(b), above.)
3) Negotiation will not be deemed to have occurred until the transferor makes the Indorsement.

(d) **Transfer of Less Than the Entire Instrument** (Note: Value will be deemed gievn even if the Instrument is sold at a discount)

1) Negotiation will not occur if the transferor purports to transfer *less than* the entire Instrument.
2) The transferee obtains no rights under Article 3; he obtains the rights of a *partial assignee*.

§3-204: Indorsement:

(a) **"Indorsement"**

1. An Indorsement is a signature that is made for the purpose of
   (i) Negotiating the Instrument.
   or (ii) Restricting Payment of the Instrument.
   or (iii) Incurring Indorser's liability on the Instrument.
2. The Indorsement may be alone or accompanied by other words.

3. **When a Signature may not be an Indorsement:**
    a) Indorsements do not include signatures by the *Maker*, *Drawer*, or *Acceptor*.
    b) Regardless of the signer's intent, a signature (and its accompanying words) will be considered an Indorsement *unless* there is an unambiguous indication that the signature was not made for the purpose of Indorsement, from looking at:
        1) The words accompanying the signature.
        or 2) Terms of the Instrument.
        or 3) Place of the signature (e.g., not on the back of the instrument, where Indorsements are normally made).
        or 4) Other circumstances.
4. A paper affixed to an Instrument is considered part of the Instrument for purposes of determining whether a signature is made on the Instrument.

(b) **"Indorser"** — a Person making an Indorsement

(c) **Holders by Indorsement:**

An Indorsement that transfers a security interest in an Instrument is effective as an *unqualified Indorsement*, when determining whether a transferee of the Instrument is a Holder.

(d) **When Holder's Name Differs from Stated Name:**

1. If an Instrument is payable to a Holder under a name different than the holder's, the holder may Indorse:
    a) In the name stated in the Instrument.
    or b) In the Holder's actual name.
    or c) Both.
2. A Person taking the Instrument (for Value or collection) may require the holder to sign both names.

§ 3-205: Types of Indorsements:

(a) **"Special Indorsements":**

1. A Special Indorsement identifies the Person to whom an Instrument (payable to an identified Person or to Bearer) is payable (e.g., "Pay to Mary Jones" or "Pay to the order of Mary Jones").
2. Special Indorsements make an Instrument an Order Instrument.
3. Special Indorsements may be negotiated only by the identified Person (as per § 3-110, since they are considered Order Instruments).

(b) **"Blank Indorsement":**

1. Indorsements that are not "Special Indorsements" (i.e., those not identifying a payee) are considered Blank Indorsements.
2. Instruments that have Blank Indorsements become Bearer instruments.

(c) **Converting Indorsements:** A Blank Indorsement may be converted into a Special Indorsement by writing, above the signature, words that identify the Person to whom the Instrument is made payable.

(d) **"Anomalous Indorsement":**

1. An Indorsement made by a Person who is *not the holder* of the Instrument is an Anomalous Indorsement.
2. An Anomalous Indorsement does not affect the manner in which the Instrument may be negotiated.

§3-206: Restrictive Indorsement:

(a) **Indorsement Prohibiting Further Transfer or Negotiation**:

An Indorsement **cannot** prevent further transfer or Negotiation of an Instrument by:

a) Limiting Payment to a particular Person

or b) Specifically prohibiting further transfer or Negotiation (e.g., "Pay to Mary Smith only")

(b) **Indorsement Stating a Condition:**

1. An Indorsement stating a condition to Payment to the Indorsee does not affect the rights of the Indorsee.
2. The Person paying the Instrument (or taking it for Value or collection) may disregard the condition. No rights or liabilities will be affected by disregarding it.

(c) **Indorsements for Deposit:**

A. Scope: This subsection applies to instruments with the following Indorsements:
   (i) Those described in §4-201(b)
   (ii) *"For deposit,"* or *"For collection,"* (or other words indicating a purpose to collect Payment for a particular Account) (in blank or to a particular Bank)

B. The following rules apply to the Indorsements described above:
   (1) *A Person* (other than a Bank) who purchases such an Indorsed Instrument will have **converted** it, *unless:*
      a. The Indorser receives the amount paid for the Instrument.

or b. The amount paid for the Instrument is applied consistently with the Indorsement.

(2) *A Depositary Bank* that purchases the Instrument or takes it for collection will **convert** it *unless:*

a. The Indorser receives the amount paid by the Bank for the Instrument.

or b. The amount paid for the Instrument is applied consistently with the Indorsement.

(3) *A Payor Bank*

a. The Payor Bank **converts** the Instrument if it:

1. Is also the Depositary Bank.

or 2. Takes the Instrument for immediate Payment over the counter (from a Person other than a Collecting Bank).

b. The Payor Bank will not be liable for conversion if:

1. The Indorser receives the amount paid for the Instrument.

or 2. The amount paid for the Instrument is applied consistently with the Indorsement.

(4) Except as otherwise provided in (3), a Payor Bank or Intermediary Bank may disregard the Indorsement, and is not liable if the proceeds are not received by the Indorser or applied consistently with the Indorsement.

(d) **Indorsements to Trustee/Fiduciary**

i) **Scope**:

1) The following rules apply if an Instrument has an Indorsement containing words indicating that Payment is to be made to an agent, trustee, or other Fiduciary, *for the benefit of the Indorser or another Person.*

2) The following rules do not apply to Indorsements made for deposit (under § 3-206(c)).

ii) **Rules Regarding Indorsements to Fiduciaries:**

(1) A Person receiving an Instrument which indicates that Payment is to be made to an agent may pay the Indorsee of the Instrument, without worrying that the Indorsee has breached a fiduciary duty to the Indorser, if:

a) The Person is *either:*

1. Purchasing the Instrument

or 2. Taking the Instrument from the Indorsee *for collection or Payment*

and b) There is no notice of a breach of fiduciary duty (as per § 3-307)

(2) Notice

a) A subsequent transferee or Person paying such an Instrument will not be deemed to have notice unless it knows that the Fiduciary dealt with the Instrument or its proceeds in breach of fiduciary duties (see § 3-307).

(e) The above restrictions do not prevent a Person from becoming an HDC unless the Person is a *converter* (under (c)) or has notice or knowledge of a breach of fiduciary duty (as stated in(d)).

(f) **Defense to Payment:**

The obligor has a defense in an action to enforce Payment of an Instrument if Payment would violate a valid restrictive Indorsement (under this section).

§ 3-207: Reacquisition:

a) **"Reacquisition"**—Reacquisition of an Instrument occurs if it is transferred to a former holder, by Negotiation or otherwise.

b) **Cancellation of Indorsements:**

1. A former Holder who reacquires the Instrument may cancel any Indorsement made *after* he *first* became a Holder of the Instrument.
2. If the cancellation causes the Instrument to be Payable to the reacquirer or "To Bearer," the reacquirer may negotiate the Instrument.
3. Discharge: An Indorser whose Indorsement is canceled is discharged of his obligations under the Instrument against any subsequent Holder.

PART 3:

Enforcement of Instruments

§3-301: Person Entitled to Enforce Instrument:

a. **"Person Entitled to Enforce"** is *either:*

(i) The Holder of the Instrument
or (ii) A non-Holder in possession of the Instrument—who has the rights of a holder
or (iii) A Person Not in possession of the Instrument—entitled to enforce the Instrument pursuant to §3-309 (lost/stolen Instrument) or §3-418(d) (Payment/Acceptance by mistake)

b. A Person may be entitled to enforce an Instrument, even if:

1. The Person is not the owner of the Instrument.
or 2. The Person is in wrongful possession of the Instrument.

§3-302: Holder in Due Course:

(a) A Holder is a **Holder in Due Course** (subject to §3-302(c) and §3-106(d)) if:

(1) The Instrument looks authentic—the Instrument when issued or negotiated to the Holder:
a. Does not bear apparent evidence of forgery or Alteration
or b. Is not otherwise so irregular or incomplete as to call into question its authenticity
(2) The Holder takes the Instrument:
(i) For **Value**
and (ii) In **Good Faith**
and (iii) Without notice that the Instrument *either:*
a. Is Overdue
or b. Has been dishonored
or c. Belongs to a series of instruments, in which there is an uncured default with respect to the Payment of another Instrument in that series
and (iv) Without notice that the instrument contains an unauthorized signature or has been altered
and (v) Without notice of any claim to the Instrument (as described in §3-306)
and (vi) Without notice that any party has a defense or claim in recoupment (as described in §3-305(a))

(b) **Notice of Discharge**

1. Notice of discharge of a party (other than in an insolvency proceeding) is not an adequate notice of a defense under § 3-302(a) (above).
2. However, discharge is effective against a Person who became an HDC with notice of the discharge.
3. Public filing or recording of a document does not, itself, constitute notice of a:
    - a) Defense
    - or b) Claim in recoupment
    - or c) Claim to the Instrument

(c) **People Who Do Not Qualify as HDCs:**

1. A Person does not acquire rights of an HDC in an Instrument if he takes the Instrument:
    - (i) By *either*:
        - a) Legal process
        - b) Purchase in a bankruptcy, execution, or creditor's sale (or similar proceeding)
    - or (ii) By Purchase as part of a bulk transaction, not in the *Ordinary Course of Business* of the transferor
    - or (iii) As the successor in interest to an estate or other organization
2. This section does not apply to the extent that the Person's transferor or predecessor in interest has rights as an HDC.

(d) **Partial Performance:**

If a Promise of performance (that is consideration for an Instrument under § 3-303(a)(1)) has been only *partially* performed, the holder may assert rights as an HDC only to the following fraction of the amount payable under the Instrument:

$$\textbf{(Face Value of the Instrument)} \times \frac{\textbf{Amount already paid}}{\textbf{Total Value Promised}}$$

(example: if discounted)

(example: Susan purchased a $1,000 Note at a discount, for $900 from Steve. If Susan is an HDC, but has only paid $500, she may only assert her rights as an HDC for $555.55 (which equals ($1,000) x ($500/$900)). This formula is designed to reward the holder with a ratable portion of the bargained-for profit).

(e) **Security Interest in Instrument:**

The Person Entitled to Enforce the Instrument may assert rights as an HDC only up to the amount of the unpaid, secured portion of the Instrument (at the time of enforcement of the Instrument) if:

(i) The Person Entitled to Enforce the Instrument has only a security interest ("S/I") in the Instrument

and (ii) The Person obliged to pay the Instrument has, against the Person who granted the S/I, *either*

a) A defense

or b) A claim in recoupment

or c) A claim to the Instrument

(f) **Notice:** In order to be effective, notice must be received at a time and manner that gives a *reasonable opportunity* to act on it.

(g) This section is subject to any law (state statutory and case law and any other similar law that may evolve in the future) limiting the status of an HDC in particular classes of transactions.

§3-303: Value and Consideration:

(a) **"Value"**—An Instrument is issued or transferred for **Value** if:

(1) It is issued or transferred for a *promise of performance* (only to the extent the Promise has been performed).

or (2) A transferee acquires an S/I or other lien on the Instrument (other than a judicial lien).

or (3) It is issued or transferred as Payment or security of a pre-existing ("antecedent") claim (against any Person), whether or not the claim was due.

or (4) It is issued or transferred in exchange for an N/I.

or (5) It is issued or transferred in exchange for an irrevocable obligation to a third party by the Person taking the Instrument.

(b) **"Consideration"**—any consideration sufficient to support a simple contract.

1. The Drawer/Maker has a defense if the Instrument is issued without consideration.
2. If an Instrument is issued for a *promise of performance*, the Maker/Drawer has a defense *to the extent* the Promise has not been performed (and is due).
3. If an Instrument is issued for Value (as stated in (a)), it will also be considered issued for consideration.

§ 3-304: Overdue Instrument:

(a) **Instruments Payable on Demand**—become overdue ("stale") at the *earlier of*:

(1) The day *after* the day a demand for payment is duly made
or (2) For Checks—90 days after its date
or (3) For other Instruments—after an unreasonable amount of time, taking into account the circumstances of the particular case, in light of:
a. The nature of the Instrument
and b. Usage/Custom of the trade

(b) **Instruments Payable at a Definite Time**:

(1) Principal Payable in Installments:
a. An Instrument becomes overdue upon default for non-payment of an installment if:
1. The principal is payable in installments
and 2. The due date has not been accelerated
b. The Instrument remains overdue until the default is cured (i.e., payment of the installment is made).
(2) Principal NOT Payable in installments: The Instrument becomes overdue on the day *after* the due date (if the due date has not been accelerated).
(3) Due date of principal has been accelerated: The Instrument becomes overdue on the day *after* the accelerated due date.

(c) **Default of Interest:**

An Instrument does not become overdue if there is a default in payment of interest (but no default in principal payment), and the due date of principal has not been accelerated.

§ 3-305: Defenses and Claims in Recoupment:

(a) Except as otherwise provided in this subsection, the right to enforce the obligation of a party to pay an Instrument is subject to:

(1) Certain defenses (These are sometimes referred to as "real" defenses):
(i) *Infancy*—of the obligor (to the extent it is a defense to a simple contract)
or (ii) *Duress, lack of legal capacity, illegality*—of the transaction (which under other law would nullify the obligor's obligation; Note: the obligation must be void, not merely voidable)

or (iii) *Fraud in the Inducement*—fraud that caused the obligor to sign the Instrument not knowing the character or essential terms of the Instrument (nor having a reasonable opportunity to learn of its character or essential terms)

or (iv) *Discharge*—of the obligor in an insolvency proceeding

and (2) Other defenses (These are sometimes referred to as "personal" defenses):

i) Obligor's defenses as stated elsewhere in Article 3

or ii) Other defenses available to the obligor under Payment of a simple contract (e.g., failure of consideration, fraud as to the underlying subject matter)

and (3) Claims in Recoupment:

a) A claim in recoupment of the obligor will arise against the original Payee of the Instrument if the claim arises from the transaction that gave rise to the Instrument.

b) The claim of the obligor may be brought only

1) Against a transferee of the Instrument

and 2) To reduce the amount owing on the Instrument at the time the action is brought (i.e., to enter a right to setoff)

(b) **Right of a Holder in Due Course:**

The HDC's right to enforce an Instrument is subject only to the "real defenses" stated in § 3-305(a)(1) (above), but not those stated in (a)(2) or (a)(3).

(c) **Obligor Using People's Defenses:**

1. An obligor cannot use another Person's defenses (3-306) against the Person entitled to Payment of the Instrument *unless* the other Person:

   a) Is joined in the action

   and b) Personally asserts the claim against the Person Entitled to Enforce the Instrument.

2. Lost/Stolen Instruments: An obligor is not obligated to pay the Instrument if :

   a) The Person seeking enforcement does not have the rights of an HDC.

   and b) The obligor proves that the Instrument is a lost or stolen Instrument.

(d) **Actions to Enforce an Instrument Against an Accommodation Party**

The Accommodation Party may assert all defenses as the Accommodated Party (original obligor), except:

1. Infancy and lack of legal capacity (§ 3-305(a)(1))

and 2. Discharge in insolvency proceedings (§ 3-305(a)(3))

Revised Article 3 (2002) adds:

(e) **Consumer Transaction:** If law (other than this Article) requires that an instrument include a statement to the effect that the "*rights of a holder or transferee are subject to a claim or defense that the issuer could assert against the original payee*," and the instruments does not include such a statement:

(1) The Instrument has the same effect as if it included such a statement

and (2) The Issuer may assert all claims and defenses that would have been available if the statement were included

and (3) Claims may be asserted against the holder or transferee as if such statement were included.

(f) This section is subject to law other than this article that establishes a different rule for consumer transactions.

§ 3-306: Claims to an Instrument:

a) A Non-HDC takes an Instrument subject to *any claim of a property or possessory right* in the Instrument or its proceeds, including:

1. Claims to rescind a negotiation

or 2. Claims to recover the Instrument or its proceeds

b) A Holder in Due Course (HDC) takes free of the claim to the Instrument.

§ 3-307: Notice of Breach of Fiduciary Duty:

(a) **Definitions** (For purposes of § 3-307):

(1) **"Fiduciary"** — A Representative owing a Fiduciary Duty with respect to an Instrument, such as:
   a. An Agent
   b. A Trustee
   c. A Partner
   d. A Corporate Officer or Director

(2) **"Represented Person"** — A Person to whom a Fiduciary Duty is owed to, such as a:
   a. Principal
   b. Beneficiary
   c. Partnership
   d. Corporation

(b) **Instruments taken from a Fiduciary who is in Breach of his Fiduciary Duty:**

A. Scope: The rules in this subsection (§ 3-307(b)) will apply if:

(i) An Instrument is taken from a Fiduciary for

a. Payment

or b. Collection

or c. Value

and (ii) The taker had knowledge of the Fiduciary status of the Fiduciary

and (iii) The represented Person makes a claim to the Instrument or its proceeds

and (iv) The claim is based on the transaction being a breach of Fiduciary duty

B. Rules relating to claims of breach of Fiduciary duty:

(1) Notice of breach of a Fiduciary duty by the Fiduciary is notice of the represented Person's claim.

(2) Instruments Payable to the represented Person or the Fiduciary (as such): The Person taking the Instrument has presumptive notice of the breach of the Fiduciary duty if the Instrument is:

(i) Taken as security for or Payment of a debt which the taker knows is a *personal debt* of the Fiduciary

or (ii) Taken in a transaction which the taker knows is for the *personal benefit* of the Fiduciary

or (iii) Deposited in an Account other than that of the Fiduciary (as such) or the represented Person

(3) Instrument Made Payable to Fiduciary personally: If such an Instrument was Issued by the represented Person or Fiduciary (as such), the taker does not have presumptive notice of the breach of Fiduciary duty *unless* the taker actually knows of the breach.

(4) Instrument Made Payable to Payee: If such an Instrument was Issued by the represented Person or Fiduciary (as such), the taker has presumptive notice of the breach of Fiduciary duty if the Instrument is:

(i) Taken as security for or Payment of a debt which the taker knows is a *personal debt* of the Fiduciary

or (ii) Taken in a transaction which the taker knows is for the *Personal Benefit* of the Fiduciary

or (iii) Deposited in an Account other than that of the Fiduciary (as such) or the represented Person

§3-308: Proof of Signature and Status as Holder in Due Course:

(a) **Admissible Evidence; Burden of Proof:**

1. Each Signature on an Instrument will be deemed admitted (i.e., authentic) in an action to determine the authenticity and authorization of a signature on an Instrument *unless* specifically denied in the pleadings.
2. Presumption of authenticity: If the validity of a signature is denied in the pleadings, the signature is presumed to be authentic and authorized unless the purported signer is dead or incompetent at the time of trial (on the Issue of the validity of the signature), and the action is to enforce that signer's liability.
3. Burden of proof:
   a. If the validity of the signature is denied in the pleadings: The burden of establishing the validity of the Instrument is on the Person claiming validity
   b. If an Instrument was Signed on behalf of an *undisclosed principal*: The burden of establishing that a Party is liable on an Instrument as a Represented Person (undisclosed principal (as per §3-402(a))) is on the plaintiff.

(b) **Plaintiff's Entitlement to Payment:**

1. A Plaintiff who can produce the Instrument will be entitled to payment if :
   a) The Plaintiff can prove that she is entitled to enforce the Instrument (under §3-301)
   and b) The validity of the signatures is admitted or proved
   and c) There is compliance with §3-308(a)
   and d) The defendant does not prove a defense or claim in recoupment
2. If the defendant proves such a claim or defense in recoupment, the plaintiff's right to Payment is subject to the defense or claim *unless* the plaintiff can prove that she has the rights of an HDC (who is not subject to such claims or defenses (as per §3-302)).

§3-309: Enforcement of Lost, Destroyed, or Stolen Instruments:

(a) A Person not in possession of an Instrument is entitled to enforce the Instrument if:

(i) The Person was in possession of the Instrument and was entitled to enforce it when he lost possession.

and (ii) The loss of possession was not the result of a transfer by the Person or a lawful seizure.

and (iii) The Person cannot readily obtain possession of the Instrument because it was *either:*

a. Destroyed

or b. Lost (i.e., its whereabouts cannot be determined)

or c. In the *wrongful possession* of a Person:

1. Whose identity is unknown

or 2. Who cannot be found

or 3. Who is not amenable to service of process

(b) **Enforcing a Lost, Stolen, or Destroyed Instrument:**

1. The Person seeking enforcement of the lost, stolen, or destroyed Instrument must prove:
   a. The terms of the Instrument
   b. Their right to enforce the Instrument
2. If Proof is brought, the party is considered to have produced the Instrument (for purposes of § 3-308 ("Proof of Signature and Status as Holder in Due Course")).
3. Adequate Protection:
   a. The court may not force a party to pay such an Instrument unless it finds that the Person required to pay the Instrument is *adequately protected* against loss (that may arise if another Person attempts to enforce the instrument).
   b. Adequate protection may be provided by any reasonable means (generally done by the posting of a bond equal to the instrument).

Amended Revised Article 3-309(a)

(a) A Person not in possession of an Instrument is entitled to enforce the Instrument if:

(1) The Person seeking to enforce the Instrument either:

(A) Was entitled to enforce the Instrument when he lost possession.

or (B) Has acquired ownership (directly or indirectly) of the instrument from a person who was entitled to enforce the instrument when it lost possession.

and (2) The loss of possession was not the result of a transfer by the Person or a lawful seizure.

and (3) The Person cannot readily obtain possession of the Instrument because it was *either*:

a. Destroyed

or b. Lost (i.e.,—its whereabouts cannot be determined)

or c. In the wrongful possession of a Person:

1. Whose identity is unknown

or 2. Who cannot be found

or 3. Who is not amenable to service of process

§ 3-310: Effectiveness of Instruments as Payment:

(a) **Effectiveness of Certified/Bank Checks**

1. Unless otherwise agreed, any of the following Checks may be used to pay off an obligation, and shall discharge the obligation as if Money had been paid:
    a. Certified Check
    b. Cashier's Check
    c. Teller's Check
2. Discharge of an obligation does not affect the obligor's liability as Indorser of the Instrument.

(b) **Effectiveness of Notes and Uncertified Checks**

i) Unless otherwise agreed, if any of the following Instruments are used to pay off an obligation, the obligation will be *"suspended"* in the amount of the Instrument (to the same extent the obligation would be discharged if paid off with Money):
   a) Note
   b) Uncertified Check

ii) This rule is subject to (a) above.

iii) Rules for Notes and Uncertified Checks:

(1) Uncertified Checks—
   a. The obligation will continue to be "suspended" until:
      1) The Check is dishonored (in which case the obligation will be revived).
      or 2) The Check is Certified (in which case the obligation will be discharged as per (a)).
      or 3) The Check is Paid (in which case the obligation will be discharged as per (a)).
   b. Payment or Certification of the Check results in discharge of the obligation in the amount of the Check.

(2) Notes—
   a. The obligation will continue to be "suspended" until:
      1) The Note is dishonored (in which case the obligation will be revived).
      or 2) The Note is Paid.
   b. Payment of the Note results in discharge of the obligation in the amount of the Payment.

(3) Dishonor of Check or Note:
   a. **Obligee Entitled to Enforce**—If the obligee of the obligation (for which the Instrument was taken) is

the Person Entitled to Enforce the Instrument, upon dishonor he may enforce either:

1) The Instrument

or 2) The obligation (may sue on the underlying obligation, most likely an action in contract)

b. **Instrument of a Third Party**—If an Instrument of a Third Person is Indorsed over to the obligee in Payment of the obligation, the obligee will be discharged; the discharge of the obligor on the Instrument also discharges the underlying obligation (but the instrument may still be enforced against the third person Maker or Drawer) (e.g., buyer delivers to seller an uncertified personal Check of X payable to the Order of buyer in Payment of the price of goods, and buyer Indorses the Check over to seller).

c. This rule (§3-310(b)(3)) is subject to (4) (below).

(4) Dishonor of Check or Note:

a. **Non-Obligee Entitled to Enforce**—If the Person Entitled to Enforce the instrument is not the obligee, the obligee may not enforce the *"suspended"* part of the obligation (i.e., the amount reflected in the Instrument).

b. **Obligee Without Possession of the Instrument**—If the obligee is the Person Entitled to Enforce the Instrument but no longer has possession of it (i.e., it was stolen, lost, or destroyed), then the following rules apply:

1. He may not enforce the *"suspended"* part of the obligation (i.e., the amount reflected in the Instrument).
2. The obligee's rights against the obligor are limited to enforcement of the Instrument, to such extent.

(c) **Other Instruments:**

1. The effect of an Instrument being used to pay for an obligation is:
   (i) That stated in §3-310(a)—if the Bank is liable for the Instrument as Maker or Acceptor
   (ii) That stated in §3-310(b)—in all other cases
2. This subsection applies only to instruments not included in §3-310(a) or (b).

§3-311: Accord and Satisfaction by Use of Instrument:

(a) **Scope:** This section will apply if a Person against whom a claim is asserted can prove that:

(i) The Person tendered an Instrument in Good Faith as full satisfaction of a claim

and (ii) The amount of the claim was unliquidated (or subject to a bona fide dispute)

and (iii) The claimant obtained payment of the Instrument

(b) **Discharge of Claim by Notice:** A claim will be discharged (unless (c) applies) if the Person against whom the claim is asserted can prove that the Instrument (or an accompanying document) contained a *conspicuous statement* stating that the Instrument was tendered *"in full satisfaction"* of the claim.

(c) **When Claim Not Dischargeable:** A claim will not be discharged (subject to §3-311(d)) under §3-311(b) if:

(1) Claimant is an Organization, and the organization proves that:

(i) The Claimant sent a *conspicuous* statement (within a reasonable time before tender) to the Person against whom the claim is asserted saying that all writings and Instruments tendered as full satisfaction must be sent to a designated Person, office, or place.

and (ii) The Instrument/Accompanying writings were not received by that designated Person, office, or place.

or (2) The Claimant, *whether or not an organization*, can prove that:

i) It tendered repayment of the Instrument to the Person against whom the claim is asserted.

and ii) Repayment was made within 90 days after Payment of the Instrument

and iii) The claimant is not an Organization that sent a statement complying with §3-311(c)(1)(i) (above).

(d) **Discharge of Claim by Knowledge:** A claim will be discharged if the Person against whom the claim is asserted can prove that any of the following people knew that the Instrument was tendered in full satisfaction of the claim within a *reasonable time before collection* of the Instrument was initiated:

1. The Claimant

or 2. An agent of the Claimant (having direct responsibility with respect to the disputed obligation)

§3-312: Lost, Destroyed, or Stolen Cashier's Check, Teller's Check, or Certified Check:[4]

(a) **Definitions** (for purposes of this section):

(1) **"Check"**—a Cashier's Check, Teller's Check, or Certified Check.
(2) **"Claimant"**—a Person who claims the right to receive the amount of a Check that was either lost, stolen, or destroyed.
(3) **"Declaration of Loss"**—a **written** statement[5] (made under penalty of perjury) claiming that:
    (i) The Person making the declaration ("The declarant") lost possession of the Check.
    and (ii) The Declarant is the:
        1. Drawer or Payee of the Check (if it is a Cashier's Check)
        or 2. Remitter or Payee of the Check (if it is a Teller's Check or Cashier's Check)
    and (iii) The loss of possession was not the result of a transfer by the declarer or lawful seizure.
    and (iv) The Person cannot readily obtain possession of the Instrument because:
        a. It was destroyed
        or b. It was lost (i.e., its whereabouts cannot be determined)
        or c. It is in the *wrongful possession* of a Person:
            1. Whose identity is unknown
            or 2. Who cannot be found
            or 3. Who is not amenable for service of process
(4) **"Obligated Bank"** includes:
    a) The Issuer of a Cashier's Check or Teller's Check
    b) The Acceptor of a Certified Check

(b) **Claim for Payment:**

A. A Claimant may assert a claim in the amount of a Check by communicating the following information to the Obligated Bank:
    a. Describing the Check with *reasonable certainty*
    and b. Requesting Payment for the amount of the Check
B. Requirements to assert claim for Payment: The Claimant may assert such a claim only if:
    (i) The Claimant is the Payee or Drawer (of a Certified Check), or remitter or Payee (of a Cashier's Check or Teller's Check)

---

[4] Note: §3-312 was not adopted as part of the 1990 Official Text of the Revised Article 3. It was officially approved and recommended for enactment in all states in August 1991 by the National Conference of Commissioners on Uniform State Laws.

[5] Revised Article 3 (2002) changes the requirement of a "Writing" to a "Record."

and (ii) The communication contains a <u>*declaration of loss*</u> (regarding the Check)

and (iii) The communication is *received* by the Bank in *reasonable time* to prevent Payment of the Check to the wrongful Person

and (iv) The Claimant provides a *reasonable identification* of himself, if the Obligated Bank so requests

C. <u>**Declaration as Warranty**</u>: Delivery of a declaration of loss will act as a <u>warranty</u> of the truth of the statements made in the Declaration.

D. If a claim is asserted in compliance with this subsection, the following rules will apply:

(1) **Time claim is Enforceable:** The claim will become enforceable at the <u>*later*</u> of:

(i) The time the claim is asserted

or (ii) <u>90 Days</u> after:

a. <u>*The check date*</u> — for Teller's Checks and Cashier's Checks

or b. <u>*The acceptance date*</u> — for Certified Checks

(2) **Payment Before Claim is Enforceable:**

a. The claim has no legal effect until it becomes enforceable.

b. The Obligated Bank may pay the Check (or permit the Drawee to pay the Check in the case of a Teller's Check) at any time before the claim becomes enforceable.

c. Payment to a Person Entitled to Enforce the Check will Discharge all of the Obligated Bank's liability on the Check.

(3) **Claim Enforceable Before Check Presented:** The Obligated Bank will <u>not</u> be obligated to pay the Check if the claim becomes enforceable before the Check is presented for payment.

(4) **Obligated Bank's Duty to Pay Claimant:**

1. The Obligated Bank must pay the Claimant when the claim becomes enforceable <u>*unless*</u> it had already paid a Person Entitled to Enforce the Check.
2. Payment to the Claimant will discharge the Obligated Bank's liability on the Check (subject to § 4-302(a)(1): "Payor Bank's Responsibility for Late Return of Items").

(c) **Claimant's Obligation to a Holder in Due Course:** If *after* the Obligated Bank pays the claimant (as per § 3-312(b)(4)) a Holder in

Due Course presents the Check for Payment, the Claimant will be obligated to *either*:

(i) Refund the Payment to the Obligated Bank if the Obligated Bank pays an HDC

or (ii) Pay the HDC the amount of the Check if the Obligated Bank refuses to pay it (i.e., it dishonors the Check)

(d) **Option to Remedies in § 3-309:** A Claimant may assert its rights under this section or § 3-309 ("Right to Enforce Lost, Destroyed, or Stolen Instruments") if:

1. The Claimant has a right to assert a claim under § 3-312(b)

and 2. The Claimant is entitled to enforce a Check which is lost, destroyed, or stolen (under § 3-309).

PART 4:

Liability of Parties

§ 3-401: Signature:

(a) **Liability on an Instrument:**

A Person will be liable on an Instrument only if:

(i) The Person has *Signed* the Instrument.
or (ii) A Representative has Signed it for the Person (and such signature is binding on the Represented Person under § 3-402).

(b) **Method of Signature:**

A signature may be made by:

(i) Any of the following means:
- a) Manually
- or b) By use of a machine or device

and (ii) The use of:
- a. A name (including a trade or assumed name)
- or b. Any of the following if they are *executed or adopted* by a Person with a *present intention to authenticate a writing*:
  - 1) Word
  - or 2) Mark
  - or 3) Symbol

§ 3-402: Signature by Representation:

(a) **Represented Person Bound**

1. A Person whose name is Signed by a Representative is bound to the same extent he would be if the signature were on a simple contract if:
   - a) The Person acting (or purporting to act) as a Representative signs the Instrument.
   - and b) Such Person either:
     - 1) Signs the name of the Represented Person
     - or 2) Signs his own name.
2. If the Represented Person is bound (under the law of agency), then the following rules apply:
   - a) The signature of the Representative is considered to be the *"Authorized signature of the Represented Person."*

and b) The Represented Person is liable on the Instrument *whether or not he is identified in the Instrument.*

(b) **Liability of the Representative**—

Scope: The liability rules in this section apply if:

a) The Representative signs an Instrument in her own name.
and b) The Representative's signature is considered the *"authorized signature of the Represented Person,"* (under § 3-402(a)).

(1) The Representative is not liable if:

a) The form of the signature shows *unambiguously* that the signature is made on behalf of the Represented Person.
and b) The Represented Person is identified in the Instrument.

(2) The Representative will be liable

a) *To HDC*—The Representative will be liable to a *Holder in Due Course* if:

1. The HDC took the Instrument without notice that the Representative was not intended to be liable on the Instrument.
and 2. *Either*:
(i) The form of the signature does not *unambiguously* show that the signature is made in a Representative capacity.
or (ii) The Represented Person is not identified in the Instrument.

b) *To Non-HDC*—The Representative will be liable to non-HDCs, *unless* he can prove that the original parties did not intend the Representative to be liable on the Instrument.

c) Subsection 3-402(b)(2) is subject to § 3-402(c).

(c) **Checks**—The Representative Signer is not liable on a Check if:

1. The signature is an "authorized signature of the Represented Person."
and 2. The Representative signs with his own name (as Drawer of a Check).
and 3. The Representative does not indicate his status as a Representative (i.e., no need to indicate status).
and 4. The Check is payable from an Account of the Represented Person.
and 5. The Represented Person is identified on the Check.

§3-403: Unauthorized Signature:

(a) **Unauthorized Signature Ineffective:** An Unauthorized signature is **ineffective** unless:

Forged check treated as thief's

1) Otherwise provided in Article 3 or 4
2) The signature is effective to impose liability upon the signer in favor of a Person who **in Good Faith**:
    a) Takes it for Value
    or b) Pays the Instrument
3) **"Ratification":** The Unauthorized signature may be retroactively adopted by the Person whose name is Signed.
    - Ratification may be found from conduct or express statements.

(b) **Multi-Person Signatures:**

If an organization requires more than one signature to constitute the organization's authorized signature, the signature is deemed unauthorized if *any* of the required signatures are absent.

(c) **Liability:** Civil or criminal liability for persons making Unauthorized signatures is not affected by any provision of this Article which makes the Unauthorized signature effective for the purposes of this Article.

§3-404: Impostors; Fictitious Payees:

(a) **Impostor's Indorsement Effective:**

1) An Indorsement of an Instrument by any Person in the name of the Payee is *effective,* as if it were the Payee, in favor of a Person who:
    a) Pays the Instrument
    or b) Takes it for Value or Collection
2) This rule applies if an impostor (by use of mail or otherwise)
    a) Induces the Issuer of an Instrument to Issue the Instrument to *either:*
        1) The impostor himself
        or 2) A Person acting in concert with the impostor
    and b) Causes the Issuer to do so by impersonating *either* the:
        1) Payee of the Instrument
        2) A Person authorized to act for the payee

(b) **Unintended or Fictitious Payee:**

A. **Scope**—These rules apply if:
    (i) A Person whose intent determines to whom an Instrument is payable (see §3-110(a) or (b)) does not intend the Person identified as payee to have any interest in the Instrument.
    or (ii) The Person identified as payee is a fictitious Person.

B. Rules of unintended or fictitious Payee (These apply until the instrument is negotiated by special Indorsement):
   (1) Any Person in possession of the Instrument is considered its holder.
   (2) An Indorsement (made by anyone) in the name of the payee stated in the Instrument is effective as the Payee's Indorsement in favor of a Person who, in **Good Faith:**
      a) Pays the Instrument
      or b) Takes it for Value or collection.

(c) **Intended Payee:** An Indorsement is made in the name of a Payee (under (a) and (b)) if:

   (i) It is made in a name *substantially similar* to that of the payee.
   or (ii) The Instrument is deposited in a Depositary Bank Account in a name *substantially similar* to that of the payee (whether or not Indorsed).

(d) Failure to Use Ordinary Care

   1) A Person paying or taking for Value or collection an Instrument (to which (a) or (b) applies) will be liable on the Instrument if:
      a) He fails to use Ordinary Care when paying or taking the Instrument for Value or collection.
      and b) His failure to use Ordinary Care *substantially contributes* to the loss resulting from Payment of the Instrument.
      and c) A Person suffers damages as a result.
   2) Such Person will be liable only to the extent of the amount lost as a result of the failure to use Ordinary Care.

§ 3-405: Employer's Responsibility for Fraudulent Indorsement by Employee:

(a) **Definitions**—the following definitions apply to this section:

   (1) **"Employee"**—includes an Independent contractor and employee of an independent contractor retained by the employer
   (2) **"Fraudulent Indorsement"**—
      (i) For Instruments Payable to employer—a forged Indorsement purporting to be that of the employer
      or (ii) For Instruments where employer is Issuer—a forged Indorsement purporting to be that of the Person identified as the payee
   (3) **"Responsibility"**
      a) "Responsibility" includes the authority to:
         (i) Sign or Indorse instruments on behalf of the employer
         or (ii) Process instruments received by the employer for

a) Bookkeeping purposes
or b) Deposit to an Account
or c) Other disposition
or (iii) Prepare or process instruments for Issue in the employer's name
or (iv) Supply information determining the names or addresses of the payees of instruments (which were to be issued by the employer)
or (v) Control disposition of instruments to be issued in the employer's name
or (vi) Act otherwise with respect to instruments in a responsible capacity

b) *"Responsibility"* does not include authority that merely allows an employee to have access to instruments or blank/incomplete Instrument forms that are being stored, transported, or are part of incoming or outgoing mail, or have similar access.

(b) **Rights and Liabilities**:

1) A <u>Fraudulent Indorsement</u> will be effective (as the Indorsement of the Person to whom the Instrument is payable) as against a Person who in **Good Faith** pays the Instrument or takes it for Value or collection if:
   a) The employer entrusted the employee with a "<u>responsibility</u>" specified in (3).
   or b) The responsible employee (or someone working with such employee) <u>makes a fraudulent Indorsement</u>.
   or c) The Indorsement is made in the <u>name of the Person to whom the Instrument is payable</u>.
2) <u>Failure to Use Due Care</u>:
   a) If the Person paying or taking for Value or collection the Instrument fails to use Ordinary Care in paying or taking the Instrument for Value or collection, he will be liable to anyone suffering as a result if it *substantially contributes* to the loss resulting from the fraud.
   b) Such Person will be liable only for the amount lost as a result of its failure to use Ordinary Care.

(c) **"Made in the Name of the Payee"** A forged Indorsement made under (b) will be considered to have been made in the name of the Person to whom the Instrument is payable if:

(i) It is made in a name *substantially similar* to the name of that Person.
or (ii) The Instrument is deposited in a Depositary Bank account in a name *substantially similar* to the name of that Person (whether or not Indorsed).

§3-406: Negligence Contributing to Forged Signature or Alteration of an Instrument:[6]

(a) **Preclusion from Defense:**

A Person will be precluded from asserting a defense of Alteration or Forgery if:

1) The Person failed to use *Ordinary Care* (see §3-103(7)).
and 2) Failure to use the Ordinary Care *substantially contributed* to the Alteration or Forgery.
and 3) Such defense is asserted against a Person who, in **Good Faith:**
   a) Pays the Instrument.
   or b) Takes it for Value or collection.

(b) **Person Asserting Preclusion also Negligent:**

1) Loss will be allocated between the Person precluded from making the defense (in (a)) and the Person asserting the preclusion if:
   a) The Person asserting the preclusion in (a) also failed to exercise Ordinary Care in paying or taking the Instrument.
   b) That failure *substantially contributes* to loss.
2) The loss will be allocated to the extent each party's failure to use Ordinary Care contributed to the loss.

(c) **Burden of Proof** ("BOP"):

1) Under (a), the BOP that Ordinary Care was not used rests on the Person asserting the preclusion.
2) Under (b), the BOP that Ordinary Care was not used is on the Person precluded from using the defenses.

§3-407: Alteration:

(a) **"Alteration"** means:

(i) An unauthorized change in an Instrument that purports to modify the obligation of a party in any respect.
or (ii) An unauthorized addition of words or numbers (or other change) to an *incomplete instrument* relating to the obligation of a party.

(b) **Effect of Alteration:**

1. An Alteration fraudulently made will discharge a party whose obligation is affected by the Alteration, *unless:*
   a) That party assents to the Alteration

[6] Former 3-406 does not provide for Comparative Negligence.

or b) That Party is precluded from asserting the Alteration (e.g., the party is precluded under § 3-406 or there is some other ground barring the defense)

or c) Otherwise provided in (c).

2. No other Alteration discharges a party, thereby allowing the Instrument to be enforced according to its *original* terms.

(c) **Payment of Altered Check:**

1. The following rule applies only to:
   a. A Payor Bank/Drawee paying a fraudulently altered Instrument

   or b. A Person taking the Altered Instrument:
      1. For Value

      and 2. In Good Faith

      and 3. Without notice of the Alteration
2. A Person paying or taking a fraudulently altered Instrument may enforce the Instrument (as against the Drawer) only:
   (i) According to its original terms

   or (ii) According to its completed/Altered terms, if it was altered by an *unauthorized completion.*

§ 3-408: Drawee Not Liable on Unaccepted Draft:

a. **Draft not an Assignment:** A Check or other Draft does not, itself, operate as an Assignment of funds in the hands of the Drawee available for its Payment.

b. **Drawee Not Liable Until Accepted:** The Drawee is not liable on the Instrument until he accepts it.

§ 3-409: Acceptance of Draft and Certified Checks:

(a) **"Acceptance"** — occurs when the Drawee signs a Draft in agreement that it be paid upon presentation.

1) Signature Rules:
   a) The Drawee's signature alone is enough to convey Acceptance.
   b) Acceptance must be written on the Draft.

2) Effective Date:
   a) When notification of Acceptance (pursuant to instructions) is given.

   or b) When the Accepted Draft is delivered—*for the purpose of giving rights on the Acceptance to any Person.*

3) Acceptance may be made at any time.

(b) **Acceptance of a Draft:** A Draft may be accepted, *even though* it:

a) Is not Signed by the Drawer
or b) Is otherwise incomplete
or c) Is overdue
or d) Has been dishonored

(c) **Undated Drafts:** The holder may complete the Acceptance by supplying a date in Good Faith if:

1) A Draft is payable at a fixed period after sight.
and 2) The Acceptor fails to date the Acceptance.

(d) **"Certified Checks"**

1) A Certified Check is a Check accepted by the Bank on which it is drawn.
2) Acceptance of Certified Checks—may be made by:
   a) Signing the Check (as indicated in §3-409(a) above)
   or b) Writing on the Check an indication that it is *Certified*
3) The Drawee of a Check does not have to certify the Check.
4) A refusal to certify is not *dishonor* of the Check.

§3-410: Acceptance Varying Draft:

(a) **Differing Terms:** If the Terms of a Drawee's Acceptance are different from the terms of the Draft (as presented):

1) The holder may refuse the Acceptance of the Draft.
2) The holder may treat the Draft as dishonored.
3) The Drawee may then cancel the Acceptance.

(b) **Place of Payment:** The terms of a Draft are not considered different if the Acceptance indicates Payment at a particular Bank or place in the U.S., *unless* the Acceptance states that the Draft can *only* be paid at that particular Bank or place.

(c) **Holder's Assent to Varying Terms:** If the Holder agrees to an Acceptance which varies the terms of a Draft, then the obligation of each Drawer and Indorser who does not expressly assent to the Acceptance is *discharged.*

§3-411: Refusal to Pay Cashier's, Teller's, or Certified Checks:

(a) **"Obligated Bank"**—*for this section*—means:

1. The Acceptor of a Certified Check
and 2. The Issuer of a Cashier's Check or Teller's Check (bought from the Issuer)

(b) **When Bank is Liable:**

1. An Obligated Bank will be liable to a Person entitled to Payment of a Check if it wrongfully:
   - (i) Refuses to pay a Cashier's Check or Certified Check
   - or (ii) Stops Payment of a Teller's Check
   - or (iii) Refuses to pay a dishonored Teller's Check
2. A Person asserting the right to enforce the Check is entitled to:
   - i) Compensation — for expenses and loss of interest *resulting from the nonpayment*
   - and ii) Consequential damages — if the obligated Bank refuses to pay after receiving notice of particular circumstances giving rise to the damages.

(c) **When Bank is not Liable:** Expenses or consequential damages (under (b) above) are NOT recoverable if the Bank refuses to pay because:

- (i) The Bank suspends Payments.
- or (ii) The Obligated Bank asserts a claim or defense of the Bank that it has reasonable grounds to believe is available against the Person Entitled to Enforce the Instrument.
- or (iii) The Obligated Bank has a reasonable doubt whether the Person demanding Payment is the Person Entitled to Enforce the Instrument.
- or (iv) Payment is prohibited by law.

§ 3-412: Obligation of Issuer:

a) This section applies only to:

1. Notes
- and 2. Cashier's Checks
- and 3. Other Drafts drawn on the Drawer (i.e., Teller/Bank Checks)

b) **Applicable Terms of Payment:** The Issuer of the above drafts is obliged to pay the Instrument according to the terms of the Draft at the time it was:

- (i) Issued, or if it was not issued, when the Holder first took possession
- or (ii) Completed (to the extent stated in § 3-115 and § 3-407) — if the Issuer Signed an Incomplete Instrument

c) This obligation is owed to:

- i) A Person Entitled to Enforce the Instrument
- and ii) An *Indorser* who paid the Instrument (under § 3-415)

§3-413: Obligation of Acceptor:

(a) **Applicable Terms of Payment:**

1. The Acceptor of a Draft must pay the Draft, according to its terms at the time the Draft was:
   - (i) Accepted — even if the Acceptance states that the Draft is payable *"as originally drawn"* (or has equivalent terms)
   - or (ii) As varied — if the Acceptance varies the terms of the Draft (see §3-410)
   - or (iii) As completed (to the extent stated in §3-115 and §3-407) — if the Draft was accepted while incomplete
2. This obligation is owed to:
   - i) The Drawer or a Person Entitled to Enforce the Draft
   - or ii) An *Indorser* who paid the Draft (under §3-414 or §3-415)

(b) **Exceptions**

1) Amount Stated: The Acceptor must pay the amount so stated on the Draft if the Acceptance of the Draft (or certification of a Check) specifically states the amount Accepted or Certified.
2) Holder in Due Course: The Acceptor must pay the amount of the Instrument at the time it was taken by an HDC if:
   - (i) The Certification or Acceptance does not state an amount.
   - and (ii) The amount of the Instrument is subsequently raised.
   - and (iii) The Instrument is then negotiated to an HDC.

§3-414: Obligation of Drawer:

(Primary obligation) - one responsible for making pymt (drawer, maker, acceptor of draft, drawee Bank who certifies check)

(a) **Scope:** This section does not apply to:

1. Cashier's Checks
2. or Other Drafts drawn on the Drawer

(b) **Obligation to Pay for Dishonored Draft** (uncertified)

1) If an Unaccepted Draft is dishonored, the Drawer is obliged to pay the Draft, according to its terms at the time it was:
   - (i) *Either:*
     - a) Issued — if the Draft was issued
     - or b) First possessed by a Holder — if the Draft was not issued
   - or (ii) Completed (to the extent stated in §3-115 and §3-407) — if the Drawer Signed an Incomplete Instrument
2) This Obligation is owed to:
   - i) A Person Entitled to Enforce the Draft
   - and ii) An *Indorser* who paid the Draft (under §3-415)

(c) **Discharge of Drawer:** If a Draft is Accepted by a Bank, the Drawer is discharged (regardless of when or by whom acceptance was obtained).

(d) **Dishonored Draft Accepted by a Non-Bank:** The Drawer has the same obligation (to pay the Draft) as an Indorser (under §3-415(a) and (c)) if:

1) The Draft is accepted by a non-Bank.
and 2) It is dishonored by the Acceptor.

(e) **Disclaimer of Liability:**

1. The Drawer will not be liable under (b) if:
   a) The Draft *either:*
      1) States that it is drawn *"without recourse"*
      or 2) Otherwise disclaims the Drawer's liability (to pay the Draft)
   and b) The Draft is not a Check
2. A disclaimer of the liability under (b) is not effective if the Draft is a Check.

(f) **Discharge of Obligation:**

1. The Drawer may discharge its obligation to pay a Check by assigning its rights against the Drawee (with respect to the funds) to the Person Entitled to Enforce the Check.
2. The Drawer may do this only *to the extent* the Drawer is deprived of funds, when:
   (i) *Either:*
      a) A Check is not presented for Payment within 30 days after its date
      or b) A Check is not given to a Depositary Bank for collection within 30 days after its date[7]
   and (ii) The Drawee suspends payments after the 30 day period expires (without paying the Check)
   and (iii) Because of the *suspension of payments*, the Drawer is deprived of funds maintained with the Drawee to cover the Payment of the Check (e.g., Bank is insolvent)
3. Limitation: The amount that may be discharged is limited to the amount of funds the Drawer is deprived of.

§3-415: Obligation of Indorser:

(a) **Obligation to Pay for Dishonored Draft:**

1) If an Instrument is dishonored, an Indorser is obliged to pay the amount due on the Instrument, according to its terms at the time it was:
   (i) Indorsed

[7] Former 3-503 did not specify a time period; it merely prescribed a reasonable time standard, which was presumed to be less than 30 days in most courts.

or (ii) Completed (to the extent stated in §3-115 and §3-407), if the Indorser Indorsed an Incomplete Instrument

2) This obligation is owed to:

i) A Person Entitled to Enforce the Instrument

or ii) A *subsequent Indorser* who paid the Instrument (under this section)

3) This subsection is subject to subsections (b), (c), (d), (e), and Section 3-419(d).

(b) **Disclaimer of Liability**: The Indorser is not liable under (a) if the Indorsement *either:*

1) States that it is made *"without recourse"*

or 2) Otherwise disclaims the Indorser's liability (to pay the Instrument)

(c) **Discharge Without Notice of Dishonor:**

The Indorser's liability (under (a)) will be *discharged* if:

1) Notice of Dishonor is required (as per §3-503)

and 2) Such notice is not given to an Indorser

(d) **Discharge by Acceptance**:

The Indorser will be discharged of liability (under (a)) if a Bank accepts a Draft after an Indorsement is made.

(e) **Discharge for Checks:**

The liability (under (a)) of the Indorser will be discharged if:

a) The Draft Indorsed is a Check.

and b) *Either*:

1) The Check is not presented for Payment within 30 days after Indorsement.

or 2) The Check is not given to a Depositary Bank for collection within 30 days after Indorsement.[8]

§3-416: Transfer Warranties:

(a) **Warranties:** When a Person transfers an Instrument for Consideration, the following warranties are made to a transferee and, if the Transfer is by Indorsement, to any subsequent transferees:

(1) **Entitlement to Enforce:** The Warrantor is a Person Entitled to Enforce the Instrument.

---

[8] Under former 3-502 discharge occurred after a reasonable time passed of Indorsement; most courts presumed this to be about 7 days.

and (2) **Authentic and Authorized Signatures:** All signatures on the Instrument are Authentic and Authorized.

and (3) **No Alterations:** The Instrument has not been altered.

and (4) **No Defense of Recoupment:** The Instrument is not subject to a defense or claim in Recoupment of any party (which can be asserted against the warrantor).

and (5) **No Knowledge of Insolvency:** The Warrantor has no knowledge of any insolvency proceedings of the Maker, Acceptor, or Drawer (in the case of an Unaccepted Draft).

Revised Article 3 (2002) adds:

and (6) **Remote Consumer Item:** With respect to a Remotely Created Consumer Item, that the person on whose account the Item is drawn authorized the issuance of the Item in the amount for which the Item is drawn.

(b) **Damages for Breach of Warranty:**

1. A Person may recover (from the warrantor) the amount lost as a result of a breach of warranty, if:
   a. The transfer warranties under (a) are made to that Person.
   b. The Person took the Instrument in Good Faith.
2. Limitation: The damages cannot exceed the following:

The amount of the Instrument
\+ **Expenses and loss of interest** (incurred as a result of the breach)

(c) **Notice and Disclaimer:**

1. The warranties in (a) cannot be disclaimed for Checks.
2. If the Claimant does not notify the warrantor of the claim for breach of warranty within 30 days after the Claimant has *reason to know* of the breach (and the identity of the warrantor), the warrantor will be discharged of any amount of damages he incurs from the delay in giving notice of the claim (i.e., deductions for failure to mitigate).

(d) **Cause of Action:** A cause of action for breach of warranty (under this section) accrues when the Claimant has *reason to know of the breach.*

§ 3-417: Presentment Warranties:

(a) **Presentment Warranties:**

i) Presentment warranties will be available only if:
   1) An Unaccepted Draft is presented to the Drawee for Payment or Acceptance. The warranties will be made by:
      (i) The Person obtaining Payment or Acceptance.
      and (ii) A previous transferor of the Draft.

and 2) The Drawee Pays or Accepts the Draft in Good Faith.

ii) The Warranties include:

(1) <u>**Good Title and Rightful Transfer:**</u> The warrantor is (or was at the time the warrantor transferred the Draft):
   a) A Person Entitled to Enforce the Draft.
   or b) A Person authorized to obtain Payment or Acceptance of the Draft on behalf of a Person Entitled to Enforce the Draft.

(2) <u>**No Alteration:**</u> The Draft has not been Altered.

(3) <u>**Authentic and Authorized Signature:**</u> The Warrantor has <u>No knowledge</u> that the Drawer's signature is unauthorized.

(b) **Damages for Breach of Warranty:**

1. A Drawee making Payment may recover from any warrantor (damages for breach of warranty):

   The amount paid by the Drawee
   − **The amount the Drawee received** (or is entitled to receive) **from the Drawer** (because of Payment)
   + **Compensation for expenses and loss of interest** (resulting from the breach)

2. The Drawee's rights are not affected by any failure to exercise Ordinary Care in making Payment.
3. **Defense:** If the Drawee accepts the Draft, the Acceptor may use breach of warranty as a defense to the obligation of the Acceptor.
4. If the Acceptor makes Payment for the Draft, he may collect damages as provided in section (b).

(c) **Available Defenses:**

1. <u>Scope</u>: Section 3-417(c) applies if a Drawee asserts a claim for breach of warranty under (a) based on:
   a) An Unauthorized Indorsement of the Draft ((a)(1))
   or b) An Alteration of the Draft ((a)(2))
2. The warrantor may use the following defenses:
   a) The Indorsement is effective under §3-404 or §3-405.
   or b) The Drawer is precluded from asserting that his signature is unauthorized or that the Draft was altered (under §3-406 and §4-406).

(d) **Payment Warranties:**

1. <u>**Scope:**</u> Section 3-417(d) applies if:
   (i) A <u>dishonored Draft</u> is presented for Payment to *either*:
      a. The Drawer
      or b. An Indorser.

or (ii) Any <u>other Instrument</u> is presented for Payment to a party obligated to pay the Instrument.

and (iii) Payment is Received.

2. **Warranties**

(1) The Person obtaining Payment (and a prior transferor of the Instrument) warrants to the Person making Payment that the warrantor is (or was at the time the Draft was transferred):

a) A Person Entitled to Enforce the Instrument

or b) A Person authorized to obtain Payment on behalf of a Person Entitled to Enforce the Instrument.

(2) The Person making Payment may recover the following from *any* warrantor for breach of warranty:

The amount paid
+ **Expenses and loss of interest** (resulting from breach of warranty)

(e) **Notice and Disclaimer:**

1. The Warranties in (a) and (d) cannot be disclaimed for Checks.
2. If the claimant does not notify the warrantor of a claim for breach within <u>30 days</u> after the claimant has *reason to know* of the breach and the identity of the warrantor, the liability of the warrantor under (b) and (d) is discharged of any amount of damages he incurs from the delay (i.e., deductions for failure to mitigate).

(f) **Cause of Action:** A cause of action for breach of warranty (under this section) accrues when the claimant has *reason to know of the breach.*[9]

§ 3-418: Payment or Acceptance by Mistake:

(a) **Drawee's Right to Revoke or Recover:**

1) <u>Power to Recover</u>: The Drawee may recover the amount of the Draft from the Person who received Payment if the Drawee:

a) Pays the Draft.

and b) Acted on the <u>mistaken</u> belief that:

(i) Payment of the Draft had not been stopped (pursuant to § 4-403).

or (ii) The drawer's signature on the Draft was authorized.

2) <u>Power to Revoke</u>: If the Drawee Accepts the Draft (instead of paying for it), and the above conditions are met, he may Revoke Acceptance.

3) These rights are not affected by the Drawee's failure to exercise Ordinary Care in paying or accepting the Draft.

4) This subsection is subject to (c) below.

[9] Under former Article 3, the warrantor had to be the owner of the Check, and not a "Person Entitled to Indorse Check."

(b) **Person Paying or Accepting Party's Rights:**

1. If an Instrument was Accepted or Paid by *mistake*, the Person Paying or Accepting may (to the extent permitted by the law governing mistake and restitution, i.e., common law and other statutes):
   - (i) Recover Payment from the Person who received Payment (i.e., Restitution)
   - or (ii) Revoke Acceptance.[10]
2. Section 3-418(b) applies only to cases not covered by (a).
3. This subsection is subject to (c) below.

(c) **Defenses:**

1. Remedies in (a) and (b) may not be asserted against a Person who:[11]
   - a. Took the Instrument:
     - 1. In Good Faith
     - and 2. For Value
   - or b. Changed his position:
     - 1. In Good Faith
     - 2. In Reliance on the Payment or Acceptance (example: taking Money out of Bank Account)
2. This subsection does not limit remedies provided by §3-417 or §4-407.

(d) **Effect of Revocation or Recovery**:

1. This section applies if:
   - a) An Instrument is Paid or Accepted by mistake
   - and b) The Payor or Acceptor either:
     - 1. Recovers Payment (under (a) or (b))
     - or 2. Revokes Acceptance (under (a) or (b)).
2. Effect of Revocation or Recovery: If the above conditions are fulfilled, then:
   - a) The Instrument is deemed not to have been Paid or Accepted.
   - and b) The Instrument is treated as dishonored.
   - and c) The Person from whom Payment is recovered obtains the same rights as a Person Entitled to Enforce the dishonored Instrument.
3. Even though a Payor Bank may have paid an Item under §4-215, it may have a right to recover the Payment under §3-418.

[10] This provision was not part of former Article 3.
[11] Former Article 3 limited these defenses to HDCs.

§ 3-419: Instruments Signed for Accommodation:

(a) **Accommodation Party's Signature:**

1. **"Accommodation Party"** — An Accommodation Party is a party to the Instrument who *signs* the Instrument (thereby incurring liability for the Instrument) without becoming a direct beneficiary of the Value given for the Instrument (example: A surety, who ensures Payment on the Instrument, but does not receive the Value given for the Instrument (see also Off. Comm. 1)).
2. **"Accommodated Party"** — The Accommodated Party is the party who gets the benefit of the Accommodation Party's signature (i.e., the Accommodated Party is the one whose Instrument is guaranteed by the Accommodation Party).
3. An Instrument Signed by an Accommodation Party will be considered to be Signed *"for accommodation."*

(b) **Accommodation Party's Liability:**

1. The Accommodation Party may sign the Instrument as *either*:
   a. Maker
   or b. Drawer
   or c. Acceptor
   or d. Indorser
2. The Accommodation Party will be obliged to pay the Instrument in the capacity in which he signs the Instrument (subject to § 3-419(d)) (e.g., if the Accommodation Party Indorses the Check, it will be responsible to pay the Check as if it were the Indorser, as per § 3-415 (i.e., like an Indorser, the Accommodation Party will only be responsible to pay for the Instrument until 30 days after it Indorsed the Instrument)).
3. The obligation of an Accommodation Party may be enforced notwithstanding any statute of frauds and whether or not the Accommodation Party receives consideration for the accommodation.

(c) **Notice of Accommodation Party:**

1. A Person signing an Instrument is presumed to be an Accommodation Party only if there is notice that the Instrument is Signed for Accommodation — there is notice that an Instrument is Signed *"for Accommodation"* if the signature is:
   a) An *Anomalous Indorsement*
   b) Accompanied by *words* indicating that the party Signed as a *guarantor* or *surety* for another party's obligation under the Instrument.
2. The obligation of an Accommodation Party to pay the Instrument is not affected by the fact that the Person enforcing the obligation

had notice (when the Instrument was taken by that Person) that the Accommodation Party Signed the Instrument as an Accommodation Party (except as provided in §3-605: "Discharge of Indorsers and Accommodation Parties").

(d) **Guaranteeing Collection and Not Payment:**

If the signature of a party to an Instrument is accompanied by words *unambiguously indicating* that the party is guaranteeing *collection* (rather than Payment) of the obligation of another party to the Instrument, the signer is obliged to pay the amount due on the Instrument to the Party Entitled to Enforce the Instrument only if:

(i) Execution of Judgment against the other party has been returned unsatisfied
or (ii) The other party is Insolvent (or in an insolvency proceeding)
or (iii) The other party cannot be served with process
or (iv) It is otherwise apparent that Payment cannot be obtained from the other party.

(e) **Entitlement to Reimbursement:**

1. *Accommodation Party Pays:* An Accommodation Party who pays the Instrument is entitled to:
   a) Reimbursement from the Accommodated Party
   and b) Enforcement of the Instrument against the Accommodated Party.
2. *Accommodated Party Pays:* If the Accommodated Party pays the Instrument, it will have No right of recourse against an Accommodation Party, and will Not be entitled to contribution from the Accommodation Party.

Revised Article 3 (2002) Changes (e) and adds a new (e) making the current (e) into (f) as follows:

(e) **Entitlement to Reimbursement:** The Signer is obliged to pay the amount due on the instrument to a person entitled to enforce it in the same circumstances as an Accommodated Party would be obliged if:
1) the signature of a party to an instrument is accompanied by words indicating that the party "*guarantees payment*"
or 2) the signer signs the Instrument in some other manner that does not *unambiguously indicate* an intention to *guarantee collection* (rather than payment)

(f) **Entitlement to Reimbursement**

1. *Accommodation Party Pays:* An Accommodation Party who pays the Instrument is entitled to:
   a) Reimbursement from the Accommodated Party
   and b) Enforcement of the Instrument against the Accommodated Party

2. *Accommodation Party Required to Perform:* In proper circumstances, an accommodation party may obtain relief that requires the Accommodated Party to perform its obligations under the instrument.
3. *Accommodated Party Recourse Limitations:* If the Accommodated Party pays the Instrument, it will have No right of recourse against an Accommodation Party, and will Not be entitled to contribution from the Accommodation Party.

§ 3-420: Conversion of an Instrument:

(a) **Grounds for Conversion**

1) The law applicable to conversion of personal property also applies to instruments (i.e., common law and other statutes).
2) An Instrument is also converted if:
   a) A transferee takes it, without negotiation, from a Person not Entitled to Enforce the Instrument (i.e., a forgery or missing Indorsement).
   or b) A Bank makes or obtains Payment for a Person not Entitled to Enforce the Instrument or receive Payment.
3) An action for conversion of an Instrument may not be brought by:
   (i) The Issuer or Acceptor of the Instrument
   or (ii) A Payee or Indorsee who did not receive delivery of the Instrument either:
      1. Directly
      or 2. Through delivery to an agent or a co-payee

(b) **Amount of Liability**

1. The amount of liability in (a) is *presumed* to be the *amount payable on the Instrument.*
2. Recovery may not exceed the amount of the plaintiff's interest in the Instrument.

(c) **Representative's Liability:**[12]

A Representative (other than a Depositary Bank) will be liable only for the amount of any proceeds not paid out to a Person not entitled to enforce the Instrument, if:

1) The Representative dealt with the Instrument or its proceeds in **Good Faith.**
and 2) The Representative dealt with an Instrument on behalf of someone not entitled to enforce an Instrument.
and 3) The Representative is not a Depositary Bank.

[12] Former § 3-419 only allowed a Depositary Bank to sue under its capacity as a Depositary Bank, and not a trustee.

PART 5:

Dishonor

§3-501: Presentment:

(a) "**Presentment**"—Presentment occurs when a creditor (a "Person Entitled to Enforce an Instrument") (or his Representative) makes a demand to either:

(i) One of the following, to Pay the Instrument:
a) The Drawee
or b) A Party obliged to pay the Instrument
or c) The Bank in the case of a Note or Accepted Draft payable at a Bank

or (ii) The Drawee to Accept a Draft

(b) **Presentment Rules**

(1) **Place and Manner of Presentment:**
a) Presentment may be made:
1) At the place designated in the Instrument.
and 2) By any *commercially reasonable means* (including an oral, written, or electronic communication).
b) Presentment must be made at the place of Payment designated in the Instrument if it is payable at a Bank in the U.S.
c) Presentment is effective when the demand (for Payment or Acceptance) is received by the Person being presented with the Instrument.
d) If there are two or more Makers, Acceptors, Drawees, or other payors, demand is effective if made to any one of them.

(2) **Requirements Upon Demand**—The Person making Presentment must, upon demand:
(i) Physically exhibit the Instrument (unless agreed otherwise, as with an electronic Presentment)
and (ii) Give reasonable identification and reasonable evidence of authority to present (if the presentor is a Representative)
and (iii) *Either*:
a) Sign a Receipt for any Payment made (on the Instrument)
or b) Surrender the Instrument—if full Payment is made

(3) **Action Upon Presentment Which Will Not Constitute Dishonoring**

The party to whom Presentment is made may do the following without dishonoring an Instrument:

(i) Return the Instrument — for lack of a necessary Indorsement

or (ii) Refuse Payment or Acceptance — for failure of the Presentment to comply with:

a) The terms of the Instrument

or b) An agreement of the parties

or c) Other applicable law

(4) **"Cut-Off Hour" for Receipt of Instruments:**

The party to whom Presentment is made may treat the Presentment as if it occurred on the next business day if:

a) That party has established a "cut-off" hour (no earlier than 2:00 P.M.) for the receipt and processing of Instruments presented for Payment or Acceptance.

and b) Presentment is made after the cut-off hour.

(5) **Section 3-501(b) is subject to:**

a) Article 4

and b) Agreement of the Parties

and c) Clearinghouse rules and the like

§ 3-502: Dishonor:

(a) **Rules Governing Dishonor of a Note:**

(1) Notes Payable on Demand — A Note is considered dishonored when:

a) Presentment is duly made to the Maker.

and b) The Note is not paid on the day of Presentment.

(2) Notes Not Payable on Demand —

a) This section applies to Notes not Payable on Demand if:

1. They are payable at or through a Bank.

or 2. The terms of the Note require Presentment.

b) The Note will be considered dishonored if:

1. Presentment is duly made.

and 2. The Note is not paid by the *later* of:

a) The day it becomes payable.

or b) The day of Presentment.

(3) Other Notes Not Payable on Demand — The Note is dishonored if it is not paid on the day it becomes payable.

(b) **Rules Governing Dishonor of an Unaccepted Draft** (other than a Documentary Draft)**:**

(1) Check Presented for Payment at a later date — A Check is dishonored when:

a) The Check is duly presented for Payment to the Payor Bank.

and b) The Check is not presented for immediate Payment over the counter.

and c) The Payor Bank *either*:

1. Returns the Check in a timely fashion.

or 2. Sends a timely Notice of Dishonor or non-payment (under § 4-301 or § 4-302).

or 3. Becomes accountable for the amount of the Check under § 4-302 (Late Return).

(2) Draft Payable on Demand —

a) This section applies to drafts:

1. Payable on Demand

and 2. Not falling under (1) above (This section covers demand drafts (other than Checks) and Checks presented for immediate Payment (official comment))

b) The Draft will be considered dishonored if:

1. The Draft is duly presented to the Drawee for Payment.

and 2. The Draft is not paid on the day of Presentment.

(3) Time Draft Payable at a Specified Date (stated in the Draft) — the Draft will be considered dishonored if:

(i) **Draft Presented for Payment:**

a) The Draft is duly presented for Payment to the Drawee.

and b) Payment is not made by the *later* of:

1. The day of Presentment.

2. The day the Draft becomes payable.

or (ii) **Draft Presented for Acceptance:**

a) The Draft is duly presented for Acceptance before the Draft becomes payable.

and b) The Draft is not accepted on the day of Presentment.

(4) Time Draft Payable on elapse of a period of time after sight or Acceptance — the Draft is dishonored if:

a) The Draft is duly presented for Acceptance.

and b) The Draft is not accepted on the day of Presentment.

(c) **Rules Governing Dishonor of an Unaccepted Documentary Draft** (e.g., drafts under a Letter of Credit): The rules in § 3-502(2),(3), and (4) apply to Unaccepted Documentary Drafts *except* that Payment or Acceptance may be delayed until the end of the third business day after Payment or

Acceptance would otherwise be required (under § 3-502(2), (3), (4)) without the Draft being considered dishonored.

(d) **Rules Governing Dishonor of an Accepted Draft:**

(1) Draft Payable on Demand — the Draft will be considered dishonored if:

a. The Draft is duly presented to the Acceptor for Payment.

and b. The Draft is not paid on the day of Presentment.

(2) Draft Not Payable on Demand — the Draft will be considered dishonored if:

a. The Draft is duly presented for Payment to the Acceptor.

and b. Payment is not made by the *later* of:

i) The day of Presentment.

or ii) The day the Draft becomes payable.

(e) **Dishonor Without Presentment:**

Dishonor may occur without Presentment if:

1. Presentment is otherwise required for dishonor (under § 3-502).

and 2. Presentment is excused (under § 3-504).

and 3. The Instrument is not duly Accepted or Paid.

(f) **Consent to Late Acceptance:**

A Draft will not be considered dishonored from the time of Acceptance if:

a) Dishonor occurred because the Draft was not timely accepted (under 3-502(b)(3)(ii) or (4)).

b) The Person entitled to demand Acceptance consents to a late Acceptance.

§ 3-503: Notice of Dishonor:

(a) **When Indorser and Drawer Obligated:** The obligation of an Indorser (under § 3-415(a)) and a Drawer (under § 3-414(d)) may not be enforced *unless*:

(i) The Indorser or Drawer is given Notice of Dishonor (complying with § 3-503) of the Instrument.

or (ii) Notice of Dishonor is excused (under § 3-504(b)).

(b) **Requirements for Notice:**

1. By Whom Given — Notice of Dishonor may be given by any Person.
2. Method of Notice — Notice of Dishonor may be given by any *commercially reasonable* means (including oral, written, or electronic communication).

3. Contents of notice — notice will be sufficient if it:
   a) *Reasonably identifies* the Instrument
   and b) Indicates that the Instrument has been dishonored or that it has not been Paid or Accepted
4. Return of Instrument as notice — Return of an Instrument given to a Bank for collection is sufficient notice.

(c) **Deadline for Notice:**

(i) Notice by Collecting Bank: If an Instrument is taken for collection by a Collecting Bank, Notice of Dishonor must be given by the Bank by midnight of the next Banking Day (i.e., The Bank's "Midnight Deadline") after the Bank received Notice of Dishonor from the Payor Bank.

(ii) Notice by other Person: If an Instrument is taken for collection by a Collecting Bank, Notice of Dishonor may be given by any Person other than the Bank within 30 days from the date that Person received Notice of Dishonor.

(iii) Other Instruments: Notice of Dishonor must be given within 30 days after the date on which dishonor occurred.

(iv) This subsection is subject to § 3-504(c).

§ 3-504: Excused Presentment and Notice of Dishonor:

(a) **Presentment Excused** — Presentment is not needed for Payment or Acceptance if:

(i) The Person entitled to present the Instrument cannot make Presentment with *reasonable diligence.*

or (ii) The Maker or Acceptor *either:*
   1. Repudiated his obligation to pay the Instrument.
   or 2. Died.
   or 3. Is in insolvency proceedings.

or (iii) The Instrument's terms do not require Presentment to enforce the obligation of the Indorsers or the Drawer.

or (iv) The Drawer or Indorser (whose obligation is being enforced) *either:*
   1. Has waived the requirement of Presentment.
   or 2. Otherwise has no reason to expect that the Instrument be Paid or Accepted.
   or 3. Otherwise has no right to require that the Instrument be Paid or Accepted.

or (v) *Either:*
   1. The Drawer instructed the Drawee not to pay or Accept the Draft.
   or 2. The Drawee was not obligated to the Drawer to pay the Draft.

(b) **Notice of Dishonor Excused:**

1. A Notice of Dishonor is not required if:
   (i) The terms of the Instrument do not require notice to enforce the obligation of a party to pay the Instrument.
   or (ii) The party (whose obligation is being enforced) waived notice.
2. A waiver of Presentment is also a waiver of Notice of Dishonor.

(c) **Delay of Notice of Dishonor Excused:** Delay of Notice of Dishonor is excused if:

1. The delay was caused by circumstances beyond the control of the Person giving the notice.

and 2. The Person giving the notice exercised *reasonable diligence* after the cause of the delay ceased to operate.

§ 3-505: Evidence of Dishonor:

(a) **Admissible Evidence to Presume Dishonor:** The following evidence is admissible to create a presumption of dishonor and a presumption that Notice of Dishonor was conferred:

(1) Protest Documents — any document which purports to be a Protest (must be in regular form, as provided in § 3-505(b))
(2) Writing or Stamps — a purported writing or stamp of the Drawee, Payor Bank, or Presenting Bank, on the Instrument or accompanying the Instrument stating that Acceptance or Payment has been refused (unless the reasons for refusal of Payment/Acceptance are not consistent with dishonor)
(3) Books or Records — the Drawee, Payor Bank, or Collecting Bank may provide books or records which show dishonor, if the Books/Records were kept *in the ordinary course of business* (even if there is no evidence of who made the entry)

(b) **Protest:**

1. **"Protest"** — a protest is a certificate of dishonor made by *either*:
   a) A United States Counsel
   or b) A United States Vice Counsel
   or c) A Notary Public
   or d) Another Person authorized to administer oaths by the law of the place where dishonor occurs.
2. The protest may be made upon providing information *satisfactory* to that Person.
3. Requirements of protest — The protest must:
   a) Identify the dishonored Instrument

and b) Certify that *either*:

i) Presentment has been made

or ii) If Presentment was not made, the reason why it was not made

and c) Certify that the Instrument has been dishonored by nonacceptance or nonpayment

4. The protest may also certify that notice of dishonor has been given to some or all of the parties.

PART 6:

Discharge and Payment

§ 3-601: Discharge and Effect of Discharge:

(a) **When Discharge Occurs:** The obligation of a Party to pay an Instrument will be discharged:

1. By an act or agreement between the parties that would discharge an obligation to pay Money under a simple contract

or 2. As stated elsewhere in Article 3

(b) **Discharge from HDCs:** Discharge of the obligation is effective as a defense against a Holder in Due Course only if the holder had notice of the discharge when Holder in Due Course status was acquired.

§ 3-602: Payment:

(a) **When Payment Is Made:**

1. An Instrument is paid (subject to (b) below) *to the extent* Payment is made:
   - (i) By or on behalf of the obligated party
   - and (ii) To a Creditor
2. The obliged party's obligation to pay the Instrument is discharged to the extent of such Payment, *even if* the Instrument was paid with knowledge of a claim to the Instrument under § 3-306 by another Person.

(b) **When Obligation Not Discharged:** The obligation to pay an Instrument will not be discharged under (a) (above) if:

(1) The following defenses apply:

a) There is a § 3-306 claim on the Instrument that is *enforceable* against the party receiving Payment.

and b) *Either*:

(i) Payment is made with knowledge by the Payor that Payment is prohibited (by injunction or similar court process)

or (ii) The party making Payment accepted indemnity (from the Person having a claim to the Instrument) against loss resulting from refusal to pay the creditor

and c) *The Instrument was not:*

1. A Cashier's Check

or 2. A Teller's Check
or 3. A Certified Check
or (2) The Person making Payment knows the Instrument is a stolen Instrument and pays a Person it knows is in wrongful possession of the Instrument.

Revised § 3-602: Payment:

(a) **When Payment is Made:** An Instrument is paid (subject to (e) below) *to the extent* Payment is made:
i) By or on behalf of the obligated party
and ii) To a Person Entitled to Enforce the Instrument

(b) **Payment to Former Payee:** Subject to section (e), above:
1) *When Payment to a Former Payee is Considered Payment:* A Note is considered to be paid to the extent that Payment is made by or on behalf of a party obliged to Pay the Note to a person that *formerly* was entitled to enforce the note only if:
a) The party obliged to pay has not received *adequate notification* that the note has been transferred, at the time of the payment
and b) Such payment is to me made to the transferee.
2) *Adequate Notification:* Notification is deemed "*adequate*" only if:
a) It is signed by the transferor or transferee
and b) Reasonably identifies the transferred note
and c) Provides an address at which payments subsequently are to be made
3) *Proof of Transfer:* Upon request, the transferee shall *seasonably* furnish proof that the note has been transferred.
4) *Eligibility for Discharge:* A payment to the person that formerly was entitled to enforce the note is effective for purposes of discharge (per subsection (c)) even if the party obliged to pay the note has received a notification under this paragraph.

(c) **Discharge:** The obliged party's obligation to pay the Instrument is discharged to the extent of such Payment (in sections (a)-(b) above), *even if* the Instrument was paid with knowledge of a claim to the Instrument under § 3-306 by another Person (subject to section (e), below).

(d) **Parties Deemed to have Notice:** The following are deemed to have notice of any payment that is made under (b) above *after* the date that the note is transferred to the transferee, but *before* the party obliged to pay the note received *adequate notification* of the transfer:
1) A transferee
or 2) Any party that has acquired rights in the instrument directly or indirectly from a transferee
or 3) any party that has the rights of a Holder In Due Course

(e) **When Obligation Not Discharged:** The obligation to pay an Instrument will not be discharged under (a)-(d) (above) if:

(1) The following defenses apply:

a) There is a § 3-306 claim on the Instrument which is *enforceable* against the party receiving Payment.

and b) *Either:*

(i) Payment is made with knowledge by the Payor that Payment is prohibited (by injunction or similar court process)

or (ii) The party making Payment accepted indemnity (from the Person having a claim to the Instrument) against loss resulting from refusal to pay the Person Entitled to Enforce the Instrument

and c) *The Instrument was not:*

1. A Cashier's Check

or 2. A Teller's Check

or 3. A Certified Check

or (2) The Person making Payment knows the Instrument is a stolen Instrument and pays a Person it knows is in wrongful possession of the Instrument.

(f) **"Signed"**—as used in this section, with respect to a record that is not in writing, includes the attachment to or logical association with the record of an electronic symbol, sound, or process with the present intent to *adopt* or accept the record.

§ 3-603: Tender of Payment:

(a) **Effect of Tender:** The effect of tender of Payment on an Instrument is governed by the principles of law applicable to tender of Payment under a simple contract if the tender was made to a creditor.

(b) **Tender Refused:** If a creditor *refuses* a tender of Payment, the obligation of any Indorser or Accommodation Party having a right of recourse against the party making the tender is discharged *to the extent* of the amount of the tender.

(c) **Interest Payable After Tender; Date of Tender:**

1. Interest Payable After Tender: If tender is made to a creditor, the obligor's obligation to pay interest *after* the due date on the amount tendered is discharged.
2. Date of Tender: If the obligor is "able and ready" to pay an Instrument (at every place of Payment stated in the Instrument) by its due date, the obligor will be deemed to have tendered Payment on the due date (even though Presentment was required for Payment and the obligee has not yet presented the Instrument).

§3-604: Discharge by Cancellation or Renunciation:

(a) **Expressions of Discharge:** A creditor may discharge the obligation of a party to pay the Instrument (with or without consideration) by *either*:

(i) An intentional voluntary act, such as:

1. Surrender of the Instrument to the Party
2. Destruction or mutilation of the Instrument
3. Cancellation of the Instrument (see (b) below)
4. Cancellation or striking out of the Party's signature (see (b) below)
5. Adding Words to the Instrument that indicate Discharge

or (ii) Agreeing not to sue or otherwise renouncing his rights against the party by a **signed writing.**[13]

(b) **Rights Derived from Indorsement Unaffected:** Cancellation or striking out of an Indorsement (pursuant to (a)(i) above) does not affect the status and rights a party may derive from the Indorsement (e.g., Warranties).

Revised Article 3 (2002) adds:

(c) "**Signed**" as used in this section, with respect to a record that is not in writing, includes the attachment to or logical association with the record of an electronic symbol, sound, or process with the present intent to adopt or accept the record.

§3-605: Discharge of Indorsers and Accommodation Parties:

(a) **"Indorser"**—For purposes of this section, the term "Indorser" includes a Drawer having the obligation described in §3-414(d).

(b) **Effect of Discharge under §3-604:** A discharge under §3-604 (i.e., by cancellation or renunciation) does not discharge the obligation of an Indorser or an Accommodation Party having a right of recourse against the discharged party under §3-419.

(c) **Extension of Due Date:** If a creditor agrees (with or without consideration) to extend the due date of the Instrument, an Indorser or Accommodation Party with a right of recourse against the obligor is discharged *to the extent* the Indorser or Accommodation Party can prove that the extension caused him loss.

---

[13] Revised Article 3 (2002) changes the requirement of a "Writing" to a "Record."

(d) **Material Modification:**

1. If a creditor agrees (with or without consideration) to make a *material modification* of a party's obligation (other than an extension of the due date), an Indorser or Accommodation Party with a right of recourse against the obligor is discharged *to the extent* it can prove that the modification caused him loss.
2. "Loss Suffered" = **The Amount of the Right of Recourse,** *unless* the Person enforcing the Instrument proves:
   a) That no loss was caused by the modification.
   or b) That the loss caused by the modification was less than the amount of the right of recourse.

(e) **Discharge of Sureties by Impairment of Collateral:**

1. An Indorser or Accommodation Party with a right of recourse is discharged *to the extent* of an impairment in collateral, if:
   a. The Instrument is secured by a security interest in collateral.
   and b. A creditor impairs the Value of the interest in the collateral.
2. Impairment—The Value of the interest in the collateral will be considered *impaired* to the extent:
   (i) The Value of the interest is reduced to an amount *less than* the right of recourse of the party asserting discharge.
   or (ii) The reduction in Value of the interest causes an increase in the amount by which the right of recourse *exceeds* the Value of the interest (i.e., the unsecured interest increases while the secured amount decreases).
3. Burden of Proof: The party asserting the discharge has the burden of proving impairment.

(f) **Impairment of Secured Collateral Affecting Jointly and Severally Liable Parties:**

1. Any party who is jointly and severally liable on an obligation will be discharged *to the extent* of an impairment in collateral if:
   a. The Instrument is secured by a security interest in collateral that is not provided by an Accommodation Party.
   and b. A creditor impairs the Value of the interest in collateral.
   and c. The Impairment caused the jointly and severally liable party to pay more than it would have if the impairment had not occurred (taking into account rights of contribution).
2. Assertions by Accommodation Party: If the party asserting discharge is an Accommodation Party not entitled to discharge under subsection (e), the party is deemed to have a right to contribution (based on joint and several liability), rather than a right to reimbursement.

3. Burden of proof: The party asserting the discharge has the burden of proving Impairment.

(g) **Methods of Impairing Value:** For purposes of (e) or (f) (above), Impairment can occur by:

(i) The failure to obtain or maintain perfection (or recordation) of the interest in the collateral

or (ii) The release of collateral without substitution of collateral of equal value

or (iii) The failure to perform a duty to preserve the Value of the collateral owed to a debtor or surety (or other Person secondarily liable) (owed under Article 9 of the UCC or other law).

or (iv) The failure to comply with applicable law in disposing of collateral

(h) **Knowledge of Accommodation Party for Discharge:** An Accommodation Party is not discharged under § 3-605(c), (d), or (e) unless the creditor *either*:

1. Knows of the Accommodation

or 2. Has notice (under § 3-419(c)) that the Instrument was Signed *"for Accommodation"*

(i) **When Party Not Discharged:** A Party will not be discharged under this section if:

(i) The party asserting discharge consents to the event or conduct that is the basis of the discharge (e.g., the Accommodation Party consents to a material modification (as per § 3-605(d))).

or (ii) The Instrument (or separate agreement of the party) provides for waiver of discharge under this section either *specifically* or by *general language* indicating that parties waive defenses based on suretyship or impairment of collateral.

2. Inference of Consent By Secondary Obligor:

a. Consent by the principal obligor to an act that would discharge of a secondary obligor constitutes the secondary obligor's consent to that act if the secondary obligor either:

i. controls the principal obligor

or ii. deals with the creditor on behalf of the principal obligor

b. Exception: If the circumstances indicate otherwise.

(g) **When the terms of a release or extension "preserve the secondary obligor's recourse":** The terms of the release or extension must provide:

1. that the creditor retains the right to enforce the instrument against the secondary obligor

and 2. that the recourse of the secondary obligor continues as though the release or extension had not been granted.

(h) **Rules for Burden of Persuasion — When Burden is on the Secondary Obligor:**

1. A secondary obligor asserting discharge under this section has the burden of persuasion.
2. This applies with respect to both:
   a. the occurrence of the acts alleged to harm the secondary obligor
   and b. loss or prejudice caused by those acts
3. Exception: As otherwise provided in subsection (i).

(i) **Rules for Burden of Persuasion — When Burden is on the Creditor:**

1. It is presumed that an act impairing recourse causes a loss or impairment equal to the secondary obligor's liability if:
   a. the secondary obligor demonstrates prejudice caused by an impairment of its recourse
   and b. the circumstances of the case indicate that the amount of loss either:
      i. is not *reasonably susceptible* of calculation
      or ii. requires proof of facts that are not ascertainable.
2. In this case, the burden of persuasion is on the creditor to show any lesser amount of loss.

ARTICLE 4

PART 1:

General Provisions and Definitions

§4-101: Short Title:

This Article may be cited as "Uniform Commercial Code—Bank Deposits and Collections."

§4-102: Applicability:

(a) **Conflicts with other Articles:**

1. Items in Article 4 that are also discussed in Articles 3 and 8 are subject to those Articles.
2. Article 4 Governs: If Article 4 conflicts with Article 3, Article 4 governs.
3. Article 8 Governs: If Article 4 conflicts with Article 8, Article 8 governs.

(Note: Applicable Federal law may supersede provisions of Article 4. Such laws include the Expedited Funds Availability Act ("EFAA"), 12 U.S.C. §4001 et seq., and its implementing Regulation CC (12 CFR Pt. 229).)

(b) **Governing Local Law for Banks:**

1. The law of the place where the Bank is located governs the liability of a Bank for action or non-action on an Item handled for Presentment, Payment, or collection.
2. Branch Offices: Liability of local Bank branches or separate offices is governed by the law of the place where the branch or separate office is located.

§4-103: Variation by Agreement:

(a) **Non-Waivable Responsibilities:**

1. This Article's provisions may be varied by agreement of the parties.
2. **Exception:** Parties to such an agreement may not do the following:

a) Disclaim the Bank's responsibility for
   1) Lack of Good Faith
   or 2) Failure to exercise *ordinary care*
b) Limit the measure of damages for lack of Good Faith or failure to use Ordinary Care.

3. Parties may agree upon the *standards* by which the Bank's responsibility will be measured, as long as they are not *"manifestly unreasonable."*

(b) **Other Regulations:** The following have the same effect as agreements under subsection (a) (whether or not specifically assented to by all parties interested in the items handled):

1. Federal Reserve regulations and operating circulars
and 2. Clearinghouse rules
and 3. Other similar official rules

(c) **Ordinary Care:**

1. Action or non-action will be considered exercised with *ordinary care* if it is approved by *either:*
   a. Article 4
   or b. Federal Reserve regulations or operating circulars
2. Action or non-action will be considered *prima facie* exercised with *ordinary care* if it is consistent with:
   a. Clearinghouse rules and the like
   or b. A general banking usage (not inconsistent with Article 4)

(d) **Other Procedures:** The specification or approval of certain procedures by this Article is not considered disapproval of other procedures that may be reasonable under the circumstances.

(e) **Damages:**

1) Damages for failure to exercise ordinary care in handling an Item =

$ Amount of Item
+ Any other proximate damages resulting from Bad Faith
- Amount that could not have been realized by the exercise of Ordinary Care

§4-104: Definitions:

(a) The following definitions apply to Article 4, unless the context requires otherwise:

(1) **"Account"**—Any deposit or credit Account with a Bank, not evidenced by a Certificate of Deposit, *including:*

a. Demand Account
b. Savings Account
c. Time Account
d. Passbook Account
e. Share Draft Account

(2) **"Afternoon"**—Period of day between noon and midnight
(3) **"Banking Day"**—Part of the day when a Bank is open to the public for carrying on *substantially all* of its banking functions
(4) **"Clearinghouse"**—An association of Banks (or other Payors) who regularly clear items
(5) **"Customer"**—
a. A Person who has an Account with a Bank
or b. A Person for whom the Bank has agreed to collect items, including a Bank that maintains an Account with another Bank
(6) **"Documentary Draft"**—A Draft presented for Acceptance or Payment, that requires the receipt of *either* of the following items before Acceptance/Payment:
a. Specified Documents
or b. Certificated securities (as per §8-102)
or c. Instructions for uncertificated securities (as per §8-308)
or d. Other Certificates, statements, or the like
(7) **"Draft"**—
a. A Draft as defined in §3-104
or b. An "Item" (other than an Instrument) that is an Order
(8) **"Drawee"**—A Person ordered in a Draft to make Payment (example: Bank)
(9) **"Item"**—
a. An Item is an Instrument or a Promise or Order to Pay Money, which is *handled by a Bank* for Collection or Payment.
b. Does not include:
1. Payment Order governed by Article 4A
or 2. Debit or Credit Card slips
(10) **"Midnight Deadline"**—for a Bank is the *later* of:
a. Midnight on the next Banking Day after it receives the relevant Item or notice
or b. Midnight on the next Banking Day from which the time for taking action begins to run
(11) **"Settle"**—
a. To Pay in Cash, or to pay through the following:
1. By Clearinghouse Settlement
or 2. In a charge or credit
or 3. By remittance
or 4. As otherwise agreed
b. A Settlement may either be provisional or final.

(12) **"Suspends Payment"** — A Bank suspends payments when:
1. It has been closed by Order of the *"supervisory authorities"*
or 2. A public officer has been appointed to take it over
or 3. It ceases or refuses to make payments ~~in~~ the *ordinary course of business*

(b) Other definitions applying to this Article and the sections in which they appear are:

"Agreement for Electronic Presentment" §4-110
"Bank" §4-105
"Collecting Bank" §4-105
"Depositary Bank" §4-105
"Intermediary Bank" §4-105
"Payor Bank" §4-105
"Presenting Bank" §4-105
"Presentment Notice" §4-110

(c) The following definitions in other Articles apply to this Article:

"Acceptance" §3-409
"Alteration" §3-407
"Cashier's Check" §3-104
"Certificate of Deposit" §3-104
"Certified Check" §3-409
"Check" §3-104
"Good Faith" §3-103
"Holder in Due Course" §3-302
"Instrument" §3-104
"Notice of Dishonor" §3-503
"Order" §3-103
"Ordinary Care" §3-103
"Person Entitled to Enforce" §3-301
"Presentment" §3-501
"Promise" §3-103
"Prove" §3-103
"Teller's Check" §3-104
"Unauthorized Signature" §3-403

(d) In addition, Article 1 contains general definitions and principles of construction and interpretation applicable throughout this Article.

§4-105: Definitions:

The following definitions apply for purposes of this Article:

(1) **"Bank"** — A Person engaged in the business of banking, including:

a. Savings Banks
and b. Savings and Loan Associations
and c. Credit Unions
and d. Trust Companies

(2) **"Depositary Bank"** — The first Bank to take an Item (even if it is also the Payor Bank), *unless* the Item is presented for immediate Payment over the counter.

(3) **"Payor Bank"** — A Bank that is the Drawee of a Draft

(4) **"Intermediary Bank"** — A Bank to which an Item is transferred in the course of collection (except the Depositary or Payor Bank)

(5) **"Collecting Bank"** — A Bank handling an Item for collection (except the Payor Bank)

(6) **"Presenting Bank"** — A Bank presenting an Item to the Payor Bank (a Presenting Bank cannot also be the Payor Bank)

§4-106: "Payable Through" or "Payable At" Bank; Collecting Bank:

(a) ***"Payable Through"*:** If an Item states that it is *"payable through"* a Bank identified in an Item, the following rules apply:

(i) The Item designates the Bank as a Collecting Bank, and does not, itself, authorize the Bank to pay the Item.
and (ii) The Item may be presented for Payment only by or through the specified Collecting Bank

(b) ***"Payable At"*:**

- **ALTERNATIVE DEFINITION A**
If an Item states that it is *"payable at"* a Bank identified in the Item, the Item is considered a <u>Draft</u> drawn on the specified Bank.

- **ALTERNATIVE DEFINITION B**
If an Item states that it is *"payable at"* a Bank identified in the Item:
(i) The Item designates the Bank as a Collecting Bank, and does not, itself, authorize the Bank to pay the Item.
and (ii) The Item may be presented for Payment only by or through the specified Collecting Bank.

(c) **Draft with Two Names:** If a Draft names a non-Bank Drawee, as well as a Bank, but it is unclear whether the Bank named in the Draft is a <u>Co-Drawee</u> or a <u>Collecting Bank</u>, it will be considered a Collecting Bank.

§4-107: Separate Office or Bank Branch:

A branch or separate office of a Bank will be considered a separate Bank for purposes of:

a) Computing the time in which action may be taken or notices or Orders shall be given (Under Articles 3 & 4)

and b) Determining the place where action may be taken or notices or Orders shall be given (Under Articles 3 & 4)

§4-108: Time of Receipt of Items:

(a) **Cut-Off Hour:**

1. A Bank may fix an hour after 2:00 P.M. as a cut-off hour for purposes of:
   a) Handling Money and Items
   b) Making entries on its books
2. The cut-off hour has been allowed in order to allow banks time to:
   a) Process Items
   and b) Prove balances
   and c) Make the necessary entries on its books (to determine its position for the day)

(b) **Deferral of Receipt:**

An Item or deposit of Money may be treated as being received at the opening of the next Banking Day if it is received *after:*

1. The cut-off hour

or 2. The close of the Banking Day

§4-109: Delays:

(a) **Delay for an Item with Non-Bank Payors:** A Collecting Bank may (unless otherwise instructed) waive, modify, or extend time limits imposed or permitted by this Act (with or without approval from anyone involved) for up to **2 days** without discharging the Drawers or Indorsers, and without liability to its transferor or a prior party *if:*

1. The Collecting Bank does so in a *Good Faith effort* to secure Payment of the Item.

and 2. The Item is drawn on a non-Bank Payor (i.e., the Drawee is not a Bank).

(b) **Delay Excused:** If a Collecting Bank or Payor Bank delays beyond any time limit permitted by Article 4 (or by instructions), the Bank will be excused if:

(i) The delay is caused by:
a. Interruption of communication or computer facilities
or b. Suspension of Payments by another Bank
or c. War
or d. Emergency conditions
or e. Failure of equipment
or f. Other circumstances *beyond the Bank's control*
and (ii) The Bank exercises such diligence *as the circumstances require*

§4-110: Electronic Presentment:

(a) **"Agreement for Electronic Presentment"** is an agreement, clearinghouse rule, or Federal Reserve regulation or operating circular allowing Presentment of an Item to be made by transmitting an image of the Item (or "Presentment notice," information describing the Item) rather than actually delivering the Item itself. The agreement may provide for procedures governing:

1. Retention
and 2. Presentment
and 3. Payment
and 4. Dishonor
and 5. Other matters concerning Items subject to the agreement

(b) **Time of Presentment:** Presentment of an Item pursuant to an agreement for Presentment is made when the Presentment notice is *received.*

(c) **Checks by Presentment Notice:** If Presentment is made by "Presentment notice," a reference to "Item" or "Check" in this Article will mean the Presentment notice (unless the context otherwise indicates).

§4-111: Statute of Limitations:

Three-Year Limit: An action to enforce an obligation, duty, or right arising under this Article must be commenced within **3 years** after the cause of action (or claim for relief) *accrues.*

PART 2:

Collection of Items: Depositary and Collecting Banks

§ 4-201: Status and Rights of Collecting Bank; Item Indorsed "Pay Any Bank":

(a) **Rights and Status of Collecting Bank:**

1. **Collecting Bank Presumed to be Agent:** The Collecting Bank is an agent (or sub-agent) of the Item's owner unless a *contrary intent* clearly appears and *before* a Collecting Bank settlement becomes final.
2. **Settlement Presumed to be Provisional:** Any settlement given for the Item is provisional unless a *contrary intent* clearly appears and *before* a Collecting Bank settlement becomes final.
3. The above rules apply:
    a. Regardless of the form of Indorsement
    b. Regardless of a lack of Indorsement
    c. Even if credit given for the Item is subject to immediate withdrawal as of right (or is actually withdrawn).
4. The owner's continuance of ownership of the Item and the owner's rights to its Proceeds are subject to the rights of the Collecting Bank (example: rights of recoupment, setoff, or rights resulting from outstanding advances on the Item).
5. If an Item is handled by a Bank for purposes of Presentment, Payment, collection, or return, the relevant provisions of this Article will apply (even though the parties' actions clearly establish that a particular Bank has purchased the Item and is the owner of it).

(b) ***"Pay Any Bank"*:** After an Item has been Indorsed "*pay any bank*" (or the like), only a Bank may acquire the rights of a Holder until the Item has been *either:*

(1) Returned to the Customer initiating collection
or (2) Specially Indorsed by a Bank to a Person who is not a Bank.

§ 4-202: Responsibility for Collection or Return; When Action Timely:

(a) **When Ordinary Care Required:** A Collecting Bank must exercise *ordinary care* when:

(1) Presenting an Item or sending an Item for Presentment (Ordinary Care is required with respect both to the time and manner of Presentment).
and (2) Sending notice of dishonor or nonpayment, or returning an Item (other than a Documentary Draft) to the Bank's transferor after learning that the Item has not been paid or accepted.
and (3) Settling for an Item when the Bank receives final settlement.
and (4) Notifying its transferor of any loss or delay in transit (within a reasonable time after discovering it).

(b) **Manner of Exercising Ordinary Care:**

1. A Collecting Bank exercises *Ordinary Care* (required by § 4-202(a), above) by taking *"proper action" after* receiving an Item, notice, or settlement, and *before* its Midnight Deadline.
2. If the Bank takes proper action within a *reasonably* longer time (past its Midnight Deadline), the action may still constitute *Ordinary Care*, but the Bank will have the burden of proving that it acted *timely.*

(c) **When Bank Not Liable:**

1. A Bank is not liable for another Bank's or Person's
   a) Insolvency
   or b) Neglect (although its own Ordinary Care and Good Faith cannot be waived (§ 4-103(a))
   or c) Misconduct
   or d) Mistake
   or e) Default.
2. A Bank is not liable for loss or destruction of an Item in the possession of others or in transit.
3. § 4-202(c) is subject to (a)(1) (above).

§ 4-203: Effect of Instructions:

a. **Who May Give Notice or Instructions:** Only a Collecting Bank's transferor can give instructions that *affect* the Bank or *constitute notice* to the Bank.

b. A Collecting Bank is not liable to prior parties for any action taken:

   1. Pursuant to such instructions.
   2. In accordance with any agreement with its transferor.

c. This section is subject to § 3-420 (conversion) and § 3-206 (restrictive Indorsements).

§4-204: Methods of Sending and Presenting:

(a) **Method of Sending Items:**

1) A Collecting Bank shall send items by a *reasonably prompt method.*
2) Banks are expected to take into account:
    a) The nature of the Item
    and b) The number of items on hand
    and c) The cost of collection involved
    and d) The usual method used by the Bank or other banks to present those items.

(b) **A Collecting Bank May Send an Item:**

(1) Directly to the Payor Bank
(2) To a Non-Bank Payor—if authorized by the Collecting Bank's transferor
(3) To a Non-Bank Payor (without authorization of transferor) if:
    a) The Item is not a Documentary Draft
    and b) It is Authorized by *either:*
        1. A Federal Reserve regulation or an operating circular
        or 2. A Clearinghouse rule
        or 3. The like

(c) **Place of Presentment:**

A Presenting Bank must make <u>Presentment</u> at a place where the Payor Bank (or other Payor) has requested that Presentment be made.

§4-205: Depositary Bank as Holder of Unindorsed Item:

- <u>**Scope**</u>: The following rule applies if a Customer delivers an Item to a Depositary Bank for collection:

    (1) **Depositary Bank as Holder:**
        a. <u>Lack of Indorsement Irrelevant</u>: The Depositary Bank becomes a Holder at the time it receives the Item for collection if the Customer was a holder of the Item (at the time of delivery), *regardless* of whether the Customer Indorses the Item.
        b. <u>Bank as Holder in Due Course</u>: The Bank is an HDC if it satisfies the other requirements of §3-302.
    (2) **Depositary Bank's Warranty:**
        a. The Depositary Bank warrants that the amount of the Item was paid to the Customer (or deposited in the Customer's Account).

b. The Depositary Bank makes this warranty to:
   1. Collecting Banks.
   and 2. The Payor Bank (or other Payor).
   and 3. The Drawer.

§4-206: Transfer Between Banks:

Any agreed method that identifies the Transferor Bank is sufficient for the Item's further transfer to another Bank.

§4-207: Transfer Warranties:[14]

(a) **Warranties:**
The following warranties are made to a Transferee and any *subsequent* Collecting Banks by a Customer or Collecting Bank when it transfers an Item for a Settlement or other Consideration:

(1) **Entitlement to Enforce:** The warrantor is a Person Entitled to Enforce the Item (see §3-301).
and (2) **Authentic and Authorized Signatures:** All signatures on the Item are Authentic and Authorized.
and (3) **No Alterations:** The Item has not been altered.
and (4) **No Defense of Recoupment:** The Item is not subject to a defense or claim in recoupment (as per §3-305(a)) of any party (which can be asserted against the warrantor).
and (5) **No Knowledge of Insolvency:** The warrantor has no knowledge that the Maker, Acceptor, or Drawer (in the case of an Unaccepted Draft) is involved in insolvency proceedings (see §1-201(22)).

Revised Article 3 (2002) adds:
and (6) **Remote Consumer Item:** With respect to a Remotely Created Consumer Item, that the person on whose account the Item is drawn authorized the issuance of the Item in the amount for which the Item is drawn.

(b) **Item Dishonored:**

1. If an Item is dishonored, a Customer or Collecting Bank (which transfers the Item and receives settlement for it) is obligated to pay the amount due on the Item:
   (i) According to the terms of the Item (at the time it was transferred).

---

[14] Note: §4-207 is almost identical to §3-416's Transfer Warranty section, except for §4-207(b).

or (ii) If an Incomplete Item: according to the terms of the Item when completed (as per § 3-115 and § 3-407).

2. The obligation of a transferor is owed to:
   a) The transferee—who takes the Item in *Good Faith.*
   and b) Any subsequent Collecting Banks taking the Item in *Good Faith.*
3. Transferor Cannot Disclaim: A transferor cannot disclaim these obligations by indorsing the Item *"without recourse"* or otherwise disclaiming liability.

(c) **Damages for Breach of Warranty:**

1. A Person may recover from the warrantor the amount he lost as a result of the breach of warranty, if:
   a. The warranties (in (a) above) are made to him.
   and b. He took the Item in *Good Faith.*
2. Limitation: The damages cannot exceed:

   The amount of the Item
   + Expenses and loss of interest (incurred as a result of the breach)

(d) **Notice and Disclaimer:**

1. The warranties in (a) cannot be disclaimed for Checks.
2. If the claimant does not notify the warrantor of the breach within 30 days after the claimant had *reason to know* of the breach (and the identity of the warrantor), the warrantor will be discharged of any damages he incurs from the delay in notice.

(e) **Cause of Action:** A cause of action for breach of warranty (under this section) accrues when the claimant has *reason to know* of the breach.

§ 4-208: Presentment Warranties:[15]

(a) **Presentment Warranties:**

I. Presentment warranties are made to the Drawee by the following Persons:
   (i) The Person Obtaining Payment or Acceptance (at the time of Presentment) if:
      a) An Unaccepted Draft (as defined in § 4-104) is presented to the Drawee for Payment or Acceptance
      and b) The Drawee Pays or Accepts the Draft (as defined in § 4-104) in Good Faith

[15] This section is almost identical to § 3-417's Presentment Warranty section.

(ii) A Previous Transferor of the Draft (at the time the previous transferor made its transfer) if:

a) An Unaccepted Draft (as defined in §4-104) is presented to the Drawee for Payment or Acceptance

and b) The Drawee Pays or Accepts the Draft (as defined in §4-104) in Good Faith

II. Presentment Warranties include:

(1) **Good Title:** The warrantor is (or was at the time the warrantor transferred the Draft) either:

a) A Person Entitled to Enforce the Draft (see §3-301).

or b) A Person authorized to obtain Payment or Acceptance of the Draft (on behalf of a Person Entitled to Enforce the Draft).

and (2) **No Alteration:** The Draft has not been altered.

and (3) **Authorized signature:** The warrantor has no knowledge that the Signature (of the purported Drawer) is unauthorized.

Revised Article 3 (2002) adds:

and (4) **Remote Consumer Item:** With respect to a Remotely Created Consumer Item, that the person on whose account the Item is drawn authorized the issuance of the Item in the amount for which the Item is drawn.

(b) **Recovery:**

1) **Payment:** If the Drawee paid for the Draft it may recover from the warrantor:

a) Damages for breach of warranty—equal to:

The Amount Paid by the Drawee

—**The Amount the Drawee received** (or is entitled to receive) **as Payment from the Drawer because of Payment**

plus b) Compensation for Expenses and loss of interest (resulting from the breach)

2) **Acceptance:** If the Drawee Accepted the Draft, then the following rules apply:

(i) The Acceptor may use "breach of warranty" as a defense not to pay the Draft (or to fulfill any of his other obligations under the Draft).

and (ii) If the Acceptor already paid he may recover the amounts specified above for breach of warranty damages.

3) The Drawee's right to recover these damages is not affected by the Drawee's lack of *Ordinary Care* in making Payment.

(c) **Warrantor's Defenses:**

1) The warrantor may defend a claim for breach of warranty by proving that:

a) The Indorsement is effective under §3-304 ("Impostors; Fictions Payees") or §3-405 ("Employer's Responsibility for Employees Fraudulent Indorsements")

or b) The Drawer is precluded from asserting a claim under

1) §3-406 (Contributory Negligence)

or 2) §4-406 (Contributory Negligence)

2) These defenses may be used only if the Drawee asserts a claim for breach of warranty (as per (a)) for the following breaches:

a) Unauthorized Indorsement of the Draft

b) Alteration of the Draft

(d) **Warranty for Dishonored Drafts:**

1. The warranties in this subsection are made by the Person obtaining Payment and any prior transferor of the Item if:

a. *Either:*

(i) A dishonored Draft is presented for Payment to the Drawer or an Indorser

or (ii) Any other Item is presented for Payment to a party obligated to pay it

b. The Item is paid in Good Faith

2. Dishonored Draft warranty:

The warrantor warrants that he is (or was at the time the warrantor transferred the Draft) either:

A) A Person Entitled to Enforce the Draft (see §3-301)

or B) A Person authorized to obtain Payment or Acceptance of the Draft (on behalf of a Person Entitled to Enforce the Draft)

3. **Recovery:**

a) The Person making Payment may recover for breach of warranty from *any warrantor.*

b) Recovery Amount =

The Amount Paid

+ **Expenses and loss of interest** (resulting from the breach)

(e) **Limitations:**

1. Non-waivability for Checks: The warranties in (a) and (d) cannot be disclaimed with respect to Checks.

2. Time Limit: The claimant must give notice of a claim within 30 days after the claimant has *reason to know* both

a) The Identity of the warrantor

and b) That the breach occurred.

3. If the notice is given after the 30-day time limit, the warrantor is discharged *to the extent* of any loss caused by the delay of notice.

(f) **Accrual of Action:**

A cause of action for breach of warranty begins to accrue when the claimant has *reason to know* of the breach.

§ 4-209: Encoding and Retention Warranties:

(a) **Warranty for Encoding an Item:**

1. Encoder Liable — A Person who encodes information on an Item (after it was issued) warrants to any subsequent Collecting Bank (and to the Payor Bank or other Payor) that the information is correctly encoded.
2. Depositary Bank also liable — If the Customer of a Depositary Bank encodes an Item, that Depositary Bank also makes the warranty.

(b) **Warranty for Retaining an Item:**

1. Retainer Liable — If a Person undertakes to retain an Item under an electronic Presentment agreement (§ 4-110), he warrants to any subsequent Collecting Bank (and to the Payor Bank or other Payor) that retention and Presentment of the Item comply with the agreement.
2. Depositary Bank also liable — If the Customer of a Depositary Bank undertakes to retain an Item, that Depositary Bank also makes the warranty.

(c) **Availability of Damages:**[16]

1. Limitation on damages available for breach of the above warranties: Damages are limited to an amount equal to:

The loss suffered as a result of the breach
+ Expenses incurred as a result of the breach
+ Loss of interest incurred as a result of the breach

2. A Person may collect damages if:
    a) The warranties were made to him under this section.
    and b) A warranty was breached.
    and c) He took the Item in Good Faith.

[16] Under the former Article 4, one could sue only under § 4-202's Breach of Due Care. The revised § 4-209's actions were not available.

§4-210: Security Interest of Collecting Bank in Items:

(a) A Collecting Bank has an S/I in an Item and any accompanying documents (or the proceeds of either) if:

(1) Credit given for an Item deposited into an Account has been withdrawn or applied, to the extent that credit has actually been applied/withdrawn.

or (2) The Bank has given credit available for withdrawal as of right for an Item, the Collecting Bank has an S/I to the extent Credit is given (regardless of whether or not the credit is drawn upon or there is a right to charge back).

or (3) The Bank makes an advance on or against the Item.

(b) Credit given for several Items received at one time:

1. If credit given for several Items received at one time (or pursuant to a single agreement) is either withdrawn or applied, the S/I remains on all the items and accompanying documents (or their proceeds).
2. **Credits first given are first withdrawn** for purposes of this section ("first in, first out" rule).

(c) **The Bank's Security Interest:**

i) When a Collecting Bank receives *final settlement* for an Item, the settlement is considered a realization of the S/I (in the Item, documents, and proceeds).

ii) As long as the Bank does not receive final settlement (or give up possession of the Item, documents, or proceeds for purposes other than Collection) an S/I will continue to the extent not paid.

iii) The Bank's security interest ("S/I") will be subject to Article 9, except that:

(1) No security agreement is necessary to make the S/I enforceable (see §9-404)).

and (2) No filing is required to perfect the S/I.

and (3) The S/I has priority over conflicting (perfected) S/Is in the Item, accompanying documents, or their proceeds.

§4-211: When Bank Gives Value for Purposes of Holder in Due Course:

- For purposes of determining a Bank's status as Holder in Due Course:

  A Bank gives Value *to the extent* it has a security interest (as per §4-210) in an Item (assuming the Bank complies with the other requirements of §3-302 ("Holder in Due Course")).

§4-212: Presentment:

(a) **Presentment by Notice:**

1. If an Item is not payable by, through, or at a Bank, then (unless otherwise instructed) a Collecting Bank may "present" the Item by sending a ***written***[17] notice indicating that the Bank is holding the Item for Acceptance or Payment.
2. Notice Requirements:
   a) Must be in writing
   b) Must be sent to the party to Accept or Pay
   c) Must be sent in time to be received by the time Presentment is due
3. Honoring Party's Request: The Bank must honor any request of the party to Accept or Pay (under §3-501) by the close of the next Banking Day following the day it receives the request.

(b) The Presenting Bank may treat an Item as dishonored and charge any Drawer (or Indorser) by sending notice of the facts, if:

1. Presentment is made by notice.

and 2. Payment, Acceptance, or Request for Compliance (with a requirement under §3-501) is not received by:
   a) **Demand Items:** 3 Banking days after notice was sent (at the close of business on the third day).
   or b) **Other Items:** The Close of the business day after maturity.

§4-213: Settlement by Bank:

(a) **Time and Medium:**

i) The time and medium of settlement may be prescribed by:
   a) Federal Reserve regulations or circulars
   and b) Clearinghouse rules and the like
   and c) Agreement

ii) Default Rule: If there are no such prescriptions of time or medium, the following shall apply:
   (1) **Medium of Settlement:**
      a) Cash
      or b) Credit to an Account (in a Federal Reserve Bank) of or specified by the Person receiving the settlement
   (2) **Time:**
      (i) When the settlement is sent or delivered — for settlements tendered by

[17] Revised Article 3 (2002) changes the requirement of a "Writing" to a "Record."

a) **Cash**
or b) **Cashier's Check**
or c) **Teller's Check**

(ii) When Credit is made—for settlements tendered by **credit in a Federal Reserve Bank** Account

(iii) *Either*:
a) When a credit or debit is made—for settlements tendered by a **credit** or **debit to an Account** in a Bank
b) When Authority is sent or delivered—for settlements tendered by **authority to charge an Account**

(iv) When Payment is made to the Person receiving the settlement—for tender made by **Funds Transfer** (under §4A-406(a))

(b) **Other Mediums of Settlement:** Settlement occurs when it is accepted by the Person receiving the settlement, if the settlement is not by a medium or time authorized by (a).

(c) **Finality for Cashier's or Teller's Check:**

(1) Settlement is final when the Check is finally paid if:
a) Settlement is made by Cashier's Check or Teller's Check.
and b) The Person receiving the settlement Presents or forwards the Check for collection *before* the Midnight Deadline (of the Person receiving Payment) (see §4-104(10)).

(2) Settlement is final at the *Midnight Deadline* (of the Person receiving Payment) if:
a) Settlement is made by Cashier's Check or Teller's Check.
and b) The Person receiving the settlement fails to Present or forward the Check for collection *before* the Midnight Deadline (see §4-104(10)).

(d) **Finality for Authority to Charge Account**:

Settlement is final when the Account charged has available funds to cover the amount of the Item, if:

1. There is an agreement that permits the Bank giving settlement to give an authority to charge an Account as settlement.
and 2. Settlement is made by giving authority to charge the Account of the Bank making settlement in the Bank receiving settlement (and the Bank accepts the authority).

§4-214: Provisional Settlement:

(a) **Bank's Power to Charge Back:**

1. Options available: If a Collecting Bank makes a *provisional settlement* for a Check (i.e., advances its Customer Money for an Item (see §4-104(12) and §4-213) or credits a Customer's Account), and that Check is later dishonored or suspended, resulting in the Bank's failure to receive a final settlement, the Bank may:
   - a) Revoke the settlement it gave
   - or b) Charge back the Customer's Account for the amount of credit given
   - or c) Obtain a refund from its Customer
2. The Bank must *either:*
   - a) Return the Item (i.e., Check)
   - or b) Send the Customer a notification of the facts
3. **Time Limit:**
   - a) To avoid liability, the Bank must send the notification or return the Item:
     - 1) By its Midnight Deadline
     - or 2) Within a *reasonable time* after it learns the facts
   - b) If the Bank misses the above deadline, it may still revoke, charge back the credit or obtain a refund from the Customer, but it will be liable for any loss *caused by the delay.*
4. Termination of options: These options will terminate if and when a settlement for the Item received by the Bank is or becomes final.

(b) **Returning Items**—An Item is returned by a Collecting Bank when it is sent or delivered to:

1. The Bank's Customer

or 2. The transferor

or 3. Pursuant to instructions

(Note: This subsection does not apply to Checks—see Regulation CC.)

(c) If a Depositary Bank is also a Payor, it may:

1. Charge back the amount of an Item to its Customer's Account

or 2. Obtain a refund (in accordance with §4-301)

(d) **The Right to Charge Back Is Not Affected By:**

(1) Previous use of a credit given for the Item

or (2) Any Bank's failure to use Ordinary Care (although a Bank failing to use Ordinary Care remains liable; see §4-103(e) for measure of damages)

(e) **Failure to Charge Back:** A failure to charge back or claim a refund from the Customer does not affect other rights of the Bank against its Customer (or any other party). (Note: These might include warranty causes of action or enforcement of the Instrument).

(f) **Determining Foreign Exchange Rate:**

If the Bank advanced dollars for an Item payable in foreign currency, the dollar amount of the charge-back or refund is calculated using the Bank-offered spot rate for the foreign currency on the day that the Person entitled to the charge-back or refund learns that it will not receive Payment in ordinary course (unless otherwise fixed by the parties).

§4-215: Finality and Availability of Items:

(a) **Finality of an Item:** An Item is considered *finally paid* by the Payor Bank once it has *either:*

(1) Paid the Item in cash
or (2) Settled for the Item, *without* having a right to revoke the settlement under:
a) Statute
or b) Clearinghouse rule
or c) Agreement
or (3) Made a **Provisional Settlement** (as per §4-214) and failed to revoke the settlement in the time and manner permitted by:
a) Statute
or b) Clearinghouse rule
or c) Agreement

(b) **Finality of Provisional Settlement:**

If provisional settlement for an Item does not become final, the Item is not finally paid.

(c) **Finality of Provisional Payments Between Banks:**

Provisional settlements become final (i.e., "firms-up") upon final Payment of an Item by the *Payor Bank* if:

1. The provisional settlement for the Item (between the Presenting and Paying banks) is made *either:*
a) Through a Clearinghouse
b) By debits and credits in an Account between the banks
and 2. Provisional debits or credits for the Item are entered in Accounts between *either:*

a. The Presenting and Payor Banks
or b. The Presenting Bank and successive prior Collecting Banks in a series

(d) **Responsibility to Customer for Final Settlements:**

1) If a Collecting Bank receives settlement for an Item (which is or becomes final), the Bank is accountable to its Customer for the amount of the Item.
2) If the Bank previously gave its Customer a provisional credit for the Item in an Account, the Bank's receipt of final settlement for the Item makes the provisional credit final ("firms up" the provisional credit).

(e) **Availability of Provisional Settlements and Items — Bank's Time Limit:**

I. This subsection is subject to:
    (i) Any applicable law stating a time for availability of funds (Checks, for example are controlled by Regulation CC or similar applicable state law)
    and (ii) Any right of the Bank to apply the credit to an obligation of the Customer (right of setoff, such as a credit card balance owed to the Bank)

II. When a Bank credits a Customer's Account for an Item, the Customer will have a right to withdraw those funds, when the following conditions are met:
    (1) **Provisional Settlements:** If the Bank received a provisional settlement for the Item, the credit becomes available when:
        a) The settlement becomes final.
        and b) The Bank has had a *reasonable time* to receive return of the Item (this could depend on the distance the Item has to travel, the number of banks through which it has to pass, and other pertinent facts).
        and c) The Item has not been received within that time.
    (2) **The Bank is Both the Depository and Payor Bank** — In this case, if the Item is finally paid, the credit becomes available 2 Banking Days after the Bank receives the Item (at the opening of the second Banking Day).

(f) **Availability of Money Deposits:**

1. A deposit of Money becomes available for withdrawal, as of right, at the opening of the next Banking Day after the Bank receives the deposit.
2. This subsection is subject to:
    a) Any applicable law stating a time for availability of funds (example: Regulation CC).

b) Any right of a Bank to apply a deposit to an obligation of the depositor.

§4-216: Insolvency and Preference:

(a) **Closed Bank:** When a Bank closes (i.e., becomes Insolvent), its Trustee, Receiver, or Agent must return any Item to its Customer or Presenting Bank if:

1. The Item is in or comes into possession of the Payor or Collecting Bank

and 2. The Bank Suspends Payment of the Item

and 3. The Item has not been finally paid

(b) **Owner's Preferred Claim Against Payor Bank:** The owner of an Item will have a preferred claim against a Payor Bank if:

1. The Payor Bank finally pays the Item

and 2. The Payor Bank Suspends Payments without making a settlement for the Item with:

a) Its Customer

or b) The Presenting Bank that has made final settlement

(c) **Suspension After Provisional Settlement:** A suspension of payment will have no effect on a settlement becoming final, if:

a) The finality of the settlement occurs *automatically* upon the lapse of a certain time/happening (example: Midnight Deadline).

and b) The Payor or Collecting Bank gives (or receives, in the case of a Collecting Bank) a provisional settlement for an Item.

and c) The Bank Suspends Payment of the Item after giving the provisional settlement.

(d) **Owner's Preferred Claim Against Collecting Bank:** The owner of an Item will have a preferred claim against a Collecting Bank if:

1. The Collecting Bank receives a final settlement of the Item from *subsequent parties.*

and 2. The Collecting Bank Suspends Payments without making a settlement for the Item with its Customer.

and 3. The Customer's provisional settlement from the Collecting Bank becomes final.

PART 3:

Collection of Items

§4-301: Recovery and Return:

(a) **Revoking and Recovering Settlement:** A Payor Bank may revoke and recover a settlement if:

a) The Payor Bank tendered the settlement before midnight of the Banking Day of receipt of a demand Item (other than a Documentary Draft)

and b) The demand Item was not Presented for immediate Payment (i.e., over the counter)

and c) Before its Midnight Deadline and before it has made Final Payment, the Bank

(1) Returns the Item

or (2) Sends a ***written*** notice[18] of dishonor or nonpayment if the Item is unavailable for return (example: when Presentment is made by a Presentment notice and the Item is retained by the Collecting Bank). (For Checks, Regulation CC governs method of giving notice.)

Revised Article 3 (2002) adds:

or (3) Returns an image of an Item, if the party to which the return is made has entered into an agreement to accept an image as a return of the Item, and the image is returned in accordance with that agreement.

(b) **Recovery and Revocation when Payor Bank is also Depositary Bank:**

1. A Payor Bank may:

a) Return the Item

and b) Send notice of dishonor

and c) *Either:*

1) Revoke any credit given

or 2) Recover the amount of credit given

or 3) Recover the amount withdrawn by its Customer

2. **Availability:** In order to take the above actions:

a) A demand Item must be received by a Payor Bank for credit on its books.

b) The Payor Bank must act within the time limit and in the manner specified in (a).

[18] Revised Article 3 (2002) changes the requirement of a "Writing" to a "Record."

(c) **Time Limit for Notice of Dishonor:**

Unless a previous notice of dishonor has been sent, an Item is dishonored when:

1) The Item is returned (for purposes of dishonor)
or 2) Notice is sent (in accordance with this section)

(d) **When an Item is Considered "Returned":**

(1) Items Presented through a Clearinghouse:
 a) When the Item is *delivered* to:
  1. The Presenting Bank
  or 2. The Last Collecting Bank
  or 3. The Clearinghouse
 or b) When the Item is *sent* (see § 1-201(38)) or *delivered* in accordance with Clearinghouse rules

(2) All other Cases: When the Item is *sent* (see § 1-201(38)) or *delivered:*
 a) To the Bank's Customer
 or b) To the transferor
 or c) Pursuant to instructions

§ 4-302: Payor Bank's Responsibility:

(a) **Bank's Liability:** If an Item is presented to and received by a Payor Bank, the Bank is accountable for the amount of:

(1) **A Demand Item Other than a Documentary Draft** (whether properly payable or not) if:
 a. The Payor Bank retains the Item beyond the Midnight Deadline (of the Banking Day of receipt without settling) and it is not also the Depositary Bank.
 or b. The Payor Bank does not pay or return the Item (under § 4-301) until after the Midnight Deadline (regardless of whether it is also the Depositary Bank).
 or c. The Payor Bank does not send Notice of Dishonor until after the Midnight Deadline (regardless of whether it is also the Depositary Bank).

or (2) **Any Other Properly Payable Item** — *unless:*
 a. The Bank Accepts or Pays the Item within the time allowed for Acceptance or Payment (of that Item).
 or b. The Bank Returns the Item and its accompanying documents within the time allowed for Acceptance or Payment (of that Item).

(b) **Exceptions to Liability of Payor Bank to Pay:**

The liability in (a) is subject to defenses based on:

1. Breach of Presentment warranty (under § 4-208)

or 2. Proof that the Person seeking enforcement of the liability either Presented or transferred the Item in order to defraud the Payor Bank

§ 4-303: Time Limit for Stop Payment Orders:

(a) **Time Limit:**

1. **Scope; "The Four Legals":** This section applies if a Payor Bank, while processing an Item presented for Payment, *either:*
   a. Receives legal notice: The Payor Bank receives knowledge or a legal notice affecting the Item (example: that the Drawer has filed a petition in bankruptcy; the Drawer made an assignment for the benefit of creditors).
   or b. Receives a stop payment order: The Payor Bank receives an Order of the Drawer stopping Payment on the Item.
   or c. Is served order of attachment: The Payor Bank is served an attachment of the Drawer's Account ("legal process").
   or d. Exercises a setoff: The Payor Bank exercises a right of setoff against the Drawer's Account.

(Note: These are sometimes called **"The Four Legals."**)

2. **Time Limit for Bank to Terminate, Suspend or Modify:** If any one of the four events listed above takes place, and a reasonable time for the Bank to act on it expires (or the setoff is exercised), then:
   a. Such event has priority.
   and b. The knowledge, notice, stop payment order, legal process, or setoff is deemed too late to terminate, suspend, or modify the Bank's right or duty to:
      1) Pay the Item.
      or 2) Charge its Customer's Account for the Item.
3. The above time limit applies provided that the event plus a reasonable time to act on it occur after one of the following, whichever is earliest:
   (1) The Bank Accepts or Certifies the Item.
   (2) The Bank Pays the Item in Cash.
   (3) The Bank Settles for the Item without having a right to revoke the settlement (under a Clearinghouse rule, statute, or agreement) (example: the Bank Settles for an Item presented over the counter for immediate Payment by a

Cashier's Check or Teller's Check, which the Person agrees to take).

(4) The Bank becomes accountable for the amount of the Item (under § 4-302).

(5) For Checks:

a. A cutoff hour between 1 hour after the opening of the Banking Day after the Bank received the Check and the close of the next Banking Day passes.

b. If no cutoff hour is fixed, the close of the Banking Day after the day the Bank received the Check comes to a close.

(b) Subject to subsection (a), items may be Accepted, Paid, Certified, or charged to the indicated Account of the Bank's Customer *in any order*.

PART 4:

Relationship Between Payor Bank and Its Customer

§ 4-401: When Bank May Charge Customer's Account:

(a) **Charging Customer's Account**

1. A Bank may charge the Customer's Account for an Item that is *properly payable* from the Account, even if the charge creates an overdraft.
2. An Item is "properly payable" if:
   - a) It is authorized by the Customer.
   - and b) It is in accordance with any agreement between the Customer and the Bank.

(b) **When Customer Not Liable**

The Customer is not liable for the overdraft if:

1. The Customer did not sign the Item.

and 2. The Customer did not benefit from the proceeds of the Item.

(c) **Post-dated Checks**

1. A Bank may charge the Customer's Account for an otherwise *properly payable* Check even though the Check is post-dated.
2. If the Customer gives the Bank *reasonable* notice of the post-dating, the Bank may not charge the Account before the Check date.
3. Requirements for Customer's Notice:
   - a) Must describe the Check with *reasonable certainty.*
   - b) Must be received within a *reasonable time and manner* before the Bank takes action as described in § 4-303.
   - c) Notice will be effective for the period stated in § 4-403(b) for stop payment orders.
4. Bank's liability for charging post-dated Checks before date: If a Bank charges the Customer's Account for a post-dated Check before the date in the notice, then the Bank is liable for any damages for the loss resulting from the early charge, including damages for dishonor of subsequent items (under § 4-402).

(d) **Terms of Charge:**

i) A Bank may charge the Customer's Account if:
   - 1) The Bank makes **Payment**
   - and 2) Payment is made to the **Holder**
   - and 3) Payment is made in **Good Faith**

ii) The Bank may charge the indicated Account of its Customer according to:
   (1) Altered Item — the Original terms of the Altered Item
   (2) Completed Item — the terms of the Completed Item unless the Bank *has knowledge* that the completion was improper. (Note: It is okay if the Bank knows that the Item was completed.)

§ 4-402: Bank's Liability for Wrongful Dishonor:

(a) **"Wrongful Dishonor"**

A Payor Bank will have **wrongfully dishonored** an Item if the Bank dishonors:

a) A *properly payable* Item

or b) An Item that would create an overdraft and the Bank had *agreed* to pay the overdraft

(b) **Liability of Payor Bank**

1. A Payor Bank is liable to its Customer for damages *proximately caused* by the wrongful dishonor.
2. Limitation of Liability:
   a) Liability is limited to *actual damages proved.*
   b) Liability may include damages for:
      1) An arrest of the Customer.
      or 2) Prosecution of the Customer.
      or 3) Other consequential damages.
3. Whether damages were *"proximately caused"* by the wrongful dishonor is a question of fact (to be determined on a case-by-case basis).

(c) **Time of Determining Insufficiency of Account**

1. A Payor Bank may determine the Customer's Account balance (on which to base a decision not to Honor an Item) at any time between the time the Item is received by the Payor Bank and *either:*
   a) The time the Payor Bank returns the Item.
   or b) The time the Payor Bank gives notice (instead of return).
2. Only one determination need be made.
3. Redetermination: If the Bank decides to redetermine the Customer's Account balance (to determine sufficiency of funds), the later Account balance is the one used to determine whether an Item is wrongfully dishonored.

§ 4-403: Customer's Right to Stop Payment:

(a) **The Stop Payment Order Process:**

1. A Customer (or anyone authorized to draw on the Account (if there is more than one Person)) may:
    - a) Stop Payment of any Item drawn on its Account.
    - or b) Close its Account.
2. Procedure:
    - a) The Customer must order the Bank to stop payment or close the Account.
    - b) The Customer must describe the Item or Account with *reasonable certainty.*
    - c) The order and description must be received by the Bank at a time and in a manner that affords the Bank a *reasonable opportunity* to act on it before it takes an action described in § 4-303.
3. If more than one signature is required to draw on an Account, any of the signatories may stop Payment or close the Account.

(b) **Effectiveness of a Stop Payment Order:**

1. A Stop Payment Order ("SPO") will remain in effect for:
    - a) ***Written*** SPO[19]—6 months
    - b) Oral SPO—effective for 14 days (unless confirmed in *writing* before the 14 days are over)
2. Renewal: An SPO may be renewed for additional 6-month periods with a ***writing*** to the Bank (while the SPO is still in effect)

(c) **Burden of Proof; Damages:**

1. The Customer has the burden of establishing the fact and amount of loss resulting from the Payment of an Item (contrary to an SPO or order to close an Account).
2. The loss from Payment of an Item contrary to an SPO may include damages for dishonor of subsequent items (under § 4-402).

§ 4-404: Bank Not Obliged to Pay Stale Checks:

a. A Bank is under no obligation to pay a Check that is Presented more than 6 months after its date (unless it is a Certified Check, which is the primary obligation of the certifying Bank under § 3-409 and § 3-413).

b. The Bank may pay the *"stale"* Check in *Good Faith* and charge its customer's Account for the Check amount.

[19] Revised Article 3 (2002) changes the requirement of a "Writing" to a "Record."

§ 4-405: Death or Incompetence of Customer:

(a) **Bank Unaffected Until Knowledge of Death or Incompetence:**

1. A Bank's authority to Accept, Pay, or collect an Item (or to Account for proceeds of its collection) will not be affected by a Customer's death or incompetence before the Bank has *actual knowledge* of the Customer's death or incompetence (example: the Bank did not know of an Adjudication of Incompetence when it took the Item for collection).
2. Neither death nor incompetence will revoke the Bank's authority to Accept, Pay, or collect an Item (or to Account for its proceeds) until the Bank *actually knows* of the death or adjudication of incompetence and has a *reasonable opportunity* to act.

(b) A Bank may pay or certify Checks drawn on or before the date of death up to 10 days after the Customer's death, even if the Bank had knowledge of the death, *unless* ordered to stop Payment by a Person claiming an interest in the Account (e.g., executor, administrator).

§ 4-406: Customer's Duty to Discover and Report Unauthorized Signature or Alteration:

(a) **Statement of Account**

If a Bank that has paid a Check or other Item sends its Customer a statement of account showing Payment of the Item, it must *either:*

1) Return the Item or make it available to the Customer.
2) Provide information in the statement, sufficient to allow the Customer to *reasonably* identify the Item paid. (If the Item is described by number, amount, and date of Payment, sufficient information is provided; no need to return the Item, absent an agreement otherwise.)

(b) **Items Not Returned**

1) If the Items are not returned to the Customer, the Person retaining them shall *either:*
   a) Retain the items for at least 7 years after receipt of the Items
   or b) Retain legible copies of the Items for at least 7 years after receipt of the Items (if they have been destroyed)
2) Upon request by a Customer, a Bank must provide the Item paid (if destroyed it must send a copy) within a *reasonable* time after the request.

(c) **Customer's Duty**

1) If a Bank sends such a statement of Account, the Customer has a duty to examine it with *reasonable promptness*, and must check to see if a paid Item was unauthorized due to *either:*
   a) An unauthorized signature (e.g., forgery or agent acting outside the scope of authority)

   or b) Alteration
2) The Customer must *promptly* notify the Bank of any unauthorized payment if he should have *reasonably discovered it* based on the statement or Items provided.

(d) **Preclusion of Customer's Claims**

(1) A Customer is precluded from asserting the Alteration or the Customer's Unauthorized signature (against the Bank) if the Bank proves:
   a) The Customer *should reasonably have discovered* the unauthorized Payment and did not notify the Bank.

   and b) It suffered a loss as a result of the Customer's failure.

(2) Checks in a Scheme: A Customer is precluded from asserting the Alteration or the Customer's Unauthorized signature (against the Bank) if the Bank proves:
   a) The Customer *should reasonably have discovered* the unauthorized Payment and did not notify the Bank.

   and b) The Bank subsequently pays other items of the Customer that have Unauthorized signatures or Alterations by the same wrongdoer.

   and c) Such Payments occurred after the Customer had been given a *reasonable* time, not more than 30 days, in which to examine the Items or statement and notify the Bank of the first Item.

(e) **Allocation of Loss**

1) Loss will be allocated between the Customer precluded from making the claims (under (d)) and the Bank asserting the preclusion if:
   a) The Customer proves that the Bank failed to exercise *Ordinary Care* in paying the Item (see §4-104(c) and §3-103(a)(7)).

   and b) That failure *substantially contributed* to the loss.
2) The loss will be allocated according to the amount each party's failure contributed to the loss (under subsection (d) for the Customer and Ordinary Care for the Bank).
3) If the Customer proves that the Bank did not pay the Item in *Good Faith* (see §3-103(a)(4)) then the Customer is not precluded under (d).

(f) **Absolute Time Limit:**

1) Regardless of the care or lack or care of the Customer or the Bank, in order to assert any defense that a signature was Unauthorized or an Item was altered, the Customer must discover and report the problem within 1 year after the Statement or Items are made available to the Customer (according to §4-406 (a)).
2) If the Customer is precluded under this subsection, the Payor Bank may not recover for breach of warranty under §4-208 (with respect to the Unauthorized signature/Alteration to which the preclusion applies) (i.e., the Payor Bank may not choose to recredit the Drawer's Account and pass the loss to the Collecting Banks on the theory of breach of warranty).

§4-407: Payor Bank's Right to Subrogation on Improper Payment:

a) The Payor Bank will obtain **subrogation rights** if a Payor Bank has paid an Item *either:*

1) After the Drawer or Maker had placed a stop payment order on the Item

or 2) After the Drawer or Maker's Account had been closed

or 3) Under circumstances otherwise giving the Drawer or Maker a basis for objection

b) The Payor obtains subrogation rights only to prevent unjust enrichment and only *to the extent necessary* to prevent loss to the Bank because of paying the Item.

c) **Payor Bank's subrogated rights** — The Payor Bank is subrogated to the rights of:

(1) Any HDC on the Item, against the Drawer or Maker

and (2) The Payee (or any other Holder of the Item) against the Drawer or Maker *either:*

a) On the Item

or b) Under the transaction from which the Item arose

and (3) The Drawer or Maker against the Payee (or any other Holder of the Item) with respect to the transaction from which the Item arose

PART 5:

Collection of Documentary Drafts

§4-501: Handling Documentary Drafts; Duty of Presentment and Notice:

a. **Bank's Duty:** A Bank that takes a Documentary Draft (defined in §4-104) for collection shall present or send the Draft (and accompanying documents) for Presentment.

b. **Notice of Non-Payment or Non-Acceptance:** After learning that the Draft has not been paid or accepted in *due course*, the Bank shall *seasonably* notify its Customer of the occurrence, even if:

1. The Bank had discounted the Draft

or 2. The Bank had bought the Draft

or 3. The Bank extended credit (which was available for withdrawal as of right)

§4-502: Presentment of "On Arrival" Drafts:

a. The Collecting Bank does not have to Present a Documentary Draft until, in its judgment, a *reasonable time* for the arrival of goods has expired, if the Draft (or the relevant instructions) requires Presentment as follows:

1. *"On arrival"*

or 2. *"When goods arrive"*

or 3. The like

b. Refusal to Pay or Accept a Draft because the goods have not arrived is not dishonor.

c. The Collecting (Presenting) Bank must notify its transferor of the refusal but need not Present the Draft again, until:

1. It is instructed to do so

or 2. It learns of the arrival of the goods

§4-503: Responsibility of Presenting Bank:

a. **Presenting Bank's Obligations:** The following rules apply to a Bank Presenting a Documentary Draft (unless otherwise instructed and except as provided in Article 5):

(1) **Time for Delivery:** The Bank must deliver the documents to the Drawee:
   a. On Acceptance of the Draft, if the Draft is payable more than 3 days after Presentment.
   b. On Payment of the Draft, for all other Drafts

(2) **Dishonor:** Upon dishonor (either upon Presentment for Acceptance or Presentment for Payment), the Presenting Bank may *either:*
   a) Seek and follow instructions from any referee (as designated in the Draft) in a case of need

   or b) Choose not to use the referee, and then must:
      1. Use *diligence* and *Good Faith* to ascertain the reason for dishonor
      and 2. Notify its transferor of the dishonor
      and 3. Notify its transferor of the results of its effort to ascertain the reason for the dishonor
      and 4. Request Instructions on how to proceed

b. **Dealing with Goods:** The Presenting Bank is only obligated to follow *reasonable* instructions it *seasonably* receives with respect to the goods represented by the Documents.

c. **Right to Reimbursement:** The Presenting Bank has a right to reimbursement for any expense incurred in following such instructions.

d. **Right to Prepayment or Indemnification:** The Presenting Bank also has a right to prepayment of the expenses or indemnity for the expenses incurred in following such instructions.

§4-504: Privilege of Presenting Bank to Deal with Goods; Security Interest for Expenses:

(a) **Presenting Bank's Rights to Deal with Goods:** The Presenting Bank may sell, store, or otherwise deal with goods (represented by the Draft) in any *reasonable manner* (in the light of business factors and the judgment of a business man (e.g., "commercially reasonable")) if:

   1. The Documentary Draft covering the goods is dishonored.
   and 2. After the dishonor, the Bank *seasonably* requests instructions on what to do with the goods.
   and 3. The Bank does not receive the instructions within a *reasonable* time.

(b) **Security Interest for Expenses:**

   1. The Presenting Bank has a lien upon the goods or their proceeds represented by the Draft (or their proceeds) for its reasonable expenses incurred under (a).
   2. The lien may be foreclosed by the Bank in the same manner as an unpaid seller's lien (under §2-706).

SELECTED STATUTES FROM ARTICLES 2, 5 & 7 OF THE UCC

§2-514: When Documents Deliverable on Acceptance; When on Payment:

1) Documents Delivered Upon Acceptance—Documents (against which a Draft is drawn) are to be Delivered to the Drawee upon *Acceptance* of the Draft if:

   a) The Draft is payable more than 3 days after Presentment.

   and b) The Parties do not otherwise agree.

2) Documents Delivered Upon Payment—Documents (against which a Draft is drawn) are to be Delivered to the Drawee upon *Payment* of the Draft if:

   a) The Draft is not payable more than 3 days after Presentment.

   or b) The Parties so agree.

§7-104: Negotiable and Non-Negotiable Documents of Title:

(1) **Requirements for Negotiability:** A Document of Title (including a Bill of Lading) will be considered negotiable if:

   (a) The goods under the document are to be delivered *to Bearer or Order* of a named Person (according to the terms of the document).

   or (b) It *runs to a named Person or assigns*, where recognized in overseas trade.

(2) **Non-Negotiable Documents:**

   1. Any other Document not fulfilling the requirements of §7-104(1) will be considered non-negotiable.
   2. A Bill of Lading will not be made negotiable by simply stating that the goods are consigned to a named Person, providing that the goods are to be Delivered only against a written Order Signed by the named Person.

§7-403: Obligations of Warehouseman or Carrier to Deliver:

(1) **Bailee's Obligations and Defenses:** The bailee must deliver the goods to the Person entitled to them under the Document of Title ("DOT") if:

i) The Person entitled under the document complies with sections (2) and (3) (below)

and ii) NO DEFENSES: The bailee cannot establish the following defenses:

(a) **Goods Already Delivered:** That the bailee already delivered the goods to a Person whose receipt was *rightful* against the claimant, or

or (b) **Bailee Not Liable:** That the bailee is not liable for any:

1. Damage to the goods

or 2. Delay

or 3. Loss

or 4. Destruction

Note: Some States include Burden of Proof. The Person entitled to the Document has the burden of proving that the bailee was negligent in order to preclude the bailee's liability defenses.

or (c) **Previous Sale or Disposition:** that there was a previous sale or disposition of the goods, either:

1. In lawful enforcement of a lien

or 2. On the Warehouseman's lawful termination of storage

or (d) **Seller's Right to Stop Delivery:** That the seller exercised his right to stop delivery (as per §2-705)

or (e) **Disposition:** Pursuant to §7-303 (or a tariff relating to such right) there was *either:*

1. A diversion

or 2. A reconsignment

or 3. Other disposition

or (f) **Personal Defense**: The bailee had a personal defense against the claimant resulting from *either:*

1. A release

or 2. A satisfaction

or 3. Any other fact affording a personal defense

or (g) **Any Other Lawful Excuse**

(2) A Person claiming goods covered by a DOT ("Claimant") must satisfy the bailee's lien if:

a) The bailee so requests

or b) The bailee is prohibited by law from delivering the goods until the charges are paid.

(3) **Receipt of Delivery:**

a) Upon receipt of the goods, the Claimant must surrender the Documents of Title (or any other outstanding negotiable documents covering the goods) and the bailee must:
   1) *Cancel* the Document — if *complete delivery* is made
   or 2) *Conspicuously* note the quantity delivered — if *partial delivery* is made

b) If the bailee does not do this, he will be liable to whom the Note is duly negotiated

c) **Exception:** If the Claimant is a Person against whom the DOT offers no right (as per §7-503(1))

(4) **"Person Entitled Under the Document"** — means, *either*

a) Negotiable Instrument — A Holder of a Negotiable Instrument

or b) Non-Negotiable Instrument — A Person to whom delivery is to be made, pursuant to *written* instructions under a non-negotiable Instrument

§7-404: Not Liable for Good Faith Delivery:

1) A bailee is not liable for misdelivering or disposing of goods if he:

a) Acted in Good Faith

and b) Observed *reasonable commercial standards*

and c) Delivered (or otherwise disposed of) goods according to the terms of the Document of Title (or pursuant to Article 7)

2) **Scope** — This rule applies even though:

a) The Person who gave the bailee the goods had no authority to:
   1. Acquire the Document
   or 2. Dispose of the goods

or b) The Person to whom the bailee delivers the goods had no authority to receive them

§7-501: Due Negotiation:

(1) **Manner of Negotiation:**

a) Named Person: A *Negotiable* Document of Title "running" to the Order of a named Person can be negotiated only if:
   1) Indorsement — The identified Person in the document Indorses it.
   and 2) Delivery — The document is delivered into the possession of the holder.

b) Bearer: If the Instrument is Indorsed in blank (i.e., "to Bearer" or with a "Blank Indorsement"), it can be negotiated by *delivery* alone.

(2) **Delivery as Negotiation:**

(a) A Negotiable Document of Title may also be negotiated by delivery alone if it "runs" to Bearer (by its original terms).
(b) A Document of Title will be considered as if it had been negotiated if it is delivered to the *identified Person.*

(3) Special Indorsement: If a Negotiable DOT has been Indorsed to an identified Person, the special Indorsee must Indorse and Deliver it to negotiate it.

(4) **"Due Negotiation":** Requirements for a Negotiable Document of Title to be *"duly negotiated"*:

a) It is Negotiated (in the manner stated above in this section) to a **Holder** (as per §1-201(20))
and b) The Holder takes by ***Purchase*** (as per §1-201(32))
and c) It is Purchased:
1. In **Good Faith** (as per §1-201(19))
and 2. **Without any notice** of another Person's claims or defenses against the document
and 3. For **Value** (as per §1-201(44))
and 4. In the *regular course of business or financing* (i.e., from a merchant)
and d) The negotiation does not involve receiving the document in settlement or Payment of a Money obligation

(5) **Non-Negotiable Documents:** Indorsement of a non-negotiable Document neither makes it negotiable nor adds to the transferee's rights.

(6) **Naming Person to Notify upon Arrival:** The naming of a Person (in a negotiable DOT) to be notified when goods (represented by the DOT) arrive does not:

a) Limit the negotiability of the bill
or b) Constitute notice to a Purchaser of the bill that the named Person has any interest in the goods

§7-502: Rights Acquired by Due Negotiation:

(1) **Rights by Due Negotiation:** A Person acquires the following rights if a Negotiable Document has been *Duly Negotiated* to him (subject to §7-205 and §2-703):

(a) Title to the Documents
and (b) Title to the goods

and (c) All rights accruing under the law of agency and estoppel (including rights to goods delivered to the bailee after the document was issued)

and (d) *Either*:

1. The direct obligation of the *Issuer* to hold or deliver the goods according to the terms of the Document free of any defense or claim by the Issuer (except those arising under the terms of the Document or under Article 7)

or 2. Delivery Orders: The bailee's obligation accrues only when:

a) The bailee accepts its obligation.

and b) The obligation acquired by the Holder is that the Issuer (and any Indorser) will procure the Acceptance of the bailee.

(2) **Title and Rights** (subject to §7-503):

a) Title and rights acquired by negotiation will not be defeated by:

1) Any stoppage of goods (represented by the document)

or 2) Surrender of the goods by the bailee

b) Title and rights acquired by negotiation will not be impaired, even if:

1. Negotiation (or any prior negotiation) constituted a breach of duty

or 2. Any Person has been deprived of possession of the document by:

a) Misrepresentation

or b) Fraud

or c) Accident

or d) Mistake

or e) Duress

or f) Loss

or g) Theft

or h) Conversion

or 3. A previous sale (or other transfer of the goods or document) has been made to a third Person

§7-503: Defeated Documents of Title:

(1) Interests before Issuance: A DOT confers no right in goods against a Person who:

(a) Didn't deliver or entrust such goods (or DOT covering them) to a merchant (as per §2-403)

and (b) Didn't acquiesce title in the procurement by the bailor (or his nominee) of any DOT and (c) Had a legal or perfected S/I in the goods *before* the Document was issued

(2) Unaccepted Delivery Orders:

a) Title to goods based upon an *unaccepted delivery order* is subject to the rights of anyone to whom a negotiable warehouse receipt or BOL (covering such goods) has been *Duly Negotiated.*
b) Such a title may be defeated under § 7-504 to the same extent as the rights of the Issuer or a Transferee from the Issuer.

(3) BOL issued to a Freight Forwarder:

a) Title to goods based on a BOL issued to a freight forwarder is subject to the rights of anyone to whom a bill issued to the freight forwarder is *duly negotiated.*
b) Delivery by the carrier (in accordance with Part 4 of Article 7) pursuant to its own BOL discharges the carrier's obligation to deliver.

§ 2-323: Bill of Lading:

(1) **Requirements of the Bill of Lading:**

a. The seller must obtain a negotiable Bill of Lading (unless otherwise agreed) if:
   1. The contract involves an *overseas* shipment.
   and 2. The terms are FOB (vessel), CIF, or C&F.
b. Contents of the negotiable Bill of Lading:
   1. FOB — must state that goods have been loaded on board
   2. CIF or C&F — must state that the goods have been received for shipment

(2) **Multi-Part Documents**

i) When a Bill of Lading has been issued in a set of parts, only one part need be tendered *unless:*
   a) The agreement expressly requires that a full set be tendered.
   or b) *Both:*
      1. The buyer demands that a full set be tendered.
      and 2. The documents are not to be sent from abroad.
ii) The following rules apply even if the contract expressly requires a full set of documents to be tendered:
   (a) Due tender of a single part of the BOL is acceptable to cure improper delivery (as per § 2-508(1)).
   and (b) Documents sent from abroad: If the documents are sent from abroad, the Person tendering an incomplete set of documents may still require Payment upon furnishing an

indemnity (which the buyer deems to have been made in Good Faith), even if the full set is demanded.

(3) **"Overseas"**—an "overseas" contract or shipment is one:

a) Involving shipment by water or air

and b) That is subject to commercial, financial, or shipping practices characteristic of *international deep water commerce,* either by usage of trade or agreement

§ 2-325: Letter of Credit:

(1) Failure of a buyer to seasonably provide an agreed Letter of Credit is a breach of the contract for sale.

(2) **L/C as Payment:**

a) The delivery of a proper L/C to the seller *suspends* the buyer's obligation to pay.

b) If the L/C is dishonored, the seller may require Payment directly from buyer upon *seasonable notification.*

(3) Definitions:

a) **"Letter of Credit"** (or "banker's credit")—means (unless otherwise agreed) an irrevocable credit issued by a financing agency of good repute.

b) **"Confirmed Credit"**—means that the credit carries the direct obligation of a financing agency that does business in the seller's financial market.

§ 5-109: Issuer's Obligation to Its Customer:

(1) **Issuing Bank's Obligations:**

i) An Issuer Bank's obligation to its customers include:

1) Good Faith

2) The observance of any general banking customs/usage

ii) The issuing Bank's obligations do not (unless otherwise agreed) include any liability or responsibility for:

(a) Performance of the underlying sales contract (or other transaction between the Customer and the Beneficiary)

(b) Any act or omission of any Person (other than itself) for loss or destruction of a:

1. Draft

or 2. Demand

or 3. Document in transit

or 4. Document in the possession of others

(c) Knowing or complying with any customs or usage of any particular trade

(2) **Duty to Examine:**

1. An Issuer must examine the documents with care to determine whether they appear to comply with the terms of the Letter of Credit—*on their face* (see § 5-103).
2. The Issuing Bank assumes no liability or responsibility (unless otherwise agreed) for the genuineness, falsification, or effect of any document that appears regular *on its face* when examined (see § 5-114 for each party's duties, privileges, and responsibilities).

(3) A non-Bank Issuer is not bound by any banking usage (i.e., terms/customs of the trade) of which it does not know.

§ 5-114: Issuer's Duty to Honor; Right to Reimbursement:

(1) **Independent Significance:**

a) An Issuer must Honor a Draft or Demand for Payment if it complies with the terms of the L/C, regardless of whether the goods or documents conform to the underlying contract.

b) The Issuer is not excused from its duty to Honor such a Draft or demand if the L/C has a general term requiring *all* documents to be satisfactory to the Issuer (example: Bill of Lading, Inspection Certificate, Invoice).

(2) **When Bank Does Not Have To Honor L/C:**

i) The Bank may not have to Honor the L/C when documents appear on their face to comply with the terms of the L/C if:

a) A required document does not conform to the warranties made on Negotiation or Transfer of

1) A Document of Title (as per § 7-507)

or 2) A certified security (as per § 8-306)

or b) A required document is forged or fraudulent

or c) There is fraud in the transaction

ii) In such cases, the following rules determine when the Issuing Bank may Honor or Dishonor the L/C:

(a) Holder in Due Course: An Issuer must Honor the Draft or demand for Payment if Honor is demanded by a Negotiating Bank or other Holder of the Draft who has become:

1) A **Holder in Due Course** of a Draft (as per §3-302)

or 2) A **Holder by Due Negotiation** of a Document (as per §7-502)

or 3) A **Bona Fide Purchaser** of a Certified security (as per §8-302)

(b) All other cases:

1. Court Order: A court order (from the appropriate jurisdiction) may enjoin the Issuing Bank from honoring such an L/C.
2. Customer's Notice: An Issuer acting in **Good Faith** *may* Honor the Draft or demand for Payment, even if its Customer notifies it of fraud, forgery, or other defects not apparent on the face of the documents without a court order.

(3) An Issuer which has duly honored a Draft or demand for Payment is entitled to:

a) *Immediate Reimbursement* of any Payment it made under the L/C (unless otherwise agreed)

and b) Have funds effectively available no later than the day *before* maturity of any Acceptance made under the L/C

* * *

§9-404: Rights Acquired by Assignee; Claims & Defenses Against Assignee:

(a) **Defenses Against Assignees:** Unless the Account debtor has made an enforceable agreement not to assert defenses or claims arising out of a sale (as per (b) and (e) below), the rights of an assignee are subject to:

(1) **Contractual terms:** All terms of the contract between the Account debtor and assignor, *including* any claim or defense arising from the contract

and (2) **Setoffs of Defenses or Claims** (outside contact): Any other defense or claim that the Account debtor has against the assignor, as long as it accrues *before* the Account debtor received notification of the assignment.

(b) **Setoffs for Amounts Owed to Assignee:** The claim of an Account debtor against an assignor may be asserted against an assignee under (a), but *only* to reduce the amount the Account debtor owes (subject to (c) and except as provided in (d)).

(c) **Exception for Individuals:** This section is subject to the law (other than this article) which establishes a different rule for an Account debtor who

1) Is an *Individual*
and 2) Who incurred the obligation primarily for personal, family, or household purposes.

(d) **Omission of Required Statement in Consumer Transaction:** If a record evidencing the Account debtor's obligation is required by law to include a statement to the effect that the *account debtor's recovery against an assignee* (with respect to claims and defenses against the assignor) *may not exceed amounts paid by the Account debtor*, and such Record does not include such statement, it will be deemed to contain such statement for purposes of an Account debtor asserting a claim against an assignee.

(e) **Inapplicability to Health-Care-Insurance Receivable:** This section does not apply to an assignment of a health-care-insurance receivable.

§ 9-405: Modification of Assigned Contract:

(a) **<u>Effect of Modification of Assigned Contract</u>:**

a. Any Modification of or substitution for the contract will be effective against the assignee if it is *<u>made in Good Faith</u>*.
b. The assignee acquires the assignor's corresponding rights under the Modified or substituted contract.
c. The Assignment may provide that such a modification or substitution is a breach by the assignor.

(b) **Applicability:** Section (a) above will only apply *<u>to the extent that</u>* the right to payment has:

(1) Not been fully earned by performance under an assigned contract
or (2) Been fully earned by performance *<u>and</u>* the Account debtor has not received notification of the assignment under § 9-406(a).

(c) **Exception for Individuals:** This section is subject to other laws which establish a different rule for an Account debtor who

1) Is an individual
and 2) Who incurred the obligation primarily for personal, family, or household purposes.

(e) **Inapplicability to Health-Care-Insurance Receivable:** This section does not apply to an assignment of a health-care-insurance receivable.

§ 9-406: Discharge, Restrictions, and Proof of Assignment:

(a) **Discharge of Account Debtor; Effect of Notification:**

1. An Account debtor (on an account, chattel paper, or Payment Intangible) may *discharge* its obligation by paying the *assignor* until, *but not after*, the Account debtor received a notification.
2. Requirements for notification:
   a. Authenticated by the assignor or assignee
   and b. States that the amount due (or to become due) has been assigned
   and c. Payment is to be made to the assignee
3. Effect of notification: After receiving such notification, the Account debtor may discharge its obligation by paying the assignee.
   - It can no longer discharge its obligation by paying the assignor.

(b) **Ineffective Notification:** Notification is ineffective under (a) if

(1) It does not *reasonably identify* the rights assigned.
or (2) An agreement between the Account debtor and the assignor (i.e., the seller of the payment intangible) specifically limits the Account debtor's duty to pay a person other than the seller (and such limitation is effective under law (other than this Article)).
or (3) The notification notified the Account debtor to make less than the full amount of any installment or other periodic payment to the assignee (at the option of the Account debtor), *even if:*
(A) Only a portion of the receivable has been assigned.
or (B) A portion has been assigned to another assignee.
or (C) The Account debtor knows that the assignment to the assignee is limited.

(c) **Proof of Assignment:**

1. An assignee shall *seasonably* furnish reasonable proof of an assignment upon request by the Account debtor.
2. If the assignee does not comply with giving notice, then the Account debtor may discharge its obligation by paying the assignor (even if it received notification under (a) above).

(d) **Term Prohibiting Assignment Ineffective:** A term in any Promissory Note or contract between an Account debtor and an assignor is *ineffective* if it:

(1) Prohibits the Assignment of an account by:
a. Prohibiting assignments

b. Restricting assignments
c. Requiring the consent of the Account debtor or person obligated under the Promissory Note to the assignment
or d. Prohibiting the creation of an S/I in a general intangible for money due or to become due

or (2) Provides that a default, breach, or other claim will occur upon:
a. Assignment
b. Transfer
c. Creation, Attachment, perfection, or enforcement of a security interest

(e) **Exceptions:** Subsection (d) does not apply to the sale of a Payment Intangible or Promissory Note.

(f) **Ineffectiveness of Legal Restriction on Assignment:** A rule of law that prohibits, restricts, or requires consent (by Account debtor or a governmental body) to the transfer, assignment, or creation of an S/I in a payment intangible, will be *ineffective* to the extent that the law:

(1) Prohibits the Assignment of an account by:
a. Prohibiting assignments
b. Restricting assignments
c. Requiring the consent of the Account debtor or person obligated under the Promissory Note to the assignment
or d. Prohibiting the creation of an S/I in a general intangible for money due or to become due

or (2) Provides that a default, breach, or other claim will occur upon:
a. Assignment
b. Transfer
c. Creation, attachment, perfection, or enforcement of a security interest

(g) **No Waiver:** An Account debtor may not waive or vary its option under Subsection (b)(3) above.

(h) **Exception for Individuals:** This section is subject to other laws which establish a different rule for an Account debtor who is an individual and who incurred the obligation primarily for personal, family, or household purposes.

(i) **Inapplicability to Health-Care-Insurance Receivable:** This section does not apply to an assignment of a health-care-insurance receivable.

* * *

APPENDIX

WRONGFUL DISHONOR

OBLIGATIONS OWED TO VARIOUS PARTIES

Liable Party	Drawer
Payor Bank	The Payor Bank (Drawee) is liable to its Customer (as per §4-104(a)(5)) only for actual damages incurred as a result of a wrongful dishonor of a check (§4-402(b)).
Drawer	
Indorser	

Payee/Holder	Payor Bank
The Payor Bank (Drawee) is not liable to the holder because it is not liable on an unaccepted draft (§3-408), and the check has not been Accepted (since the Bank hasn't signed the check as per §1-201(39) (see §3-401 and §3-409(a)—signature needed for acceptance), but rather dishonored it (as per §3-409; §3-502).	
a) The Drawer has an obligation to pay the Draft if it is dishonored (§3-414(b)) (unless the bank fails (i.e., goes bankrupt) and the check has not been presented within 30 days of the check date (§3-414(e)). b) Contract Liability to Payee: The suspension of the contract will be lifted once the check is dishonored (as per §3-310(b)(3)), allowing the Payee (i.e., Obligee on the Contract) to enforce the contract. c) Certified Check Exception: Check Certification discharges the Drawer/Obligor (as per §3-414(c)—Drawer discharged when check accepted; §3-409(d): Certification is considered acceptance). The Certifying Bank will be liable to pay.	The Drawer will have No liability to the Payor Bank.
a) The Indorser has an obligation to pay the Draft if it is dishonored (§3-415(b)), unless it was presented 30 days after the Indorser indorsed the check (§3-415(e)). b) Contract Liability to Payee: If the Indorser is obligated to pay the Payee under contract, the suspension will be lifted since the check was discharged (as per §3-310(b)(3)), allowing the contract to be enforced by the obligee. c) Transfer Warranty (§3-416) is usually insufficient to cover Wrongful Dishonor (i.e.,—the Transfer Warranty really deals only with forgeries and alterations (see §3-416(a))).	No liability

COUNTERMANDED CHECKS (SPOs)

	Drawer	Payee/Holder
Payor Bank— for ignoring SPO	The Payor Bank will be responsible to pay its Customer for: a) The value of the Draft arising out of its non-observance of a Stop Payment Order (§4-403) (i.e., the bank can't charge the customer's account if it did not obey the SPO (since the check is not properly payable (§4-401))) and b) Any subsequent damages resulting from the wrongful payment (example: loss from bounced checks if an overdraft occurs from the wrongful payment (§4-403(c))), but not if the Stop Payment Order comes too late (§4-303(a)) (Note: A Bank may stop payment even if the SPO was late)	
Drawer		The Drawer will be responsible to pay an HDC the value of the dishonored check (as per §3-302) (Note: The Depositary Bank will usually want to prove that it is an HDC; and, thus, the Payee will be responsible to pay the Depositary Bank for the value of the check (see Banks as HDC)).
Payee/Holder		

Depositary Bank	Payor Bank
If the Depositary Bank paid the check, it may be compensated by the Payor Bank for the value given to the Payee/Holder since both the Payee and Depositary Bank are HDCs (Note: It may also claim from Payee under § 4-318 (payment by mistake)).	
If Depositary/Collecting banks pay the check, they'll acquire rights of subrogation (as per § 4-407) against the Drawer (on behalf of the payee) (but note, this is only effective if the payee has a valid claim against the Drawer, and will be subject to setoff)	
May claim from Payee under § 4-318 (payment by mistake)	The Payor Bank may recover the value it paid for the check from Holder (as per § 3-417(b)) even if it paid the check without using ordinary care (example: by not complying with the Drawer's Stop Payment Order) if the Payee breached a Transfer or Presentment Warranty (example: if the Payee forged an Indorsement or signature)

ALTERATION BY PAYEE (in the hands of a third-party holder)

	Payee/Holder	Payor Bank
Payor Bank	The Payor Bank may refuse to pay the altered amount of the check, but it must pay the holder the original check amount (§ 3-407(c)); The Holder will bear liability for the rest of the altered amount.	
Drawer	Drawer is responsible to give payee the original amount of the check (not the altered amount).	The Payor Bank has a right to charge back the Drawer only for the original amount of the check.

If the Payor Bank Pays, it may charge back only the *original amount* to the Drawer (§ 4-401(d)(1)) and can recover the rest from Holder/Depositary Bank (as per § 3-417(a)(2)/§ 4-208(a)(2)) since The Holder breached its *Presentment Warranties.*

FORGERY

	Forged "Drawer's" Signature:
"Drawer's" (Owner's) Liability	The "owner" of the check is not liable for a forged check (§ 3-401; § 3-403(c)) since he never signed it; however, the forger is liable on the check as if he were the Drawer (§ 3-401).
Indorser's Liability	If someone indorses a Forged check, he will be liable to subsequent Payee/Holders (under § 3-416(a)(2) (Transfer Warranties)).
Payor Bank's Liability	a) Payor Bank does Not Pay: The Payor Bank will Not be responsible to pay the forged check (§ 4-401, because it is not properly payable); if it does not pay the check, the Holder will bear the loss. b) Bank Paid Forged Check: The Payor Bank cannot recover for breach of Presentment Warranty from the Depositary Bank if the Depositary Bank didn't have knowledge of the forgery (§ 3-417(a)(3); § 4-208(a)(3) — banks warrant "no knowledge" of forgery); the Payor bank must remain liable (bears the loss) since it can't charge the drawer for it (§ 3-401; § 3-403(a)§ 4-401(a)).
Depositary Bank's Liability	
Payee's/Holder's Liability	
Forger's Liability	The forger is liable for the amount of the check as if it were the Drawer (§ 3-401).
Forged Indorsement of Payee (when in the hands of the Drawer); (example: the Drawer prepares a Check to the Payee, and before it reaches the Payee, one of the Drawer's employ-	**Forged Indorsement of Payee (once in the hands of the payee)** (example: the Drawer prepares a check for the Payee. Once the Payee receives it, one of the Payee's employees (the

FORGERY

	Forged "Drawer's" Signature:
ees (the "Holder") steals the Check and indorses it to himself)	"Holder") steals the check and indorses it to herself)
The Drawer will be responsible to give the Payee another check (§3-310), since the Payee never got the check and never got paid on its contract	The Drawer will not be responsible to give the Payee a new check (§3-309; §3-308).
If the Payor Bank pays: a) The Payor Bank cannot hold the Drawer liable since it can't charge the Drawer for a check that is not properly payable (§3-401; §3-403(a)§4-401(a)). b) The Payor Bank Can charge the Holder (Presenter) or Depository Bank (under Presentment Warranties (as per §3-417(a)(1); §4-208(a)(1)). The Holder (Presentor) will be liable (as if check can't be cashed). c) The Payor Bank may recover the value it paid for the check from the Holder (as per §3-417(b)) even if it paid the check without using ordinary care (example: by not complying with the Drawer's Stop Payment Order).	If the Payor Bank pays: a) To Payee: The Payee may sue the Payor Bank or Depositary Bank for Conversion (§3-420); b) To Drawer: The Payor Bank may not charge the Drawer's account since the check was not properly payable (§4-401). If the Payor Bank didn't pay: The Drawer should Stop Payment, and should seek indemnification from Payee (if it made a blank Indorsement on the check, the Payee may be liable for negligence).
The Drawer can't sue the Depositary Bank for Conversion (§3-420 comments); it can only sue Payor Bank for wrongly charging its account (§4-401).	
a) Since the Payor bank is not responsible to pay the forged check (§3-403(a)), the Holder will normally bear the loss. b) The Payee cannot sue Payor or Depositary Bank for Conversion (§3-420), because it never had title to it. It may sue the Drawer for nonpayment (since the check was stolen before the Payee obtained possession of it).	

OBLIGATIONS OF PARTIES

Obligated Party	Maker/Issuer of a Promissory Note and Cashier's Check	Drawer of a Check or Draft
General Obligations	• The Maker is responsible for paying the amount on the instrument. • The Maker's liability arises only if he *signs* the instrument. • If the Maker negligently leaves parts of the draft blank, he is bound to any terms later filled in (§3-412(ii)) (Note: this applies only to Notes and Drafts drawn by the Drawer (including cashier's checks)).	• The Drawer will always be liable on a check unless: 1) He signs *"without recourse"* (§3-414). or 2) The Payor Bank (i.e., Drawee) is insolvent as a result of a delay in presentment (§3-404(f)). or 3) He doesn't sign the instrument (§3-401). or 4) The Draft is changed/altered (§3-410) but only *to the extent of the Alteration.* • The Drawer promises to pay the amount of the Instrument to any Payee/Holder ONLY if it has been DISHONORED by the Payor Bank (§3-414).
Obligation Owed To	a) All Indorsers b) Anyone entitled to enforce the instrument	a) Payee b) All subsequent Indorsers
Defenses Available	§3-502 defenses are available to the Maker/Issuer (only "real defenses" if an HDC takes it).	§3-502 defenses are available to the Drawer (only "real defenses" if an HDC takes it).
Rights to Recourse		—
Extent of Liability	The Maker/Issuer will be liable for the full amount of the Instrument.	• The Drawer will not be primarily responsible to pay a check directly to the Payee *unless* the Bank first Dishonors the check (§3-414(b)). • Extent of liability: The Drawer's contractual obligation to tender payment will be discharged upon the Payor Bank's Acceptance or Payment of the check (§3-414(c); see §3-409 to determine when acceptance occurs).
Warranties Made		None

Indorser	Drawee/Acceptor or Payor Bank
The Indorser promises to pay the amount of the Instrument to any *Subsequent Indorser* (or creditor) ONLY if it has been DISHONORED (§3-415).	• The Drawee has only a Contractual Duty with the Drawer to pay the Payee/Holder upon demand, and will be liable for wrongful dishonor and ignoring a Stop Payment Order, as per its contract with the Drawer. • Once the Drawee (i.e., Payor Bank) *indorses* the instrument, it becomes an **Acceptor**, and is subject to obligations under §3-413 (i.e., it is obligated to pay the amount on the check).
Only to subsequent Indorsers/Holders.	Drawer or Maker
§3-502 defenses are available to the Indorser (only "real defenses" if an HDC takes it).	
• The Drawer: If an Indorser is sued for the value of an instrument, he may sue the Drawer for the Value of the check (§3-414). • Previous Indorsers: The Indorser may also hold any *previous* Indorsers liable for the value of the check. (but note: he may not sue Indorsers who indorsed the instrument *after* he did (§3-415)).	Right of Subrogation and Payment by Mistake
• The Indorser will be liable for the face value of the Check up to 30 days after he indorsed the check. • The Indorser may limit liability by *qualifying* or *restricting* her Indorsement (example: signing "without recourse")	• The Drawee has no liability on a Draft until it Signs it (the fact that its name appears on the Draft as Drawee does not hold the Payor Bank liable to pay the Check to the Holder).
1) Transfer Warranties 2) Presentment Warranties—if given to the Payor Bank	None

DEFINITIONS

Acceptance	§ 3-409
Acceptor	§ 3-103(a)(1)
Accommodated Party	§ 3-419
Accommodation Party	§ 3-419
Alteration	§ 3-407
Anomalous Indorsement	§ 3-205
Bank	§ 1-201(4)
Bank	§ 4-105
Banking Day	§ 4-104
Bearer	§ 1-201(5)
Bill of Lading	§ 1-201(6)
Blank Indorsement	§ 3-205
Branch	§ 1-201(7)
Cashier's Check	§ 3-104
Certificate of Deposit	§ 3-104
Certified Check	§ 3-409
Check	§ 3-104
Clearinghouse	§ 4-104
Collecting Bank	§ 4-105
Consideration	§ 3-303
Consumer Account	§ 3-103(a)(2) (only in amended Article 3)
Consumer Transaction	§ 3-103(a)(3) (only in amended Article 3)
Depositary Bank	§ 4-105
Document of Title	§ 1-201(15)
Documentary Draft	§ 4-104
Draft	§ 3-104
Drawee	§ 3-103(a)(2) ((a)(4) in Amended Article 3)
Drawer	§ 3-103(a)(3) ((a)(5) in Amended Article 3)

DEFINITIONS (continued)

Good Faith	§ 1-201(19), § 1-203: Good Faith
Good Faith	§ 3-103(a)(4) ((a)(6) in Amended Article 3)
Holder	§ 1-201(20)
Holder in Due Course	§ 3-302
Honor	§ 1-201(21)
Incomplete Instrument	§ 3-115
Indorsement	§ 3-204
Indorser	§ 3-204
Instrument	§ 3-104
Intermediary Bank	§ 4-105
Issue	§ 3-105
Issuer	§ 3-105
Item	§ 4-104
Maker	§ 3-103(a)(5) ((a)(7) in Amended Article 3)
Money	§ 1-201(24)
Negotiable Instrument	§ 3-104
Negotiation	§ 3-201
Note	§ 3-104
Order	§ 3-103(a)(6) ((a)(8) in Amended Article 3)
Ordinary Care	§ 3-103(a)(7) ((a)(9) in Amended Article 3)
Party	§ 3-103(a)(8) ((a)(10) in Amended Article 3)
Payable at a Definite Time	§ 3-108
Payable on Demand	§ 3-108
Payable to Bearer	§ 3-109
Payable to Order	§ 3-109
Payment	§ 3-602
Payor Bank	§ 4-105
Person	§ 1-201(30)

DEFINITIONS (continued)

Person Entitled to Enforce	§3-301
Presentment	§3-501
Principal Obligor	§3-103(a)(11) (only in amended Article 3)
Promise	§3-103(a)(9) ((a)(12) in Amended Article 3)
Prove (a Fact)	§3-103(a)(10) ((a)(13) in Amended Article 3)
Purchase	§1-201(32)
Purchaser	§1-201(33)
Reacquisition	§3-207
Record	§3-103(a)(14) (only in amended Article 3)
Remitter	§3-103(a)(11) ((a)(15) in Amended Article 3)
Remotely Created Consumer Item	§3-103(a)(16)
Representative	§1-201(35)
Secondary Obligor	§3-103(a)(17)
Signed	§1-201(39)
Special Indorsement	§3-205
Suspends Payments	§4-104
Teller's Check	§3-104
Transfer of Instrument	§3-203
Traveler's Check	§3-104
Unauthorized	§1-201(43)
Value	§1-201(44), §3-303 (for purposes of Article 3: Negotiable Instruments) and §4-208 and §4-209 (for purposes of Article 4: Bank Collections)
Value	§3-303
Warehouse Receipt	§1-201(45)

INDEX

LaVergne, TN USA
30 March 2010
177689LV00003B/14/P